Senior Language

SADLER

HAYLLAR

POWELL

M

© R. K. Sadler, T. A. S. Hayllar, C. J. Powell 1981

First published 1981 by
THE MACMILLAN COMPANY OF AUSTRALIA PTY LTD
107 Moray Street, South Melbourne 3205
6 Clarke Street, Crows Nest 2065
Reprinted 1982

Associated companies in
London and Basingstoke, England
Auckland Dallas Delhi Hong Kong
Johannesburg Lagos Manzini Nairobi
New York Singapore Tokyo Washington Zaria

National Library of Australia
cataloguing in publication data
Sadler, R. K. (Rex Kevin)
    Senior language.
    For secondary school students.
    ISBN 0 333 33763 8.
    1. English language. I. Hayllar, T. A. S. (Thomas Albert
    S.). II. Powell, C. J. (Clifford J.). III. Title.
428

Set in Plantin by Savage & Co. Pty Ltd, Brisbane
Printed in Hong Kong by South China Printing Co.

Contents

Acknowledgements

The authors and publishers are grateful to the following for permission to reproduce copyright material:

Ernest Benn for the extract from *Social Life in the Insect World* by J. H. Fabre; Victor Gollancz Ltd for the extract from *Profiles of the Future* by Arthur C. Clarke; Harvey Unna & Stephen Durbridge Ltd for the extract from the play *Billy Liar* by Willis Hall and Keith Waterhouse; Bob Huntley for the extract 'Blood on the Shamrock' from *Bomb Squad*; Martin Secker & Warburg Limited for the extract from 'The Childhood Stories of Christy Allen' published under the title *My Left Foot* by Christy Brown; Routledge & Kegan Paul Ltd for 'The Worst Ever Actor' and 'The Worst Macbeth' from *The Book of Heroic Failures* edited by Stephen Pile; Turnstone Press Limited for the extract from *Jonathan Livingston Seagull* by Richard Bach; Jonathan Cape Ltd for the extract from *The Caine Mutiny* by Herman Wouk; The Executors of the Ernest Hemingway Estate and Jonathan Cape Ltd for the extracts from *For Whom the Bell Tolls* and *The Old Man and the Sea* by Ernest Hemingway; Ian Mudie for the poem 'My Father Began as a God'; Penguin Books Australia Limited for the extract from *Damned Whores and God's Police* by Anne Summers, and the extract from *The Loved One* by Evelyn Waugh; Mrs Laura Huxley and Chatto & Windus Ltd for the extract from *Brave New World* by Aldous Huxley; Taylor-Type Publications for the extracts from *How Did Things Start?* by Timothy Hall; Faber and Faber Limited for the poems 'Grandparents' from *Selected Poems* by Robert Lowell and 'The Jaguar' from *The Hawk in the Rain* by Ted Hughes; Curtis Brown (Aust.) Pty Ltd for the extract from *The Ghost Train* by Lawrence Durrell and for the extract from *The Education of Young Donald* by Donald Horne; The Currency Press for the extract from the play *The Club* by David Williamson; Rigby Publishers Limited for the extract from *Reflections of Reality — The Media in Australia* by Trevor Barr, and the poem 'Bert Schultz' by Colin Thiele from *Australian Poets Speak* ed. by Colin Thiele and Ian Mudie; Longman Cheshire Pty Ltd for the poem 'The Not-So-Good Earth' by Bruce Dawe from *Sometimes Gladness* by Bruce Dawe; Gentry Books for the extracts from *Unmentionables and Other Euphemisms* by Fritz Spiegl; Australian Consolidated Press for 'Never Needle a Drug-Fiend When He's Got a Knife' by Ron Saw; John Fairfax and Sons Pty Ltd for 'No Smoking' by Robin Robertson, and 'Street-Talk' (compiled by Mandy Oakham); Richards Publishing Ltd for the article 'Jogging Is Fun (Or Is It?)' by Phil Gifford from *Span* magazine; John Murray Publishers Ltd for the extracts from *The Goebbels Experiment* by Derrick Singleton and Arthur Weidenfeld; Young Men's Christian Association for the extract from *God is for real, man* by Carl Burke; Cassell Aust. Ltd for the letter to Winston Churchill from George VI from *The Second World War — Winston Churchill* edited by Andrew Scotland; *The Bulletin* for 'Pity does damn-all for the paraplegic' by Phillip Adams; The Australian Institute of International Affairs for the extract from *Uranium — Energy Source of the Future?* by E. W. Titterton and R. P. Robotham; Methuen & Co Ltd for the extract 'Pitying Animals' from *King Solomon's Ring* by Konrad Lorenz; The Hutchinson Group for the extract 'Adland — the Magic Mountain' from *Soft Soap, Hard Sell* by R. R. Walker; *The Australian* for 'Death of Ronald Ryan' by Patrick Tennison; *The Age* for 'If these were the best years of our lives, why did we feel so caged?' by Phillip Adams; Sun Books for the extract from *Adams with Added Enzymes* by Phillip Adams; Angus & Robertson Publishers for the poems 'Woman to Man' and 'The Surfer' from *Collected Poems 1942-1970* by Judith Wright, 'Standardization' from *Collected Poems 1930-1970* by A. D. Hope, 'Children' from *Showground Sketchbook* by Nancy Keesing, 'The Widower in the Country' from *Selected Poems — The Vernacular Republic* by Les A. Murray, and also for the extracts from *The Yarns of Billy Borker* by Frank Hardy and *Because a White Man'll Never Do It* by Kevin Gilbert.

Cartoon strips, advertisements, photos, clippings and other original pictorial matter reproduced: Alan Foley Pty Ltd pp. 7, 12, 42, 54, 92, 104, 130, 242, 245, 259, 272; British Leyland pp. 210-11; Broken Hill Proprietary Co Ltd pp. 212-13; Frederick Muller Ltd for the puzzle from *Supermazes No. 1* by Bernard Myers pp. 152-3; E. C. Publications p. 228; Herald and Weekly Times Pty Ltd pp. 29, 140; Hoover Australia Pty Ltd pp. 44-5; Imperial War Museum p. 194; Inter Continental Features pp. 6, 39, 68, 98, 129, 161, 191 (top), 227, 258; John Fairfax & Sons Pty Ltd p. 137; Mansell Collection Limited p. 56 (right); Melbourne Theatre Company pp. 85, 86, 87; New South Wales Teachers' Federation magazine *Education* pp. 131; News Ltd p. 106; Penguin Books Limited p. 56 (left); Pickering Promotions Pty Ltd p. 73; Rip Curl p. 90; Museo Civico 'Luigi Bailo', Treviso, Italy p. 196; John Spooner, *The Age* p. 34; Taylor-Type Publications (Australia) pp. 53 (bottom), 81 (bottom), 115, 145, 241; Yaffa Syndicate Pty Ltd p. 162.

Drawings by Rick Amor

Cover: Jim Lim

While every care has been taken to trace and acknowledge copyright, the publishers tender their apologies for any accidental infringement where copyright has proved untraceable. They would be pleased to come to a suitable arrangement with the rightful owner in each case.

Preface

Senior Language is a comprehensive, integrated language and literature text for English students in years 11 and 12. Teachers and students will find here a solid coverage of the areas of importance in any senior English course. The language work includes usage, vocabulary, comprehension, practical grammar and punctuation, and a thorough treatment of important language concepts. The clear-thinking strands examine aspects of language-use requiring particularly close scrutiny. The writing workshops, with their emphasis on the development of essay-writing skills, meet a major need that many texts ignore or treat superficially. The literature strands provide a rich and stimulating treatment of the principal areas of literature, leading students into their own encounter with selected forms and styles and working towards the development of evaluation skills. A special short dictionary at the back of the book provides a valuable vocabulary and spelling reservoir, while acting as a handy reference/refresher list of many of the words introduced in the vocabulary sections of each Unit.

The book is divided into 18 Units, each of which contains six strands:

- **Comprehension.** A passage chosen for its high interest level, and for aspects of its style and language. Questions accompanying the passage probe the student's understanding, response and sensitivity.

- **Working with Words.** The practical vocabulary and word-skills strand, it contains a broad range of exercises and activities designed to foster the student's knowledge, control and mastery of words.

- **Language in Action.** This strand focuses on important aspects of language with which all senior students should become familiar — bias, tone, cliché, connotation, slang, jargon, euphemism, tautology, etc.

- **The Language of Literature.** Concepts and considerations important to the study and appreciation of novel, poetry and drama are presented in a meaningful way, and related to a variety of examples drawn from past and contemporary writing.

- **Thinking and Reasoning** (Units 1–10). The clear-thinking and argument-assessment strand is of special relevance and deals with such concepts as generalization, analogy, cause-and-effect, etc. The aim is to help students identify emotive and manipulaive uses of language, and to develop the capacity for clear, critical assessment.

- **Writers' Workshop** (Units 11–18). This is a practical writing course designed to help students to construct clear and coherent sentences, and to build paragraphs that develop sequentially. Particular attention is paid to the planning, organizing and writing of essays.

- **Language Basics.** The final strand in each Unit, devoted to basic grammar, punctuation and kindred areas. Essential rules, with examples and exercises, are designed to equip students with basic knowledge necessary for writing correctly and effectively.

We have built this book on the conviction that the study of English should be enjoyable, and believe that teachers and students alike will find *Senior Language* an engaging and highly practical text and resource book.

Unit One

Comprehension (1)

The Worst Ever Actor

The worst actor ever to appear on a stage anywhere was Robert 'Romeo' Coates (1772–1842). Hardly ever did a production in which he figured end without riot.

His total incapacity to play any part whatever, combined with his insistence upon wearing diamonds from head to foot, regardless of role, and his tendency to 'improve' upon Shakespeare as he went along, made him immensely popular with astonished audiences up and down Britain.

His specialization was death scenes, which he used to preface by spreading a white silk handkerchief on the stage. These scenes were so protracted and so deliriously received that he frequently did encores, dying again.

Born in the West Indies, the son of a wealthy American sugar planter, he dabbled there in amateur dramatics.

When he inherited the estate at 35, Romeo Coates felt that he needed a larger platform and that he owed it to England to perform there. His belief in his own theatrical genius was unshakable. Criticism he put down to envy.

He arrived in Bath in 1807 in a diamond-encrusted carriage, shaped like a seashell and emblazoned with a gilt cockerel bearing his appropriate family motto, 'While I live, I'll crow'. His habit of declaiming 'improved' passages of Shakespeare ('I fancy that is rather better') over breakfast at his inn soon brought him to the attention of the manager of the Theatre Royal.

While Coates awaited his British début with pleasure, word got around as to the likely standard of his performance and all the tickets sold rapidly.

On that blustery November night he appeared in his greatest role — Romeo — a part which he was later forced to abandon because no actress would agree to play Juliet opposite him.

It started quietly enough, but when he entered the audience gave way to ecstatic cheers (which he stopped to acknowledge). Visually, Coates was always surprising and, on this occasion, he chose to dress his Romeo in a spangled sky-blue coat, bright crimson pantaloons and a white hat, excessively trimmed with feathers. Over all this was spattered a multitude of diamonds and the total effect ran quite counter to Shakespeare's description of the character as a 'quiet, virtuous and well-governed youth'.

The play continued in a hail of orange peel and whenever the audience crowed 'cock-a-doodle-do' at Coates he would break off, regardless of Juliet on the balcony, and crow back at them.

At one point the audience joined in a delighted chant of 'Off! Off! Off!' at which Coates, the gifted amateur, crossed his arms and stared at them with scorn and withering contempt.

That night the play got as far as the last act, but ended in riot when Coates suddenly re-entered with a crowbar, which was quite unnecessary and not mentioned in Shakespeare's text, to prize open the Capulets' tomb.

Of course, an actor of this calibre was soon in demand by London theatres and he arrived at the Haymarket Theatre on 9 December 1811. Here, playing Lothario in the first night of *The Fair Penitent*, Coates took longer to die on stage than anyone before or since. The audience sat politely, as his writhing figure was gripped by spasm after spasm, happy in the knowledge that it was only Act IV and that Coates would soon be dead, leaving a clear act to run without him. He died and the curtain fell.

After the interval, the gifted amateur came out before the curtain, dressed in regimental uniform, and announced that there would not be a fifth act that night. He would instead be reciting his favourite monologue.

After delighting London audiences for a further few years he retired from the stage due to bankruptcy.

[from *The Book of Heroic Failures* by STEPHEN PILE]

Check Your Understanding

(1) What was Coates's method of playing death scenes? How did the audience react to them?

(2) Why did Coates decide to come to England to further his acting career?

(3) What is the writer's attitude to Coates as an actor?

(4) What did Coates feel about his ability as an actor?

(5) Why do you think 'no actress would agree to play Juliet opposite him'?

(6) What evidence can you find to suggest that Coates's Romeo was not according to Shakespeare's intentions?

(7) Can you suggest why an actor of Coates's calibre was soon in demand by London theatres?

(8) What was unusual about Coates's performance in *The Fair Penitent*?

(9) After reading this article, what evaluation would you make of Coates as a person?

(10) Explain the meaning of: (a) he dabbled in amateur dramatics;
(b) criticism he put down to envy;
(c) his habit of declaiming 'improved' passages of Shakespeare.

(11) What is the meaning of: (a) encores (b) gilt (c) début (d) virtuous (e) blustery?

The Worst Macbeth

William McGonagall's first stage appearance was as Macbeth at Mr Giles's Theatre in Dundee. Realizing what a talent McGonagall had, Mr Giles said that he could only appear if a large sum of money was paid to the theatre in cash before the performance.

McGonagall said he considered this 'rather hard', but his fellow workers at the Seafield Handloom Works in Dundee had a whip round. They had heard him reciting Shakespeare at work, in his own unique way, and were keen to see him turned loose amidst professional actors.

'When the great night arrived,' McGonagall wrote in his diary, 'my shopmates were in high glee with the hope of getting a Shakespearian treat from me. And I can assure you, without boasting, they were not disappointed.'

When he appeared on stage, he was received with a perfect storm of applause. When he uttered his first line — 'So foul and fair a day I have not seen' — there was a deafening ovation.

The high spot came in the final scene, when Macduff is supposed to kill Macbeth in a sword fight. Unwisely, the actor playing Macduff told McGonagall to 'cut it short'.

Suspecting that the actor was jealous of the acclaim he was receiving, McGonagall refused to die. A new ending to *Macbeth* seemed imminent.

'I continued the combat until he was fairly exhausted, and there was one old gentleman in the audience cried out: "Well done, McGonagall! Walk into him!" And so I did until he (Macduff) was in great rage, and stamped his foot, and cried out "Fool! why don't you fall?" And when I did fall, the cry was "McGonagall! McGonagall! Bring him out! Bring him out!" Until I had to come out and receive an ovation from the audience.'

[from *The Book of Heroic Failures* by STEPHEN PILE]

Check Your Understanding

(1) Why do you think McGonagall's fellow-workers were keen to see McGonagall 'turned loose amidst professional actors'?

(2) What was unusual about the audience's response to McGonagall's playing of Macbeth?

(3) Why was the actor who was playing Macduff angry with McGonagall?

(4) What is meant by, 'A new ending to *Macbeth* seemed imminent'?

(5) What do you think is the writer's attitude to McGonagall as an actor?

(6) Did you find this article humorous? Why?

Working with Words (1)

Senior Spelling Demons	Confusing Pairs	Literature and Language		Increase Your Word Power*
scene	allowed	dialogue	suggest	eloquent
innocent	aloud	suppose	criticize	articulate
author	prophet	analysis	appreciate	coincidence
poetry	profit	theatre	character	prudent
approach	serial	rehearsal	argument	diligent
dictionary	cereal	syllable	suspense	abundance
article	councillor	synonym	anonymous	violation
audience	counsellor	abbreviation	tragedy	appeasement
determine	practise	theme	colloquial	exasperate
announce	practice	heroine	caricature	petulant

*The meanings of the words in this last column are in the back-of-the-book dictionary.

Change the Words

Change to nouns

(a) innocent ....

(b) determine ....

(c) allowed ....

(d) appreciate ....

(e) suppose ....

(f) criticize ....

(g) exasperate ....

(h) anonymous ....

Change to verbs

(a) rehearsal ....

(b) argument ....

(c) coincidence ....

(d) violation ....

(e) serial ....

(f) appeasement ....

(g) character ....

(h) analysis ....

Change to adjectives

(a) scene ....

(b) approach ....

(c) theatre ....

(d) profit ....

(e) practice ....

(f) suggest ....

(g) tragedy ....

(h) poetry ....

(i) coincidence ....

Change to adverbs

(a) criticize ....

(b) argument ....

(c) appreciate ....

Change to people

(a) criticize ....

(b) poetry ....

(c) announce ....

(d) violation ....

Confusing Pairs

Write out and complete the following sentences, selecting the correct words from the brackets.

(1) There was little .... in selling tennis balls. [**prophet/profit**]

(2) .... is a grain used for food. [**serial/cereal**]

(3) The amateur was not .... to accept money. [**aloud/allowed**]

(4) A student .... often gives invaluable advice concerning courses. [**councillor/counsellor**]

(5) Shot-putters .... regularly. [**practise/practice**]

Find the Word

Replace the words or phrases in heavy type with list-words in their appropriate form.

(1) The novel's central character was **an exaggerated representation** of a famous person.

(2) The preacher was **using language fluently and forcibly**.

(3) It is sometimes necessary to **shorten** words.

(4) The child's crying began to **strongly irritate** the mother.

(5) The **conversation** in the play was a mirror of Australian speech.

(6) Initially, England had a policy of **making concessions so as to pacify** Nazi Germany.

(7) The tired child was **impatient and irritable.**

(8) There was **plenty of** wheat for underprivileged countries.

(9) The poem was **of unknown authorship**.

(10) The schoolgirl was **hard-working** in her studies.

Antonyms

Find words in the list which are opposite in meaning to these. The first letters have been given to help you.

(1) **retreat**   a............................

(2) **guilty**   i ....

(3) **silently**   a............................

(4) **prevented**   a............,............

(5) **comedy**   t ....

(6) **scarcity**   a............................

(7) **unwise**   p ....

(8) **loss**   p ....

(9) **praise**   c............................

(10) **lazy**   d ....

Word Origins — 'Dictionary'

The word 'dictionary' is derived from the Latin verb *dicere/dictus* ('to say or tell'). Here are some more words built on this root: dictated, verdict, diction, predict, contradict, benediction, abdicate. Insert them correctly in the spaces below.

(1) A jury's finding is called a ....

(2) A person's wording and phrasing are called his ....

(3) To state what one believes will happen in the future is to ....

(4) To say the opposite is to ....

(5) A stenographer writes down what is ....

(6) To renounce the throne is to ....

(7) At the end of a church service, a minister says the ....

Language in Action (1)

Tone

In written communication, the writer's tone indicates his attitude and feelings towards his subject, his audience and often towards himself. In oral communication, our tone is indicated by our voice. If, while we are speaking, our tone is one of happiness, depression or anger, it will certainly be revealed by our vocal intonations regardless of the words we use. With the written word we do not have these intonations, but our choice of words enables us to show our attitudes and feelings.

THE WIZARD OF ID — By Parker and Hart

What is the tone of the King's message to his knights?

Here is the first paragraph of a letter written by a young business executive to a multinational car company. He is complaining about his new vehicle. As you read consider the tone of his writing.

> 'I must congratulate the .... Company on the production of what must surely be the most hopeless car on our roads today. If it is not the most hopeless then it is certainly the most faultridden vehicle in years. The model, yes of course, the now famous .... !'

His tone is sarcastic and aggressive. Why did he adopt this tone? He was aiming to provoke the car company into repairing or replacing his new car. What did his first paragraph reveal about his own feelings? Do you think his tone was the correct one for his situation?

A Tone Scale

For us as writers, there are as many tones as there are attitudes. Here are a few basic tones to give you some idea of the wide range available.

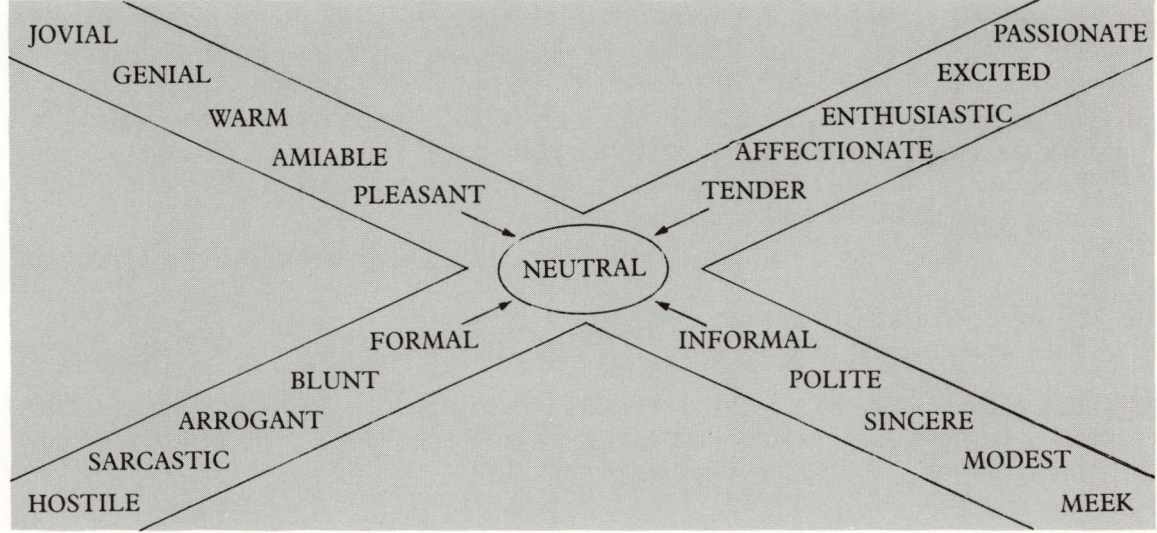

Identifying the Tone

Below is a selection of passages taken from literature and other sources. See whether you can identify the tone of the writer in each case.

(1) We shall defend our Island, whatever the cost may be. We shall fight on the beaches, we shall fight on the landing-grounds, we shall fight in the fields and in the streets, we shall fight in the hills; we shall never surrender.

> [Winston Churchill — in a radio broadcast to the British nation during World War II]

(2) *Hamlet* (taking the dead Yorick's skull):
Alas, poor Yorick. I knew him, Horatio: a fellow of infinite jest, of most excellent fancy; he hath borne me on his back a thousand times. And now how abhorred in my imagination it is. My gorge rises at it. Here hung those lips that I have kissed I know not how oft. Where be your gibes now, your gambols, your songs, your flashes of merriment that were wont to set the table on a roar? Not one now to mock your own grinning — quite chap-fallen?

> [from *Hamlet*, Act V Scene i]

(3) From your private balcony enjoy the gardens with their colourful rock-pools and immaculately kept lawns and shrubs. Crystal-clear swimming pool, poolside lounge, cardroom, sauna — all lending the mood for a carefree health-giving way of life.

> [from an advertisement for a house]

(4) Trespassers Will Be Prosecuted. [sign on a vacant block of land]

(5) There was an old woman of Ryde,
Who ate sour apples and died.
> Inside the lamented
> The apples fermented,
Making cider inside 'er inside.

(6) Paul hated his father so. The collier's small, mean head, with its black hair slightly soiled with grey, lay on the bare arms, and the face, dirty and inflamed, with a fleshy nose and thin paltry brows, was turned sideways, asleep with beer and weariness and nasty temper. If anyone entered suddenly, or a noise were made, the man looked up and shouted: 'I'll lay my fist about thy y'ead, I'm tellin' thee, if tha doesna stop that clatter! Dost hear?'

> [from *Sons and Lovers* by D. H. Lawrence]

(7) The automobile is treacherous, just like a cat is. It is tragically difficult to realize that it can become the deadliest missile. As enthusiasts tell you it makes 65 miles an hour like nothing at all. But 65 miles an hour is 100 feet a second, a speed which can instantly turn this docile luxury into a mad bull elephant.

> [from an article, ' — And Sudden Death', reprinted in *Road Safety*]

(8) My love is like a red, red rose,
That's newly sprung in June: [first lines of a poem by Robert Burns]

(9) The impudent strike by school teachers surely reveals them as pestiferous ingrates. They work a six-hour day, five-day week with three months holiday a year. Yet they are now striking for more and better working conditions!

> [from a Letter to the Editor in a newspaper]

(10) My heart leaps up when I behold
    A rainbow in the sky: [from 'The Rainbow' by William Wordsworth]

(11) She snatched her cane from the desk, and brought it down on him. He was writhing and kicking. She saw his face beneath her, white, with eyes like the eyes of a fish, stony, yet full of hate, and horrible fear. And she loathed him, the hideous writhing thing that was nearly too much for her. In horror lest he should overcome her, and yet at the heart quite calm, she brought down the cane again and again, whilst he struggled making inarticulate noises, and lunging vicious kicks at her. With one hand she managed to hold him, and now and then the cane came down on him. He writhed, like a mad thing. But the pain of the strokes cut through his writhing, vicious, coward's courage, bit deeper, till at last, with a long whimper that became a yell, he went limp.

[from *The Rainbow* by D. H. Lawrence]

(12) KILLER DOGS AT LARGE   [newspaper headline]

The Language of Literature (1)

The Greatness of Shakespeare

Shakespeare is acclaimed as the world's finest dramatist. We hope that these four passages, which we have carefully chosen, will give you an insight into the greatness of Shakespeare's talent.

THE SEVEN AGES OF MAN

Jacques:
All the world's a stage,
And all the men and women merely players;
They have their exits and their entrances,
And one man in his time plays many parts,
His Acts being seven ages. At first, the infant,
Mewling and puking in the nurse's arms.
Then the whining schoolboy, with his satchel
And shining morning face, creeping like snail
Unwilling to school. And then the lover,
Sighing like furnace, with a woeful ballad
Made to his mistress' eyebrow. Then a soldier,
Full of strange oaths and bearded like the pard,
Jealous in honour, sudden and quick in quarrel,
Seeking the bubble reputation
Even in the cannon's mouth. And then the justice,

In fair round belly, with good capon lined,
With eyes severe and beard of formal cut,
Full of wise saws and modern instances;
And so he plays his part. The sixth age shifts
Into the lean and slipper'd pantaloon,
With spectacles on nose and pouch on side;
His youthful hose, well saved, a world too wide
For his shrunk shank; and his big manly voice,
Turning again towards childish treble, pipes
And whistles in his sound. Last Scene of all,
That ends this strange eventful history,
Is second childishness, and mere oblivion,
Sans teeth, sans eyes, sans taste, sans everything.

[from *As You Like It*, Act II Scene vii]

All the World's a Stage

(1) Explain what Shakespeare means by:

> 'All the world's a stage,
> And all the men and women merely players;
> They have their exits and their entrances,'

(2) Do you find any similarity between the first age of man and the last age? Explain your viewpoint.

(3) What impression does Shakespeare give us of the schoolboy?

(4) Comment on the effectiveness of the similes, 'like the [leo]pard' and 'like furnace'.

(5) Explain what Shakespeare means by '*bubble* reputation'?

(6) What impression does Shakespeare give us of the justice?

(7) Outline the seven ages of man as Shakespeare depicts them?

(8) In the sixth age, Shakespeare brings out man's deterioration. How does he do this?

(9) Why does Shakespeare refer to the seventh age of man as 'mere oblivion'?

(10) What is the meaning of 'woeful' as it occurs in this passage? To what extent has its meaning changed through the centuries?

(11) The soldier does not receive favourable treatment from Shakespeare. Explain how Shakespeare creates an unfavourable impression.

(12) Did you notice that all the seven ages of man have their problems? Do you think Shakespeare is being unduly pessimistic? Why?

LIFE-TIDE

Brutus:
There is a tide in the affairs of men,
Which, taken at the flood, leads on to fortune;
Omitted, all the voyage of their life
Is bound in shallows and in miseries.
On such a full sea are we now afloat,
And we must take the current when it serves,
Or lose our ventures.

[from *Julius Caesar*, Act IV Scene iii]

There Is a Tide in the Affairs of Men

(1) Here is one of Shakespeare's finest metaphors, full of images from the sea. What does Brutus mean by: 'There is a tide in the affairs of men,

> Which, taken at the flood, leads on to fortune;' ?

(2) Why is Brutus suggesting that the 'current' must be taken?

TOMORROW . . .

Macbeth:
Tomorrow, and tomorrow, and tomorrow,
Creeps in this petty pace from day to day,
To the last syllable of recorded time;
And all our yesterdays have lighted fools
The way to dusty death. Out, out, brief candle!
Life's but a walking shadow, a poor player
That struts and frets his hour upon the stage
And then is heard no more. It is a tale
Told by an idiot, full of sound and fury,
Signifying nothing.

[from *Macbeth*, Act V Scene v]

Out, Out, Brief Candle!

(1) What view of life is Macbeth putting forward?

(2) How does Shakespeare create a sense of time passing quickly?

(3) What do you think is the 'brief candle'?

(4) What is the tone of this passage?

(5) Do you think the metaphor of 'a poor player' a suitable one or not? Give a reason for your answer.

THE QUESTION

Hamlet:
To be, or not to be — that is the question:
Whether 'tis nobler in the mind to suffer
The slings and arrows of outrageous fortune
Or to take arms against a sea of troubles
And by opposing end them. To die, to sleep —
No more — and by a sleep to say we end
The heartache and the thousand natural shocks
That flesh is heir to. 'Tis a consummation
Devoutly to be wished. To die, to sleep —
To sleep — perchance to dream: ay, there's the rub,
For in that sleep of death, what dreams may come
When we have shuffled off this mortal coil,
Must give us pause. There's the respect
That makes calamity of so long life.

[from *Hamlet*, Act III Scene i]

To Be or Not to Be

(1) In this passage Hamlet is contemplating suicide. He could have said something like, 'Shall I suicide or not?' Can you suggest why the line, 'To be or not to be – that is the question:' has had so much impact on audiences and readers throughout the centuries?

(2) What do you think Hamlet means by the metaphor, 'The slings and arrows of outrageous fortune'?

(3) 'Or to take up arms against a sea of troubles' is a mixture of two metaphors. Explain what each of them means.

(4) What kind of sleep is Hamlet thinking of here?

(5) What do you think Hamlet means by 'mortal coil'?

(6) Why does Hamlet have second thoughts about taking his own life?

Thinking and Reasoning (1)

This first module of the Thinking and Reasoning strand introduces some of the psychological theories about human behaviour from Eric Berne's book, *Games People Play*. While it is not our purpose to go too deeply here into Berne's theory of Transactional Analysis, his ideas will give some interesting insights into your work on reasoning and clear thinking. This module can, however, be left out if the teacher prefers. The other nine modules on reasoning and clear thinking do not depend on it.

Thinking in the Adult

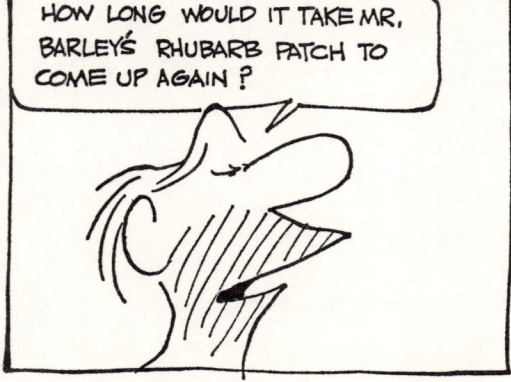

Psychiatrist Eric Berne, in his *Games People Play*, first outlined the theory that each of us is made up of three different 'personalities' or, more accurately, ego (self) states. He labelled these Parent, Adult and Child.* It's not that we have three different people running around inside us, but rather that at certain times and in certain situations we think, feel and behave quite differently, according to which self is in control.

The Personality

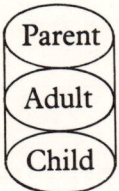

1. The Child

Our Child is the ego state which developed as a record of our *feelings* about the world around us when we were about three years old. It is that self within each of us which responds primarily at a *feeling* level — wanting recognition, showing off, arguing, feeling hurt, being afraid, becoming excited, being resentful, feeling discouraged, and so on.

Operating in our Child is not always bad! Our emotions, of course, are a very important part of us. But when we are required to weigh things up, and think clearly, it is not desirable to be thinking with our emotions. Many an advertiser, or speaker, knows that if he or she can 'hook' our Child and so entice us into reacting on the basis of our emotions, his/her job of persuading us will be much easier. Our ability to reason will be poorer if our Child is hooked.

EXAMPLES OF THE CHILD EGO STATE

Statements	**Behaviours**
I can't.	Being angry.
Wow!	Happy laughter.
Fantastic!	Day-dreaming.
I won't!	Being sulky.
Did I do all right?	Grimacing to express displeasure.

2. The Parent

Each of us also has a Parent ego state. The material in our Parent is what we learnt from our father and mother and other important adult people — a great collection of images and information that was stored in our brain in the first five years of life as these significant people spoke and acted in our world.

When we consider our task of clear thinking and reasoning, it is apparent that operating in our Parent is not the most effective or desirable mode of functioning. If we are in our Parent self we will tend to judge too quickly on the basis of what we have heard or seen in the past — failing to weigh up the evidence. We will generalize too quickly and too sweepingly. We will tend to be guided by rules and pronouncements from our past ('Honest men always get ahead') without really weighing things up. Our Parent tapes, largely taken into our brains without critical editing, will tend to prevent us looking without prejudice, deeply, at the issue.

---

*You can follow up on Transactional Analysis (T.A.) in books such as *Games People Play* by E. Berne, Penguin; *I'm O.K. — You're O.K.* by T. H. Harris, Pan; *T.A. for Teens* by A. Freed, Jalmar Press Inc. You might find it well worth while!

EXAMPLES OF THE PARENT EGO STATE

Statements	Behaviours
Oh, don't be stupid.	Laughing at someone.
That's not the way!	Pointing finger while instructing.
Girls are always talking.	Looking disgusted with someone.
You shouldn't do that.	Glaring at someone.
Never trust a _____	Correcting someone.

3. The Adult

The Adult in us begins to develop from about 10 months when we are first able to operate in our world and observe the effects. The Adult ego state is the data-processor, that self in us which figures things out. The Adult collects the facts, including the Parent's 'rules' and the Child's feelings, and proceeds to make a reasoned decision. The Adult is the ego state in which we need to operate when reasoning. We cannot erase our Parent and Child tapes, but we can choose not to operate in them in situations calling for clear thinking. That is why the aim of these sections on reasoning is to encourage you to Think in the Adult!

EXAMPLES OF THE ADULT EGO STATE

Statements	Behaviours
I think ...	Weighing evidence.
An honest estimate ...	Critically examining.
What are the facts?	Thinking through.
Who ...?	Trying to see both sides.
Probably.	Being constructive when disagreeing.

Exercises

(1) To test your mastery of the Parent, Adult, Child (PAC) concepts, separate the following statements and behaviours into P, A, and C.

Statements	Behaviours
I'll fix you!	Over-eating.
This seems to be ...	Quoting a proverb.
What ...?	Speaking in baby-talk.
Tough!	Swearing.
There, there.	Studying.
You shouldn't.	Bragging.
It's possible that ...	Teasing.
I want ...	Collecting information.
Poor old ...	Staring, in order to make someone uncomfortable.
See, it won't hurt.	
The result is ...	Being sarcastic.
Gimme!	Standing, hands on hips.
How thoughtless!	Working out priorities.
Your duty is ...	Asking questions.
Mine.	
You beaut!	

(2) Make your own summary statement about each of the three ego states, explaining how they help, or interfere with, the process of reasoning.

(3) A situation which surely should compel clear reasoned thinking is described in Reginald Rose's play, *Twelve Angry Men*. A jury of twelve has to bring in a verdict on a youth charged with murder. As the extract shows, thinking is not always reasoned. . . .

Foreman: Okay. *(To the 7th Juror.)* How about the next gentleman?

7th Juror: Me? *(He pauses, looks around, shrugs and rises.)* I don't know, it's practically all said already. We can talk about it for ever. It is the same thing. I mean, this kid is o for five. Look at his record. He was in the Children's Court when he was ten for throwing a rock at his teacher. At fifteen he was in Reform School. He stole a car. He's been arrested for mugging. He was picked up twice for trying to slash another teenager with a knife. He's real quick with switchknives, they say. This is a very fine boy.

8th Juror: Ever since he was five years old his father beat him up regularly. He used his fists.

7th Juror: So would I. A kid like that. *(He sits.)*

4th Juror: Wouldn't you call those beatings a motive for him to kill his father?

8th Juror *(after a pause)*: I don't know. It's a motive for him to be an angry, hostile kid. I'll say that.

3rd Juror: *(moving up L of the table):* It's the kids, the way they are nowadays. Angry! Hostile! You can't do a damn thing with them. Just the way they talk to you. Listen, when I was his age I used to call my father 'Sir'. That's right. Sir! You ever hear a boy call his father that any more?

8th Juror: Fathers don't seem to think it's important any more.

3rd Juror: No? Have you got any kids?

8th Juror: Three.

3rd Juror: *(moving to L of the 8th Juror):* Yeah, well I've got this one, a boy of twenty years old. You know how it is. You bring up kids. You try to do everything for them to make 'em decent. We did everything for that boy and what happened? When he was nine he ran away from a fight. I saw him. I was so ashamed I almost threw up. So I told him right out. 'I'm gonna make a man outa you or I'm gonna bust you in half trying.' Well, I made a man outa him all right. When he was sixteen we had a battle. He hit me in the face. He's big, y'know. I haven't seen

him in two years. Rotten kid. You work your heart out . . . *(He breaks off. He has said more than he intended and more passionately than he intended it. He is embarrassed. He looks around at the others. Loudly.)* All right. Let's get on with it. *(He crosses angrily above the table and stands at the window up RC.)*

4th Juror *(rising)*: I think we're missing the point here. This boy, let's say he's a product of a filthy neighbourhood and a broken home. We can't help that. We're here to decide whether he's guilty or innocent of murder, not to go into reasons why he grew up this way. He was born in a slum. Slums are breeding grounds for criminals. I know it. So do you. It's no secret. Children from slum backgrounds are potential menaces to society. Now I think . . .

10th Juror *(interrupting)*: Brother, you can say that again. The kids who crawl outa those places are real trash. I don't want any part of them, I'm telling you.

(The 5th Juror has reacted to all this. His face is angry as he tries to control himself but his voice shakes as he speaks.)

5th Juror *(rising)*: I've lived in a slum all my life . . .

(The 4th Juror sits. The 10th Juror suddenly knows he has said the wrong thing.)

10th Juror *(rising)*: Oh, now wait a second . . .

5th Juror *(furiously)*: I used to play in a back yard that was filled with garbage.

(The Foreman rises.)

Maybe it still smells on me.

10th Juror *(his anger rising)*: Now listen, sonny . . .

Foreman *(to the 5th Juror):* Now let's be reasonable. There's nothing personal . . .

5th Juror *(loudly):* There is something personal! *(He looks around at the others, then suddenly he has nothing to say, clenches his fist and sits.)*

(The 3rd Juror moves to the 5th Juror and pats him on the shoulder. The 5th Juror does not look up.)

Foreman: All right, let's stop all this arguing. We're wasting time here.

[from *Twelve Angry Men* by REGINALD ROSE]

Questions

(1) The 7th juror's use of sarcasm in 'This is a very fine boy' is an example of thinking in *which* ego state? How does sarcasm impede reasoned thinking?

(2) Which juror more than any other appears to be thinking in the Adult? What features of 'thinking in the Adult' does he display?

(3) Identify the ego state in operation behind the 3rd juror's words: 'It's the kids, the way they are nowadays.'

(4) Why is the 3rd juror unable to think in an impartial way about the young man on trial?

(5) 'Slums are breeding grounds for criminals.' (4th juror) Which ego state? Even if the statement is true, why would it be wrong to conclude that *this* boy is therefore a criminal and guilty of murder?

(6) How does the 5th juror's reaction to the comments about slums show that his Child has been 'hooked'? Does this prevent him from thinking impartially about the point being discussed? Why?

(7) 'Now listen, sonny . . .' (10th juror) is a blatant Parent statement. What effect is the word 'sonny' intended to have on the person being addressed?

(8) What aspects of the Foreman's comments and behaviour show that he is trying to operate in the Adult?

Language Basics (1)

Little Demon Errors

Here are rules that will help you avoid some constantly recurring little demons.

Rule 1 ● **Your** is the possessive of 'you' and accompanies a noun, an adjective and noun – and so on.

EXAMPLES: (a) <u>Your</u> performance, Mr Coates, is quite excessive.

(b) Mr Romeo Coates, <u>your</u> diamond-encrusted carriage awaits you.

Rule 2 ● **You're** is the abbreviated form of 'you are'.

EXAMPLE: 'Mr McGonagall, <u>you're</u> not acting fairly. <u>You're</u> the one who loses the fight not I.'

Rule 3   Make sure you know the difference between 'whose' and 'who's'.
- **Whose** is the possessive of 'who'.
- **Who's** is the abbreviated form of 'who is'.
  EXAMPLES: (a) <u>Whose</u> script is this?
  (b) <u>Who's</u> coming to see Mr McGonagall play *Macbeth*?

Rule 4 • **Their** is the possessive of 'they'.
- **They're** is the abbreviated form of 'they are'.
- **There** denotes a fact or position.
  EXAMPLES: (a) <u>Their</u> names are always going to be associated with refusals to lie down and die properly.
  (b) <u>They're</u> both outstanding comedians in the history of tragic theatre.
  (c) <u>There</u> goes Romeo, complete with diamonds.

Rule 5 • **Its** (without an apostrophe) is the possessive of 'it'.
- **It's** (with an apostrophe) is the abbreviated form of 'it is'.
  EXAMPLES: (a) The audience, <u>its</u> fervour aroused, crowed 'cock-a-doodle-do' at Coates.
  (b) <u>It's</u> a pity (perhaps) that Shakespeare wasn't around to see McGonagall murder *Macbeth*.

Using the Rules

Now use the rules to correct errors in the following sentences:

(1)   Who's way of reciting Shakespeare was unique?

(2)   Listen to that audience out their, there all for McGonagall.

(3)   Its quite plain that London audiences were delighted by the Coates method of acting.

(4)   In you're role as Macbeth your going to have to wipe the floor with Macduff — even if that was not the original intention.

(5)   I wonder whose going to object to Romeo in crimson pantaloons.

(6)   Whose making all that noise? Its Coates's audience — crowing like a cock!

(7)   They're is no doubt about it, McGonagall had talent and the audience had it's thrill.

(8)   Robert Coates, who's nickname was 'Romeo', was the worst actor ever to appear at the Haymarket Theatre, and he was their on 9 December 1811.

(9)   Its a pity that Coates had to retire from the stage due to bankruptcy, but whose to blame?

(10)   Their is the very theatre where McGonagall played Macbeth. Unfortunately, there's no way of repeating his magnificent effort.

Punctuation – Stating and asking

STATEMENT

QUESTION

The worst actor ever to appear on a stage anywhere was Robert 'Romeo' Coates.

is a statement and is ended with a full stop

Was Robert 'Romeo' Coates the worst actor ever to appear on stage anywhere?

is a question and is ended with a question mark

Exercise A: Change the following statements into questions, using the bracketed word in each case to begin your question.
  (1) Criticism he put down to envy. [**Did**]
  (2) William McGonagall's first stage appearance was as Macbeth. [**Was**]
  (3) He dabbled there in amateur dramatics. [**Did**]
  (4) They had heard him reciting Shakespeare at work. [**Had**]
  (5) His scenes were well received. [**Were**]

Exercise B: Change the following questions into statements.
  (1) Were all the tickets sold rapidly?
  (2) Was his belief in his own theatrical genius unshakable?
  (3) Did every production in which he figured end in a riot?
  (4) Have all his audiences said he was unbelievable?
  (5) Was an actor of his calibre acceptable to London theatres?

Unit Two

Comprehension (2)

No Smoking

Tobacco is a dirty weed; I like it.
It satisfies no normal need; I like it.
It makes you thin, it makes you lean,
It takes the hair right off your bean;
It's the worst darn stuff I've ever seen,
I like it.

GRAHAM HEMMINGER

Smokers know that they are addicted to cigarettes. But it doesn't feel like an addiction until they try to stop.

And only then do they experience the callousness of this addiction, which abandons them to the anguish of knowing that one cigarette — any cigarette, half a cigarette, that butt in the ashtray, just a tiny puff — will release the mind held hostage.

Smokers know too that succumbing to an addiction does not advance man as a species on the evolutionary scale. They know their lungs are dripping with slag and every cigarette is a nail in their coffin. They feel the sting of the polite sign in the doctor's waiting room — 'Thank you for not smoking' — and the cancer advertisement in the train — 'Kiss a non-smoker today — enjoy the difference'.

Thus the segregation begins. Smokers smell distinctly of nicotine which they cannot smell themselves because, as any non-smoker will tell them, tobacco dulls the senses. They have two or more orange fingers and the occasional orange tooth. Smokers who started young are stunted.

Because of a basic insecurity that is either a consequence or a cause of smoking, they always have cigarettes upon their person, and fresh packets are never far away — stacked in the pantry, behind the piano or in the sock drawer.

And always there is the problem of disposing of those major pollutants — butts, ash and smoke.

Cigarettes meet a thankless end in the ashtray, the aluminium pie plate, the empty beer can, the dregs of coffee or the toilet bowl. The smoke permeates the drapes and carpets and sours the air like a cremated memory.

Cigarette ash also burns holes in furniture, clothes and people. It falls into drinks and food and blows out of the ashtray on to the cream carpet. And so the segregation continues.

Smokers are not allowed to smoke in trains, government buses and large sections of planes. Traditionally, they have never smoked in theatres but they are always the first into the foyer, lighting up the rescuing cigarette before they suffocate.

Smoking is discouraged while others eat, but some cheat and smoke during dessert, preferring the cigarette to the sweet. They cling to the inalienable right to smoke with coffee, cup after cup after cup.

While smokers are digesting social pressures to stop smoking, they must also absorb internal shocks to their wallets. The tax on cigarettes, increasing with every Budget, is gradually pricing some low-income smokers clear out of their addiction.

But not the hardened smokers, even if they have to roll their own. They smoke on — in moments of boredom, of stress, of calm. They hold the cigarette scissored between the first two fingers and, whenever they remember, they put it in their mouths and breathe it in.

If both hands are engaged, they clench the cigarette between the teeth. The smoke wafts into the eyes, producing the famous smoker's squint. And until the filter sogs and sags, they can still talk with their lips together, although they may not pronounce their vowels as roundly as they would like.

No one really knows why smokers must

smoke. Non-smoking theorists suggest smokers were deprived of their dummies when they were babies, and this, combined with a defect in their personalities, creates a compulsion to suck something. Smokers answer that a cigarette is merely a mechanical device that stops them eating and drinking too much, or climbing the walls with tension, at the same time keeping the economy fluid and besides, everybody should mind their own business.

But it *is* everybody's business because cigarette smoke, as a pretty cloud, floats unerringly to the nearest non-smoker, whose lungs are innocent of smoke. Nature, in her wisdom, abhors a vacuum.

Some smokers smoke in bed and, if they go to sleep with the cigarette in their mouths, it falls on their nylon nighties and burns them up. Sometimes they survive.

Some smokers, with criminal apathy, drop live cigarette butts out of car windows into a forest. It is a mystery why they do that. Perhaps no one told them not to, or maybe they do not know how hard it is to extinguish a fire in a forest.

Some smokers see another smoker have a massive heart attack, and this terrifies them into giving up smoking. If this terror is stronger than the desire to smoke, the separation from cigarettes will be permanent.

Nevertheless, those first weeks of withdrawal are an agony, not only for ex-smokers, but for all who speak to them, walk by them, sit beside them, look at them, live with them or do anything that could suggest cigarettes, such as burning the toast.

Time pacifies them, and they become non-smokers, but always they are divided by two emotions: a yearning for their dear dead friend, the cigarette; and pride that they mastered their killer, the cigarette.

But, in moments of doubt, they wonder if they have really been snatched from the jaws of death. All around them they see smokers still in the grip of the addiction that kills and maims. Why don't they all, without exception, die of heart or lung failure at 35 years of age? Why do some smokers live long, full, rich, healthy lives? Is there any justice?

[by ROBIN ROBERTSON
in *The Sydney Morning Herald*]

Check Your Understanding

(1) Explain why the writer says that the ex-smokers' minds are 'held hostage'?

(2) What is the meaning of 'succumbing to an addiction'?

(3) What does the word 'segregation' mean? In what ways are smokers segregated?

(4) What evidence does the writer produce to suggest that smoking is a dirty habit?

(5) What economic pressures are brought to bear on smokers to give up smoking?

(6) What impression of smokers does the writer offer the reader?

(7) What do smokers mean when they 'argue' that smoking keeps 'the economy fluid'?

(8) What is the meaning of 'apathy'? Why does the writer refer to the dropping of live cigarette-butts out of a car window into a forest as 'criminal apathy'?

(9) How can fear influence smokers to give up smoking?

(10) Explain in your own words the meaning of 'Time pacifies them'.

(11) Explain what the writer means by 'their dear dead friend'.

(12) What evidence can you find to suggest that the writer is against smoking?

(13) What evidence can you find to suggest that the writer sympathizes with smokers?

(14) Explain the meaning of: (a) the smoke permeates the drapes and carpets;
(b) whose lungs are innocent of smoke.

(15) Would you take up smoking after reading this article? Why?

(16) Can you find any clues to suggest that the writer may have been a smoker?

Working with Words (2)

Senior Spelling Demons	Confusing Pairs	Literature and Language		Increase Your Word Power
ceremony	course	speech	unanimous	vacillate
sergeant	coarse	humorous	accuracy	dogmatic
permanent	incite	digression	persuasion	artifice
pursue	insight	summary	repetition	trite
occasion	distract	explanation	appearance	venerate
opinion	detract	sympathy	jealousy	staid
journey	moral	prejudice	villainous	taciturn
bicycle	morale	belief	desperation	insipid
sufficient	vacation	contemporary	rhythm	ardent
preparation	vocation	melancholy	deceitful	zealous

Increase Your Word Power

Insert the correct list-words.

(1) Any expression that is used so often that it becomes boring and uninteresting is ....

(2) To .... is to waver, hesitate or be undecided in an opinion.

(3) To be .... is to be silent or reserved — definitely not outgoing.

(4) Another word for a crafty trick is ....

(5) To .... is to revere, to give awed respect.

(6) A person who states opinions arrogantly or without proof is being ....

(7) Lacking character, dull, without any special flavour, spiritless — all these are covered by the word ....

(8) A .... person is one who is steady, grave and sedate.

Change the Words

Complete the table:

Noun	Adjective	Verb	Adverb
sympathy			
			rhythmically
		believe	
deceit			
	persuasive		

Confusing Pairs

Select the correct list-word to complete the following sentences.

(1) V............... time had come round again, three glorious weeks of it.

(2) He had still not come to any conclusion on his life's calling, or v................

(3) She failed because she had not completed the c.................

(4) The rug was made of c................ wool.

(5) The sails were trimmed and the c................ was set.

(6) The coach gave a pep-talk to raise the team's m..................

(7) It was a m................ question — that is, a question of right and wrong.

(8) A parable is a tale with a m.................

(9) Bad behaviour will d................ from your chances of obtaining a good reference.

(10) One policeman was able to d................ the thief while the other snapped on the cuffs.

(11) The programme is called 'I................' because it attempts to give deeper awareness and understanding.

(12) The judge said that the youth had tried to i................ his friend to commit a crime.

Opposites Using the Prefix and Suffix

Use the prefixes | in-, im-, dis-, un- |

or the suffix | -less |

to transform the following words into their opposites.

| appearance | moral | sympathetic | humour | sufficient |
| accurate | speech | prepared | belief | permanent |

Meanings

Match up the list-words on the left with their meanings on the right.

pursue	précis
prejudice	all of one opinion
summary	adequate
unanimous	act or fact of repeating
melancholy	wicked
repetition	deviation from the main course
sufficient	unreasonable opinion or attitude
contemporary	sad and depressed
villainous	chase
digression	existing or happening at the same period

Word Origins — 'Scratch'

In handicap races, a contestant who *starts from scratch* runs without any special advantages, and in golf a *scratch player* is given no free strokes. At one time the *scratch runners* started at a line scratched in the turf, while those with handicaps began at a certain distance in front of this mark; and in the days when prizefighters fought on the bare earth, a scratch would be marked on the ground which they had to toe before they began. If a person is '*up to scratch*' it means that he or she is fit to do a job. When we talk about a horse being *scratched* from a race, we mean that its name is scratched or erased from the list of entries for the race.

Language in Action (2)

Bias Words

The word 'bias' comes from the French word *biais* meaning 'a slant'. Hence, a biased person keeps 'leaning to one side'. He is unable to maintain a balanced viewpoint. It is possible to have a bias in favour of or against almost any person or thing. Could you believe that one writer, a dietitian, said this about our famous meat pie:

'The Australian meat pie is a few pieces of dead, over-cooked meat and blobs of gravy, fittingly entombed in a casket of white flour and grease.'

What bias words can you find in this description? Try writing your own description of the pie, this time with a favourable bias.

Words can sway us to one course of action in preference to another. Bias words, if accepted without question, can cloud our understanding of issues and prevent us from remaining impartial. The media people and the advertisers, of course, are very aware of this. They know only too well that some words can 'purr' and others can 'snarl'. The real safeguard that we have when confronted with a bias situation is to take up a neutral position until we can examine the bias critically and test for accuracy.

Poets, writers and speakers are constantly acknowledging the role of bias words. Samuel Taylor Coleridge (1772-1834) once wrote: 'There are three classes into which all the women past seventy that ever I knew were to be divided: 1. That dear old soul; 2. That old woman; 3. That old witch.' More recently — on a radio programme — Bertrand Russell, a famous British philosopher, humorously remarked: 'I am firm; you are obstinate; he is pigheaded.' Here are some more examples, from *The New Statesman and Nation*:

I am fastidious. You are fussy. He is an old woman.
I daydream. You are an escapist. He should seek a psychiatrist.
I am sparkling. You are unusually talkative. He is drunk.

Favourable and Unfavourable

Look at the following table. The second column has words which normally are neutral. Unless they are put in context, they convey neither approval nor disapproval. On the other hand, the words in brackets *do* convey aproval or disapproval. Your task is to place these bracket words in their correct columns. One has been done to help you.

Favourable	Neutral	Unfavourable	Your Choice
daring	confident	reckless	[daring, reckless]
	wind		[zephyr, gust]
	smell		[stench, perfume]
	economical		[thrifty, stingy]
	smart		[ingenious, cunning]
	self-respect		[dignity, arrogance]
	intensely		[fanatically, zealously]
	thin		[emaciated, slender]
	big		[monstrous, mighty]
	known		[notorious, famous]
	little		[petite, puny]
	house		[home, hovel]
	think		[brood, imagine]
	girl		[lass, hussy]
	speech		[harangue, eloquence]
	old (people)		[senile, venerable]
	old (things)		[obsolete, antique]
	young		[childish, youthful]
	planner		[schemer, strategist]
	work		[chore, career]

Biased Sentences

Give the following sentences a bias by replacing the words in heavy type with words from the box that are similar in meaning.

gloom	gullible	fat	interrogated
snarling	exploiting	bluntly	flabby
cur	inexperienced	gang	capitalists

(1) The **dog** was **growling** in the **darkness**.

(2) The boy was **overweight** and his body was **soft** from lack of exercise.

(3) He expressed his viewpoint **frankly**.

(4) The police **questioned** the **group** of teenagers.

(5) Overseas **investors** are **developing** our mineral resources.

(6) The **new** teacher was **trusting**.

The Language of Literature (2)

Understanding Poetry

Poetry deals with the whole range of human experience. Often, a poem is written because the poet has been deeply moved by an experience or emotion and wishes to share it with others. The following poem-titles will give you some idea of the limitless subject-range of poetry: 'The Flea', 'Money', 'Get Up and Bar the Door', 'Steam Shovel', 'Death Be Not Proud', 'The Corn Flake', 'Husband and Wife', 'The Day That They Shot Santa Claus', 'Abandoned Cars', 'The Talking Clothes', 'The Goldfish', 'Love'. Many of the finest human experiences and emotions are recorded in poetry.

Poetry gives the appearance of being complex because of its variety of language, subject-matter, theme, imagery, rhythm, rhyme and structure. Yet, when we begin to understand a poem we begin to enjoy it. Of course, when we read a poem for the first time we should not always expect to make immediate sense of it. Often, we have to re-read the poem and think about it before it becomes meaningful to us. Understanding a poem frequently comes with asking questions. The following poetry-appreciation guide is one approach that has given our students confidence in understanding and evaluating all kinds of poetry.

POETRY APPRECIATION GUIDE

Subject-Matter
What is the poem about? ....
....
....

Theme
What was the poet's purpose or motive in writing the poem? (What is the central idea of the poem?)
....
....
....

Moods, **Emotions** and **Experiences**
What is the predominating mood of the poem? Is the poet flippant, sad, happy, serious, dignified, angry, contemplative, satirical (etc)?
....
....
....
....

Does the mood change?
....

What are some of the feelings expressed by the poet?
....

What feelings does the poet arouse in you?
....

Does the poet succeed in conveying his emotions to you?
....
....

Technique
LANGUAGE
Are the poet's words appropriate and vivid?
....
....

What emotions are built up around certain words?

....

....

IMAGERY

What is the effect produced by the use of metaphors, similes, personification, symbolism, striking description (etc)?

....

....

SOUNDS

What about the sounds in the poem? Are the sounds in harmony with the thought and imagery? Do the sounds suggest pictures, arouse emotions or bring out qualities of character?

....

....

....

....

What is the effect produced by the poet's use of alliteration, assonance, onomatopoeia, metre?

....

....

Are the musical qualities of the poem outstanding? ....

Is rhyme used for emphasis? ....

RHYTHM

What use is made of rhythm in the poem? Is the movement slow, steady or fast? Is the rhythm constant or does it vary? Is the rhythm appropriate to the mood and thought of the poem?

....

....

....

Form

How is the poem structured? How are the stanzas organized? Is the structure itself a convention, such as sonnet, ode, elegy, ballad, epic (etc)?

....

....

A Poem to Consider

Read the following poem carefully, then answer these questions.

(1) What was the poet's purpose in writing this poem?

(2) Do you think the title suits the poem? Why?

(3) What is the poet's view of his father at the beginning of the poem?

(4) Can you suggest why the poet's attitude to his father has changed by the third stanza?

(5) When the poet says at the end of the poem, 'I see myself ... not knee-high to this long-dead god', what is his attitude to his father and to himself?

(6) Did you enjoy this poem? Why? What feelings did it arouse in you?

MY FATHER BEGAN AS A GOD

My father began as a god,
full of heroic tales
of days when he was young.
His laws were as immutable
as if brought down from Sinai,
which indeed he thought they were.

He fearlessly lifted me to heaven
by a mere swing to his shoulder,
and made of me a godling
by seating me astride
our milch-cow's back, and, too,
upon the great white gobbler
of which others went in constant fear.

Strange then how he shrank and shrank
until by my time of adolescence
he had become a foolish small old man
with silly and outmoded views
of life and of morality.

Stranger still
that as I became older
his faults and his intolerances
scaled away into the past,
revealing virtues
such as honesty, generosity, integrity.

Strangest of all
how the deeper he recedes into the grave
the more I see myself
as just one more of all the little men
who creep through life
not knee-high to this long-dead god.

IAN MUDIE

Thinking and Reasoning (2)

Generalizations

We tend to judge things according to attitudes passed on to us by significant people in early life. We don't suspend judgement and try to weigh things, but instead are inclined to generalize too much.

Generalizing is an important part of our functioning as human beings. We are bombarded with so much information in our lives that we must organize it in order to be able to make sense of our world. So when we see a horse with four legs, then another horse with four legs, and so on, we generalize — by inductive reasoning (drawing conclusions about a whole class of things by observing particular instances) we make up a broad rule: 'Horses have four legs'. Such generalizations are valid and valuable.

However, one of the pitfalls of making generalizations is that we can, and often do, over-generalize — make generalizations where there is insufficient evidence to support a general claim. Such uncertain generalizations, or sweeping statements, can be avoided, or corrected, by the use of reasoning — by weighing the evidence before accepting or rejecting.

EXAMPLE OF UNCERTAIN GENERALIZATION: People today don't listen to one another.

Exercise 1

(1) Identify the uncertain generalizations in the cartoon.

(2) Rewrite them so that they are valid.

Exercise 2

Separate the valid generalizations from the uncertain ones in the following list.

(1) Elephants are herbivorous.

(2) Country life is slower-paced than city life.

(3) A man who drinks should not drive.

(4) Man is destroying his home planet.

(5) Marriage breakups are increasing in Australia.

(6) Fat people are always jolly.

(7) Inadequate diet affects the quality of students' work in Australian schools.

(8) Women are more soft-hearted than men.

(9) Whales are a declining species.

(10) The thirty-five-hour week will prove disastrous for society.

(11) Motorists are increasingly favouring small cars over large cars.

Defining Terms and Supporting with Evidence

1. One of the things you may have realized as you looked at the preceding generalizations is that some of them, although they are sweeping statements or over-generalizations as they stand, could become quite acceptable with a little tightening of the *definition of terms*.

For example, 'A man who drinks should not drive' is one that you may have judged to be an over-generalization. Yet you would possibly accept as valid, 'A man who drinks to excess should not drive' or 'A man who drinks to excess should not drive after drinking'. The difference between an acceptable generalization and an unacceptable one may often lie simply in the tightness or looseness of definition.

It is important to remember that when a generalization is used, its terms (and their 'conditions') need to be sufficiently clear for people to judge its validity.

Exercise 3

From the list of generalizations in Exercise 2 choose those which need a clearer definition of terms in order to be acceptable. Rewrite them, tightening the definitions so that they become acceptable generalizations.

2. The other important thing needed to enable us to judge the validity of a generalization is *supporting evidence*. Sometimes a statement will correspond to a mass of evidence from our own experience, so that we will accept it on that basis. (EXAMPLE: 'Healthy dogs have wet noses.') At other times we will want to suspend judgement while we ask, 'What evidence do you have to support that?'

Exercise 4

From the generalizations in Exercise 2 identify those that need supporting evidence before they can properly be assessed.

Exercise 5

Following is a list of generalizations. Write them into your work-book and, alongside each, record one of the following three judgements: **1.** valid generalization; **2.** definition of terms needed (in order for it to be evaluated); or **3.** supporting evidence needed (in order for it to be evaluated). In some cases you may want to use two of these categories for the same generalization.

(1) There are no winners in war.

(2) Parents are reluctant to talk to their children about sex.

(3) Few spiders are really dangerous.

(4) In all fields of athletics, performances are continuing to improve.

(5) The Australian birthrate is declining.

(6) French males are the most romantic in the world.

(7) Elderly people do not have enough to do.

(8) Hang-gliding is dangerous.

(9) Government-run businesses are always inefficient.

(10) The learning of languages in Australian schools is declining.

Concluding Thoughts

Whenever you hear or see words such as 'all', 'always', 'never', or any other words that imply complete exclusion or inclusion, look very hard at the generalization. Frequently it will not stand up to an objective evaluation. However, changing the terms to 'some', 'many', 'sometimes', 'often' (and so on) could well make the statement quite acceptable.

The over-use of generalizations — both valid and uncertain — is to be avoided. Where they occur, our task is to subject generalizations to a critical and objective evaluation before we accept or reject them.

Language Basics (2)

More Little Demon Errors

Here are some more rules that will help you avoid further Little Demon Errors.

Rule 1 ● **Less** is used of quantity; **fewer** always refers to number.
    EXAMPLES: (a) There is <u>less smoking</u> today.
               (b) <u>Fewer cigarettes</u> are being sold.

Rule 2 ● **And** connects similar ideas or things.
      ● **But** connects contrasting or dissimilar ideas or things.
        EXAMPLES: (a) Cigarettes are addictive <u>and</u> dangerous.
                   (b) Smoking is a dirty habit <u>but</u> I like it.

Rule 3 ● Avoid the use of **the reason why** and **because** in the same sentence.
        EXAMPLES: (a) Some people smoke <u>because</u> they feel insecure.
                   (b) One <u>reason</u> for people's smoking <u>is</u> their insecurity.

Using the Rules

Correct the following sentences.

(1) Less people seem to be finding pleasure in smoking.

(2) He is a happy but contented customer.

(3) A good reason why people give up smoking is because their health suffers.

(4) Fewer tobacco will be produced when non-smoking advertising increases.

(5) Until the filter sogs but sags, smokers can still talk with their lips together.

(6) Theatres have prohibited smoking and one reason why is because holes are burnt in carpets, clothes and people.

(7) The less cigarettes one smokes, the better.

(8) According to popular belief, smokers who are young but inexperienced have their growth stunted.

Punctuation — More on the full stop

As well as being used to end sentences, full stops are used:
● to indicate an abbreviation
● after initials
    EXAMPLES: (a) The tobacco firm was called the Highlife Co. of U.S.A.
               (b) The Managing Director was J. N. Leaf.

Be sure *not* to use a full stop in an abbreviation when the last letter of the abbreviation is also the last letter of the full word.
    EXAMPLE: (a) Docto**r** D**r**
       but: (b) Captain Capt.

Exercise A

Rewrite the following sentences, inserting the stops.

(1) Mr R Robertson, who wrote the article on non-smoking, left for Europe in Oct last year

(2) The Prof of the Med School was head of the Dept of Physiology

(3) The mgr of the factory is from NSW

(4) Mrs L T Baldwin : secy of the Bldg Trust Hrs 9 am to 4 pm

Exercise B

Supply the abbreviations for the following and punctuate correctly.

Colonel	received
Bachelor of Arts	department
headquarters	superintendent
for example	et cetera
that is	Commanding Officer
Doctor of Medicine	Reverend
anonymous	per hundred
centimetre	latitude
Very Important Person	leg before wicket
United Kingdom	kilogram

Unit Three

Comprehension (3)

'If these were the best years of our lives, why did we feel so caged?'

Childhood was a totalitarian regime from which I was very glad to escape. Still, we sentimentalise that time, remembering it as so many sandcastles and party balloons. Too often we remember ourselves running through long grass in slow-motion, with a dog at our side, like in those lyrical television commercials for cornflakes. Yet childhood was a time of indignities and injustice. A few days ago I saw a typical scene. A mother was dragging a tired child through a big store and he was lagging, dragging. Whereupon she suddenly flared and belted him repeatedly on the backside, causing his weariness to become tears and cries of outrage. Needless to say this embarrassed the mother all the more, so she hit him harder.

That was one of the worst aspects of childhood, the fact that a kid was property. Indeed, the dominant memory of childhood was being ordered about by parents, teachers, prefects, bullies. What were school assemblies but miniature Nuremberg rallies where pompous, petty officials could indulge their egos? I well remember the way the more paranoid teachers lorded it over their diminutive, powerless populations dressed in their compulsory uniforms.

But it was just as bad at home. One was ordered to wash one's hands, clean one's teeth or to kiss some overscented friend of mummy's whose gush of affection was manifestly insincere. Then there was the way you were sent to bed just when things were getting interesting or were forced to endure the ignominy of short pants. Don't ask silly questions. Just do what you're told. Don't answer back. How dare you talk to your mother like that? If children were to be seen and not heard, adults were to be obeyed and not questioned.

You were subject to various forms of martial law, including the curfew, and had no right of appeal. There were no political parties to represent you, no trade union to protect you. You had to eat your spinach, your pumpkin and your words. Again and again grown-ups would tell us how lucky we were to be young, urging us to enjoy our childhood while we could. And most of the time this sounded to be the ravings of lunatics, given our desperation to shake off the yoke of youth. Most of us would have gladly chucked our childhood away, which is why we were so anxious to get into long pants and out of school. To us the fence around the playground was like the Berlin Wall, with teachers substituting for the provosts with their machine guns.

Then there was the ugly side to our personalities. I well remember the poor mongoloid child who lived in a flat above the local bank. On the way home from school we'd find him on the swings in the park or hanging from the rusty chains of the iron maypole. We'd begin by just talking to him, laughing at him, forcing him to answer stupid questions like a trained cockatoo. But then our goading would become cruel and we'd start to hit him. Yet he was too amiable to run away. After all these years I can still see the hurt and confusion in his eyes. And at the time I felt a vague unease and guilt about it, but it didn't stop me from doing it again.

Another dimension of our cruelty was the way we'd pick on those post-war unfortunates, the migrant kids. The term 'New Australian' had to be forced into our vocabulary and remains as ludicrous as the euphemism 'national serviceman' for conscript. Yet it was certainly better than the epithet of reffo or DP. 'Go back to your own country,' we'd chant at some bewildered victim.

Of course the pecking order in the schoolyard is as vicious as that of a fowlyard. The bullying is stratified in exactly the same way with some poor little bastard being the ultimate victim. He might be weak or weak-minded or particularly shabbily dressed. If he was especially vulnerable, he'd be the target. Years later I read *Lord of the Flies*, and when the kids killed poor Piggy it had the unmistakable ring of truth.

As well as being racist and religious bigots, kids are also snobs. I well remember times in class when we'd turn our attention to the poorest, most neglected child present; to someone who came to school in hand-me-downs, looking just a little dirtier than the rest of us. One such child, a girl called Val, was nicknamed Stinky by us all and her life must have been a crucifixion. For my own part, I suffered the nickname of Boofhead, and, although my cranium was only slightly larger than the normal, I felt as though it were a dirigible.

While I remember some of my teachers with affection and gratitude, I remember others with detestation. It's amazing the number of classroom sadists I encountered, worse bullies than any you'd find in the playground.

And I also remember the agonisingly slow progress of the classroom clock. Nowadays an hour seems a minute, a week lasts a day. But then time was interminable. Every class seemed a life sentence. I also remember the turgid rhetoric of Anzac Day speeches and the pompous lyrics of school songs. (Fancy being forced to sing stupid verses about one's undying debt to a group of prefab classrooms and a patch of broken asphalt.) Then there was the hollow mockery of the flag ceremony: 'I love God, I love God and my country, I will honour the flag, I will serve my King and cheerfully obey my parents, teachers and the laws.' And they talk of indoctrination on mainland China and tut-tut about Chairman Mao's *Little Red Book*.

Then there was the tyranny of sport, of the compulsory worship of football. And because I was no good at it, I was one of the poor devils that waited and waited to be picked for sides. Two of those odious school heroes (most of them finished up on points duty or as unsuccessful commercial travellers — there's a certain vindictive pleasure in that), would stand out in front and choose the kids they wanted, like Southern gentlemen at a slave auction. A barbarous system, because someone had to be last.

Then there was the tyranny of ignorance, not knowing about things. Of being curious about sex and not being told. I can remember one day hearing a boy I rather admired — I think his name was Lindsay Shields — saying a funny word in the school ground. For some reason it struck me as an amusing group of letters. . . . While I had no idea as to its meaning, it stuck in my mind and, that night, when cleaning my shoes, I was chanting it to myself. Whereupon my grandmother came charging through the door like a Valkyrie and boxed my ears, thus branding the word for ever in my vocabulary.

Of course, there were good things like Crosbie Morrison's nature broadcasts and hearing Grandpa and his mates sing their favourite songs like *The Rugged Cross* and *The Galloping Major*. And being given a few legs to crack from the crayfish which in those days was working man's food.

But for the most part childhood was crushing boredom. It was sitting on a kerb writing down the numbers of trams or the number-plates of cars as they came and went. It was swapping comics that you'd read twice already. It was being so limited in finance and freedom that one's options were pitifully narrow. It was being told to put on a jumper, to stay in the backyard, to do one's homework. It was being required to mow the lawn weekend after weekend, a task that seemed absurdly repetitive and ultimately meaningless.

And, increasingly, it was coping with the sufferings of puberty. Most of the time when I was a kid I felt myself on the receiving end of adult indifference or incompetence. And I remember pledging that I would be different when I grew up, that I would remember what it meant to be a kid. Yet when I think of my own impatience with my children, I know that I've forgotten.

[from *The Unspeakable Adams* by PHILLIP ADAMS]

Check Your Understanding

(1) The writer, Phillip Adams, refers to childhood as a 'totalitarian regime'. What does he mean by this phrase? (You may like to use the back-of-the-book dictionary to help you.)

(2) What do 'sandcastles' and 'party balloons' suggest about childhood? How does this picture of childhood differ from that of Adams?

(3) What is Adams's attitude to school and teachers?

(4) What does Adams mean by the 'ignominy of short pants'?

(5) The writer says: 'There were no political parties to represent you, no trade union to protect you.' What is he implying about childhood?

(6) 'To us the fence around the playground was like the Berlin Wall.' What does this statement reveal about Adams's feelings towards school?

(7) What does the simile 'like a trained cockatoo' suggest about the mongoloid child's relationship to Adams and his friends?

(8) What evidence can you find to suggest that Adams still feels guilty about his treatment of the mongoloid child?

(9) Explain the writer's 'pecking order' metaphor.

(10) Adams is certainly critical of teachers and parents. What is his attitude to the 'kids' themselves?

(11) What is his attitude now to the treatment of a girl called Val?

(12) How did the writer as a boy react to the nickname 'Boofhead'?

(13) What does Adams mean by, 'Every class seemed a life sentence'?

(14) How did Adams feel about the Anzac ceremony?

(15) What criticism did Adams have of the flag ceremony?

(16) What does Adams mean by the 'tyranny of sport'? Why do you think Adams disliked sport?

(17) Why does Adams compare the 'two odious school heroes' to 'Southern gentlemen at a slave auction'?

(18) Do you think the writer's grandmother was justified in boxing his ears? Why?

(19) What evidence can you find to suggest that Adams liked his grandfather?

(20) What is the writer's view of his own performance as a parent?

(21) This article was written for a daily newspaper. Do you think it would appeal to readers? Why?

(22) Can you find evidence to show that Adams is biased? Explain your findings. Can you find evidence that Adams tries to be impartial? Explain your findings.

(23) What is the tone of the article?

(24) Give the meanings of the following words from the article. (The back-of-the-book dictionary will help you.)

Paragraph 1: lyrical, indignity, flared
Paragraph 2: dominant, pompous, petty, paranoid, diminutive
Paragraph 3: manifestly
Paragraph 4: martial, curfew, provosts
Paragraph 5: amiable
Paragraph 6: ludicrous, euphemism, epithet
Paragraph 7: vulnerable
Paragraph 8: racist, bigot, cranium, dirigible
Paragraph 9: gratitude, sadist
Paragraph 10: interminable, turgid, rhetoric, mockery
Paragraph 11: odious, vindictive, barbarous
Paragraph 12: chant
Paragraph 15: puberty, indifference.

Working with Words (3)

Senior Spelling Demons	Confusing Pairs	Language and Literature		Increase Your Word Power
autumn	statue	literature	soliloquy	infamous
witness	stature	surprise	hilarious	adversary
favourite	sight	interrogative	comedy	sordid
resistance	cite	allusion	emphasize	diversion
neighbour	sole	interpretation	synopsis	acquiesce
commit	soul	ridicule	summary	ludicrous
refrigerator	eminent	contradiction	authentic	intercede
necessary	imminent	significance	conclusion	provocative
business	incredible	symbolic	rhyme	prolific
safety	incredulous	illiterate	subtle	turbulent

Change the Words

Change to nouns

(a) hilarious ....
(b) turbulent ....
(c) intercede ....
(d) provocative ....
(e) authentic ....
(f) infamous ....

Change to verbs

(a) summary ....
(b) interpretation ....
(c) diversion ....
(d) allusion ....
(e) significance ....
(f) necessary...............................

Change to adjectives

(a) comedy ....

(b) adversary ....

(c) ridicule ....

(d) conclusion ....

(e) contradiction ....

(f) acquiesce ....

Change to adverbs

(a) safety...

(b) emphasize ....

(c) incredible ....

Add prefixes to form opposites of

(a) necessary ....

(b) religious ....

(c) accessible ....

(d) similar ....

(e) polite ....

(f) agreeable ....

(g) legitimate ....

Confusing Pairs

Write out and complete the following sentences, selecting the correct words from the brackets.

(1) An [**imminent/eminent**] woman scientist was the [**soul/sole**] survivor of the explosion.

(2) The Chinese [**statue/stature**] was so old that visitors to the museum were [**incredible/incredulous**].

(3) The lawyer was able to [**sight/cite**] a similar case.

(4) The [**sight/cite**] of the snow falling touched the poet's [**sole/soul**].

(5) The survivor's story about the cannibals was [**incredulous/incredible**].

(6) The appearance of the dark clouds suggested that a storm was [**imminent/eminent**].

Opposites

Find list-words opposite in meaning to these words. The first letters have been given to help you.

(1) **danger**   s........................

(2) **tragedy**   c........................

(3) **friend**   a........................

(4) **calm**   t........................

(5) **disagree**   a........................

(6) **clean**   s........................

(7) **serious**   h........................

(8) **obvious**   s........................

(9) **agreement**   c........................

(10) **humble**   e........................

Find the Word

Replace the words or phrases in heavy type with words from the list which are similar in meaning.

(1) The boxer's **opponent** was formidable.

(2) A **distinguished** heart surgeon performed the operation.

(3) The chancellor of the university **consented without protest to** the lecturers' demands.

(4) Doctor Seuss is a **very productive** writer of children's books.

(5) The waves were **full of violent motion**.

(6) T. S. Eliot made an **indirect reference** to Hamlet.

(7) The pensioner lived in **dirty** surroundings.

(8) The nurse tried to **plead or act on behalf of another**.

(9) The newspaper editorial was **absurd**.

(10) He possessed a **genuine** Roman coin.

(11) The actor's performance was **very funny and merry.**

(12) The highwayman was **notorious**.

Word Origins — 'Exclusion'

If you are 'excluded' from the classroom you are shut out. 'Exclude' comes from the Latin *ex* ('out of') and *claudere/clausus* ('to shut'). Here is a list of other words derived from *claudere*: include, conclude, recluse, seclude, enclose, preclude, clause, cloister, disclose. Now match some of them with the meanings beneath.

(1) To shut in all around.

(2) A part of a sentence.

(3) One who lives in isolation.

(4) To shut off from other people.

(5) To prevent.

(6) To reveal.

Language in Action (3)

Tautology and Redundancy

Tautology is the saying of the same thing twice over in different words. For example: 'In my opinion, I think the unemployment problem can be solved.' In this case, either 'In my opinion' or 'I think' is redundant. You should avoid unnecessary repetition of this kind.

Remove the Tautologies

Many public figures in the media and elsewhere are sometimes guilty of tautology. Most of the examples beneath are from the utterances of well-established communicators. See whether you can correct the errors.

(1) I've had to change my mental thinking. (Football commentator)

(2) I have already indicated the situation in relation to the overseas ships bringing fuel to this country from other parts of the world. A satisfactory arrangement has now been made because of my direct intervention, by myself, personally. . . . (State Minister)

(3) The offender escaped on foot by running. (Radio newsreader)

(4) The unemployed who haven't got a job . . . (Leader of the Opposition)

(5) We'll see if we can get the exact facts. (Radio commentator)

(6) He left the country briefly for a short time. (Radio commentator)

(7) Everybody has unanimously agreed with the umpire's decision. (Television commentator)

(8) There have been some new innovations. (Prime Minister)

(9) Let me repeat that again. (Television sports commentator)

(10) Television has a lot of future potential. (President of the Australian Broadcasting Tribunal)

(11) There are so many vacant gaps to be filled. (Prominent playwright)

(12) It was a chance coincidence. (Television commentator)

(13) The government does not consider the explanation adequate enough. (Politician)

(14) Our new young star will be elevated up to first grade. (Football commentator)

(15) No company should have the entire monopoly. (Businessman)

(16) The soldiers had returned back to their own territory. (Newsreader)

(17) The union has no false illusions about support from its own members. (Union leader)

(18) There are several past precedents for the government's actions. (Politician)

(19) The future prospects of our client are excellent. (Industrial reporter)

(20) He was doing his club a bad disservice. (Television commentator)

The Language of Literature (3)

THE JAGUAR

The apes yawn and adore their fleas in the sun.
The parrots shriek as if they were on fire, or strut
Like cheap tarts to attract the stroller with the nut.
Fatigued with indolence, tiger and lion

Lie still as the sun. The boa-constrictor's coil
Is a fossil. Cage after cage seems empty, or
Stinks of sleepers from the breathing straw.
It might be painted on a nursery wall.

But who runs like the rest past these arrives
At a cage where the crowd stands, stares, mesmerized,
As a child at a dream, at a jaguar hurrying enraged
Through prison darkness after the drills of his eyes

On a short fierce fuse. Not in boredom —
The eye satisfied to be blind in fire,
By the bang of blood in the brain deaf the ear —
He spins from the bars, but there's no cage to him

More than to the visionary his cell:
His stride is wildernesses of freedom:
The world rolls under the long thrust of his heel.
Over the cage floor the horizons come.

TED HUGHES

The Jaguar — Points to ponder

(1) What impression does the poet give the reader of the apes?

(2) The poet does not offer the reader a very flattering picture of the parrots. Explain how he creates an unflattering picture.

(3) Why does the poet refer to the boa-constrictor's coil as 'a fossil'?

(4) At the beginning of the third stanza there is a sudden change of mood. Explain how this occurs.

(5) Why is the crowd mesmerized?

(6) Why does the poet say, 'there's no cage to him'?

(7) Explain what the poet means by, 'His stride is wildernesses of freedom'.

(8) What is the poet's message concerning the jaguar? Does the poet sympathize with the animal? Use evidence from the poem to support your viewpoint.

(9) What is your attitude to the jaguar? Do you feel he overcomes his state of captivity? Why?

(10) Did you find 'The Jaguar' an enjoyable poem? Why?

Thinking and Reasoning (3)

Emotive Language

Speakers and writers who set out to persuade us of the 'rightness' of what they have to say, often try to get us thinking with our emotions. The most common technique is to use words that pose as accurate, descriptive words, but which actually carry an emotional content as well — a bias towards approval or disapproval. Such words are called *emotive words*, *bias words*, or *coloured terms*. The term 'unemployed person' is a fairly neutral term; the term 'dole bludger' also describes an unemployed person but has strong overtones of disapproval or undesirability as well. It is an emotive term.

Exercise 1

Sort the following columns of words into their correct pairs. In each case identify the more emotive term.

Column 1	Column 2
food	compromising
overweight	work-shy
predictable	fastidious
lazy	migrant
flexible	careful
derelict	slops
unadventurous	stinginess
having principles	rigid
drab	fat
tidy	reliable
wog	homeless person
parsimony	colourless

Exercise 2

Read the following extract from *The Idiot* by Fyodor Dostoevsky, and then answer the questions.

> To kill for murder is a punishment incomparably worse than the crime itself. Murder by legal sentence is immeasurably more terrible than murder by brigands. . . . There is the sentence, and the whole torture lies in the fact that there is certainly no escape, and there is no torture in the world more terrible. You may lead a soldier out and set him facing the cannon in battle and fire at him and he'll still hope; but read a sentence of certain death over the same soldier, and he will go out of his mind or burst into tears. Who can tell whether human nature is able to bear this madness? Why this hideous, useless, unnecessary outrage?

(1) What feelings about capital punishment does Dostoevsky convey in this extract?

(2) How does he convey these feelings?

(3) Comment on the emotive force of 'murder by legal sentence' as compared with 'capital punishment'.

(4) 'Incomparably worse' and 'immeasurably more terrible'. What effect is added by the use of the adverbs 'incomparably' and 'immeasurably'?

(5) What other emotive terms are used in this extract in reference to capital punishment?

(6) 'Hideous', 'useless' and 'unnecessary' are all adjectives used to describe the legal taking of a life. To what extent do you see them as accurate descriptive words and to what extent do you see them as emotive terms?

(7) What would be lost in this extract if the writer tried to express his viewpoint without using emotive terms?

Emotion-Arousal and Advertising

Much consumer advertising makes an attempt to arouse an emotional response within us. Often the advertisement or commercial will deliberately try to create an emotion — e.g. joy, pride, carefreeness, life-loving. Once we identify that desirable emotion with the advertiser's product, we are more likely to buy. Similarly, once we identify a product with the removal of anxiety, we are more likely to buy.

At other times the advertisement will seek to remind us of a need (or even create one in us), so that it can promise satisfaction of that need by way of its product. Such attempts to arouse needs, to appeal primarily to needs, to use or appeal to our emotions, are all attempts to make us think with our emotions — to get us to suspend critical analysis and respond at a level of feeling.

Exercise 3

Study the advertisement reproduced on pp. 44–45, and then answer these nine questions.

(1) Repairmen don't 'enthuse' or 'rejoice' over the new Hoover 700 Series. What does this imply about how we consumers will feel about the product?

(2) Which of the following would you judge as being factual terms and which as emotive terms: 'reliable', 'simpler to operate', 'enormous capacity', 'love', 'good looks'?

THE REASON HE HATES IT

IS THE REASON YOU'LL LOVE IT.

It's hardly surprising that washing machine repairmen aren't too enthusiastic about our big new 700 Series washing machines.

After all, why should they enthuse over a washing machine based on anything as reliable as our old 600 Series?

And why should they rejoice over the fact that we've redesigned the console to make it not only simpler to operate, but also rust-proof?

But whilst the 700 Series is bad news for people who fix washing machines, it's good news for people who use them.

You'll love it for its enormous capacity. You'll love it for its solid construction and reliability. You'll love it for its good looks. And you'll love it because you can leave it.

Just load it, set it, forget it. Nothing could be easier.

You'll love it for its efficient system of removing lint from the wash. And for its ability to wash delicates delicately and for giving heavily soiled items a thorough going over.

Have a look at the range of washers in the new Hoover 700 Series. Big, fully automatic washers made the way they don't make washers anymore.

HOOVER 700 SERIES

HOV 8621 WW

(3) What effect does the repetition of 'You'll love it' have?

(4) The most frequently repeated emotive word in this ad is 'love'. How strong an emotive word is this? Why?

(5) Is it really possible to 'love' a washing machine?

(6) How durable are emotive words such as 'love', 'big', 'good' and 'bad'? Do they appear to have lost much impact over the years?

(7) Comment on the emotive content of 'good news'.

(8) These machines are 'made the way they don't make washers anymore'. What factual content, if any, does this statement convey?

(9) Comment on the use of 'delicately' and 'a thorough going over'. To what extent do you see them as both factual and emotive in content?

Exercise 4

(1) Write your own advertisement for a new product, Spatter-Veg, a sort of spray-pack Vegemite! Make sure you use plenty of emotion-arousing language.

(2) Write an objective, impartial, purely descriptive advertisement for the same product.

(3) Which of the two is the more effective? What criteria are you using to judge effectiveness?

Conclusion

By recognizing that emotive words and phrases are deliberately being used in the presentation of an argument, or that language is being deliberately used to create an emotional response within us, we are better able to think logically. We avoid being 'hooked' by critically examining the evidence offered, instead of allowing ourselves to be swayed emotionally.

Once again we need to emphasize that the use of emotive words and phrases is not something we can always classify as 'bad'. Without emotive terms our language would be considerably less interesting. But when we are concerned with reasoned thinking, we must guard against the impact of deliberately biased language.

Language Basics (3)

Unrelated Words and Phrases

Words and phrases are *misplaced* or *unrelated* when there is no subject to which they clearly refer, or when they give the sentence a meaning that is unclear or different from that intended. The following rules will be helpful.

Rule 1 • **Participles** must relate to definite subjects.
    EXAMPLES: (a) <u>Lagging</u> behind, <u>the child</u> followed his mother through the store.
              (b) <u>Ridiculed</u> by the teachers, the unhappy <u>students</u> could not wait to leave school.

Rule 2 • **Infinitive expressions** must relate to definite subjects.
    EXAMPLE: <u>To understand</u> your child properly, <u>you</u> need the memory of your own childhood.

Using the Rules

Use the rules to rewrite the following sentences, putting in subjects and changing the verb forms where necessary.

(1) On arriving at school, bullying became vicious.

(2) Meeting the poor mongoloid child, stupid questions would be asked.

(3) Although nicknamed Boofhead, evidence was lacking.

(4) Chanting to himself, the smack to the head came unexpectedly.

(5) While still in short pants, his parents set him contradictory standards to follow.

(6) To avoid being bored, the number-plates of cars were written down.

(7) Time seemed interminable, sitting in our classrooms.

(8) To keep control, the fence around the playground was like the Berlin Wall.

Punctuation – Using capital letters

Use capital letters:

1. To begin **sentences**.
    EXAMPLE: <u>C</u>hildhood was a totalitarian regime from which I was very glad to escape.

2. To begin the names of **people**.
    EXAMPLE: My school friend was <u>L</u>indsay <u>S</u>hields.

3. To begin the names of **countries**, **places**, and words derived from these.
    EXAMPLES: (a) They talk about a time of change in <u>C</u>hina.
             (b) The most interesting <u>C</u>hinese city is <u>P</u>eking.

4. To begin the names of the **months, days of the week, religious festivals** and **special days** or occasions.

EXCEPTION: The names of the seasons are not capitalized.

EXAMPLES: (a) The <u>C</u>hristmas holidays began on the <u>M</u>onday of the second week in <u>D</u>ecember.

(b) The <u>F</u>irst of <u>S</u>eptember marks the end of <u>w</u>inter.

5. For **titles** such as those of books or films.

NOTE: The little words such as 'of', 'the', 'and', 'in', 'by', in such titles are not usually capitalized.

EXAMPLE: By now, the author ought to be able to write a book called, perhaps, '<u>G</u>rowing <u>U</u>p and the <u>P</u>roblems of <u>P</u>arenthood'.

Exercises

Capitalize the following sentences correctly.

(1) what were school assemblies but miniature nuremberg rallies?

(2) years later i read *lord of the flies*, and when the kids killed poor piggy it had the unmistakable ring of truth.

(3) they tut-tut about chairman mao's *little red book*.

(4) of course, there were good things like crosbie morrison's nature broadcasts and hearing grandpa and his mates sing their songs.

(5) their favourite songs were: the rugged cross and the galloping major.

(6) a girl called val was nicknamed stinky by us all.

(7) i was not looking forward to anzac day, which was in april.

(8) my mother put away the easter eggs carefully.

Unit Four

Comprehension (4)

Radio

In 1956 the management of radio stations reeled back from the TV screen like so many blacksmiths confronted by a horseless carriage. Or like hand-weavers threatened by the flying shuttle. Surely they were doomed. Surely their medium would become an anachronism.

But catastrophe somehow failed to befall them. Instead, radio has enjoyed an astonishing boom with many stations earning larger profits than the major channels. In economic terms at least, the medium has gone from strength to strength.

Many factors have contributed to this apparent paradox. First of all, there was a technological breakthrough. Just as the hand-held camera revolutionized film-making, the hand-held transistor freed radio from the lounge room and kitchen.

And while TV was getting involved in the heavy costs of variety and drama production, radio had reduced its programming to what's variously described as Top Forty or Fat Fifty. The vast record libraries were no more, having been replaced by a small shelf of 45s.

Soon all dramatic presentations had been abandoned, apart from replays of old soap operas. Commercial radio had become remarkably simple and efficient.

The surprising loyalty of radio audiences was another factor in radio's favour. Whereas television consumes personalities and programme concepts voraciously, radio audiences seem willing to listen to the same breakfast announcer or DJ forever. Indeed, many of the most popular jockeys are veritable geriatric cases, having been boop-boop-a-dooping since the early 50s.

Having established itself as a juke box, radio then became a phone box as well. For it discovered that housewives were a lonely, alienated group, yearning for some form of social involvement.

Thus it introduced the dreaded talk-back show, providing group therapy for the prisoners of domestic bliss. Once again, the programme concept was simplicity itself, and remarkably inexpensive. After all, much of their airtime was now occupied by voluble amateurs.

And last but not least, radio began to benefit from the growing boredom with television, a disenchantment that's measurable in a careful analysis of rating surveys.

However, while radio is a great medium for the licensees (and for those listeners content with the obsessively repeated pops and pitiless chatter) it remains a greater wasteland than television has ever been. While television has borne the brunt of criticism, radio has been getting away with murder. Writers and actors can expect nothing from it and programme innovation is all but non-existent.

Yet radio is a medium that could well afford to make a contribution to Australian culture, and it should be required to observe drama quotas along with the TV industry. As well, it's a medium that should be required to do much more for children and for the so-called minority audiences.

Given the flexibility of audio tape, radio production costs are negligible and permit a higher degree of formal innovation than television. For example, where TV necessitates set building and costume design, the radio audience can simply imagine them. And a cast of thousands is as close as the sound-effects library.

[from *Adams with Added Enzymes* by PHILLIP ADAMS]

Check Your Understanding

(1) Why does the writer compare the managers of radio stations to blacksmiths and hand-weavers?

(2) What technological breakthrough helped save radio from catastrophe? Explain how?

(3) Explain the meaning of: (a) 'television consumes personalities and programme concepts voraciously';
(b) 'many of the most popular jockeys are veritable geriatric cases'.

(4) Why does the writer refer to radio as (a) 'a juke box', and (b) 'a phone box'?

(5) Explain why the writer should refer to housewives as 'prisoners of domestic bliss'.

(6) How did radio provide 'social involvement' for housewives?

(7) Why, according to the writer, are talkback programmes inexpensive?

(8) What evidence can you find to show that the writer is critical of radio?

(9) How does the writer believe that radio could be improved?

(10) What does the writer mean by, 'a cast of thousands is as close as the sound-effects library'?

(11) What are the main reasons the writer gives for the survival and success of radio?

(12) Work out the meanings of the following words as they are used in the passage:
(a) reeled   (c) alienated   (e) innovation
(b) veritable   (d) disenchanted   (f) therapy

Working with Words (4)

Senior Spelling Demons	Confusing Pairs	People		Increase Your Word Power
beginning	born	amazement	humility	delude
absence	borne	nuisance	irresponsible	dissuade
hindrance	recent	treacherous	similarity	docile
prosperous	resent	excellent	discretion	indulgent
vicinity	human	conscious	disapprove	escapade
answer	humane	courageous	deceive	replenish
piece	elicit	doubtful	reprimand	culprit
receive	illicit	callous	obstinate	pervade
island	industrial	passionate	impulsive	sedate
forty	industrious	reconciliation	earnest	divulge

Change the Words

Change to nouns

(a) treacherous ....

(b) conscious ....

(c) excellent ....

(d) courageous ....

(e) deceive ....

(f) irresponsible ....

(g) indulgent ....

Change to adjectives

(a) absence ....

(b) similarity ....

(c) pervade ....

(d) humility ....

(e) deceive ....

(f) resent ....

Change to people

(a) industrial ....

(b) island ....

(c) beginning ....

Change to verbs

(a) reconciliation ....

(b) industrial ....

(c) prosperous ....

(d) hindrance ....

(e) excellent ....

(f) humility ....

(g) indulgent ....

Change to adverbs

(a) conscious ....

(b) similarity ....

(c) deceive ....

(d) amazement ....

(e) earnest ....

(f) pervade ....

Increase Your Word Power

From the boxes accompanying each of the following sentences, select the word or phrase which best conveys the meaning of the word printed in heavy type.

(1) The doctors hoped that the infection would remain localized and not **pervade** the adjoining tissue.

circumscribe	diffuse or extend through	cluster	over-stimulate

(2) The spy was induced to **divulge** the secret plans.

reveal	limit	perpetrate	oppose

(3) Thorough training was needed before the animal was **docile** enough to be ridden.

powerful	stubborn	high-spirited	manageable

(4) Letting down bicycle tyres is more than an irritating prank and I hope the **culprit** will not **delude** himself or herself about that.

| innocent victim | leader | comedian | guilty one |

| deceive | congratulate | contradict |

(5) While away a tropical dream in the **sedate** surroundings of Palmbrook.

| ultramodern | habitually calm | festive | ritual |

(6) The travellers were able to **replenish** their water-supply at the oasis.

| purify | take back | medicate | fill again |

(7) The headmaster questioned the students closely about the **escapade** that had caused so much commotion during the assembly.

| mischievous adventure | terrifying experience |

| formidable confrontation | personality clash |

Antonyms

Find antonyms in the list for each of these words:

(a) give ....

(b) cautious ....

(c) persuade ....

(d) separation ....

(e) cowardly ....

(f) difference ....

(g) impecunious ....

(h) certain ....

(i) frivolous ....

(j) sensitive ....

Confusing Pairs

Use one of the words in brackets to replace the italicized word or phrase.

(1) The Olympic torch was *carried* by a marathon runner. [**born/borne**]

(2) The students are likely to *feel indignant about* having to assemble and stand about in the hot sun for more than an hour. [**resent/recent**]

(3) Nurses are members of a *kind and merciful* profession. [**human/humane**]

(4) Arms and explosives are *illegal* imports. [**elicit/illicit**]

(5) Insect life in the tropics becomes most *active and diligent* during the wet season. [**industrious/industrial**]

Prepositions

Complete the following by supplying the correct prepositions.
EXAMPLE: Deceived **by** her smile

(1) dissuaded .... trying

(2) replenish .... supplies

(3) conscious .... the temperature

(4) elicit .... him

(5) vicinity .... the church

(6) resented .... the rest of the class

(7) disapprove .... loud music

(8) absent ....work

(9) hindered .... the crowd

(10) irresponsible .... her

Origins — Kissing under the mistletoe

This old Druid superstition originally had a much more important meaning than the modern excuse for a quick kiss. As well as being a cure-all in times of sickness, mistletoe was thought to have fertility-promoting qualities that were very powerful. It also often grows in oak trees, which themselves had magical properties. To hold mistletoe over a girl's head was therefore to help her to conceive many children.

Language in Action (4)

Circumlocution and Verbosity

'Circumlocution' comes from the Latin *circum* ('around') and *loqui/locutus* ('to speak'). Thus 'circumlocution' means 'talking around the point'. 'Verbosity' comes from the Latin *verbosus* ('full of words'), which in turn is derived from *verbum* ('word). 'Verbosity' means 'the use of an unnecessary number of words'.

When sentences are longwinded and contain unnecessary words, the writer is guilty of circumlocution or verbosity. For example: 'At the present time she has her abode in a rural environment.' This sentence could be written much more simply: 'Now she lives in the country.'

Look at the comic strip below. Find an example of circumlocution and rewrite in simple terms. (Note that one word has been *misused*.)

THE WIZARD OF ID —   **By Parker and Hart**

Rewrite in Simple Sentences

The following sentences contain examples of circumlocution and verbosity. Rewrite the sentences in simple English.

(1) Because of inclement weather conditions the builders desisted from their labours.

(2) The traveller decided to fortify his constitution with good food.

(3) The teacher was made the recipient of a new roll-book.

(4) The severe injuries sustained by the motorist necessitated the summoning of a general practitioner.

(5) The child was attacked near his place of residence by a savage member of the canine species.

(6) The motorist was arrested by a law-enforcement officer because he had partaken of too much liquid refreshment.

(7) No information is available from employers as to the likelihood of a reduction in working hours for union members in the near future.

(8) After a nocturnal rest, we partook of the morning repast prepared by the cook.

(9) An early investigation by the company's director as to where the responsibility for the loss lies, is not beyond the bounds of possibility.

(10) It is anticipated with reasonable certainty that there will be a cessation of hostilities between the two countries.

(11) The listener found himself unable to believe his auditory faculties.

(12) The accident has necessitated an extension of travelling time for all vehicles.

(13) The guardians of the law were making enquiries as to the whereabouts of the two malefactors.

(14) There will be a postponement in the departure time of the train.

(15) A cessation of work by car employees has been avoided by the promptness of the decision by the management to increase the workers' monetary supply.

The Language of Literature (4)

Studying the Novel

Keep in mind the existence of the following interwoven **elements** in the novel:

Theme: the main idea(s) or intention(s) from which the novel derives and which, in turn, pervade(s) the novel. (Plot and Characters illustrate or work out the implications of the Theme.)
Examples of themes: The search for a meaning in life.
The power of nature.
Greed and unscrupulous ambition.
Fate as the prime force in human affairs.
Love — its responsibilities and its consequences.
Man's inhumanity to man.

Setting: the background of time(s) and place(s) through which the story runs and the characters move.

Plot: the novel's framework, story-line or plan of events with which the characters are involved.

Characters: the persons involved to a greater or lesser extent in the plot — usually comprising main character(s) and minor characters.

Suspense: the quality of anxious uncertainty felt by the reader about the outcome of some particular crisis concerning one or more of the characters or the events in the novel.

Climax: occurs whenever the action reaches the highest point of physical or emotional tension. Minor climaxes are often found on the way to the major climax, which usually heralds the end of the story.

Here are the elements of the novel as they appear in *The Adventures of Huckleberry Finn*, by Mark Twain.

Characters
- Huckleberry Finn – the realist.
- Tom Sawyer – the romantic.
- The innocent Jim – a runaway slave.
- Characters such as 'the duke' and 'the king' – riverside rogues.

Themes
- The moral decadence of Deep South society with its core of slavery and reliance on both deliberate and unintentional cruelty – 'human beings can be awful cruel to one another'.
- The conflict between romance and realism.
- One boy's growth to maturity.

Setting
The raft on the great brown river – the Mississippi – together with the settlements on its shores where all kinds of people are encountered.

Plot
Huck has escaped from his drunken Pap. Jim, a slave, has run away. They meet on Jackson's Island and together raft downriver.

However, after several adventures, the raft is wrecked by a steamboat and Huck is separated from Jim. Huck is witness to a family blood-feud before they manage to meet again. Then, they are imposed on by two confidence men – 'the duke' and 'the king'.

There are the faked lectures of a 'reformed pirate'; a murder witnessed by Huck; a near-lynching; and impersonations — all part of the picaresque atmosphere of the rafting trip.

The king sells Jim! Huck is despairing when Tom Sawyer arrives and concocts — true to character — a fantastic scheme to set Jim free.

In the dramatic rescue of Jim (which turns out to be quite unnecessary since Jim has already been freed in accordance with the will of his new — now late — owner), Tom is wounded by a bullet. However, while he is recuperating he reveals that he had known Jim had been freed but just wanted the 'adventure' of the rescue.

When Tom Sawyer's Aunt Sally tries to adopt Huck, he 'lights out' — because: 'Aunt Sally she's going to . . . sivilize me and I can't stand it. I been there before.'

Suspense

One instance of suspense occurs when Huck is creeping through the woods on wild Jackson's Island — out in the middle of the river.

He has successfully run away from his Pap — in fact, everybody thinks he has been drowned — and he believes himself to be alone on the island when he stumbles on a still-smoking campfire.

'My heart jumped up amongst my lungs.' Who is on the island with him? We hasten to read on and find out.

A Climax

The tension builds to a climax in the dramatic rescue of Jim by Huck and Tom:

'. . . I told Tom as quick as I could, we must jump for it, now, and not a minute to lose — the house full of men, yonder, with guns!'

Prison Life

In this passage Tom Sawyer, planning the 'rescue' of Jim the runaway slave, wants first to make sure that Jim lacks none of the 'refinements' of true prison existence. . . .

'You got any spiders in here, Jim?'

'No, sah, thanks to goodness I hain't, Mars Tom.'

'All right, we'll get you some.'

'But bless you, honey, I doan' *want* none. I's afeared un um. I jis' 's soon have rattlesnakes aroun'.'

Tom thought a minute or two, and says:

'It's a good idea. And I reckon it's been done. It *must* a been done; it stands to reason. Yes, it's a prime good idea. Where could you keep it?'

'Keep what, Mars Tom?'

'Why, a rattlesnake.'

'De goodness gracious alive, Mars Tom! Why, if dey was a rattlesnake to come in heah, I'd take en bust right out thoo dat log wall, I would, wid my head.'

'Why, Jim, you wouldn't be afraid of it, after a little. You could tame it.'

'*Tame* it!'

'Yes — easy enough. Every animal is grateful for kindness and petting, and they wouldn't *think* of hurting a person that pets them. Any book will tell you that. You try — that's all I ask; just try for two or three days. Why, you can get him so in a little while, that he'll love you; and sleep with you; and won't stay away from you a minute; and will let you wrap him round your neck and put his head in your mouth.'

'*Please*, Mars Tom — *doan'* talk so! I can't *stan'* it! He'd *let* me shove his head in my mouf — fer a favour, hain't it? I lay he'd wait a pow'ful long time 'fo' I *ast* him. En mo' en dat, I doan' *want* him to sleep wid me.'

'Jim, don't act so foolish. A prisoner's *got* to have some kind of a dumb pet, and if a rattlesnake hain't ever been tried, why, ther's more glory to be gained in your being the first to ever try it than any other way you could ever think of to save your life.'

'Why, Mars Tom, I doan' *want* no sich glory. Snake take 'n bite Jim's chin off, den *whah* is de glory? No, sah, I doan' want no sich doin's.'

'Blame it, can't you *try*? I only *want* you to try — you needn't keep it up if it don't work.'

'But de trouble all *done*, ef de snake bite me while I's a tryin' him. Mars Tom, I's willin' to tackle mos' anything 'at ain't onreasonable, but ef you en Huck fetches a rattlesnake in heah for me to tame, I's gwyne to *leave*, dat's *shore*.'

'Well, then, let it go, let it go, if you're so bullheaded about it. We can get you some garter-snakes and you can tie some buttons on their tails, and let on they're rattlesnakes, and I reckon that'll have to do.'

'I k'n stan' *dem*, Mars Tom, but blame' 'f I couldn' get along widout um, I tell you dat. I never knowed b'fo', 't was so much bother and trouble to be a prisoner.'

'Well, it *always* is, when it's done right. You got any rats around here?'

'No, sah, I hain't seed none.'

'Well, we'll get you some rats.'

'Why, Mars Tom, I doan' *want* no rats. Dey's de dad-blamedest creturs to 'sturb a body, en rustle roun' over 'im, en bite his feet, when he's tryin' to sleep, I ever see. No, sah, gimme g'yarter-snakes 'f I's got to have 'm, but doan' gimme no rats, I ain' got no use f'r 'um, skasely.'

'But, Jim, you *got* to have 'em — they all do. So don't make no more fuss about it. Prisoners ain't ever without rats. There ain't no instance of it. And they train them, and pet them, and learn them tricks, and they get to be as sociable as flies. But you got to play music to them.... play The Last Link is Broken — that's the thing that'll scoop a rat, quicker'n anything else; and when you've played about two minutes, you'll see all the rats, and the snakes, and spiders, and things begin to feel worried about you, and come. And they'll just fairly swarm over you, and have a noble good time.'

'Yes, *dey* will, I reck'n, Mars Tom, but what kine er time is *Jim* havin'? Blest if I kin see de pint. But I'll do it ef I got to. I reck'n I better keep de animals satisfied, en not have no trouble in de house.'

[from *Huckleberry Finn* by MARK TWAIN]

Some Questions

(1) What evidence can you find from Jim's speech to suggest he is a Negro?

(2) 'I jis' 's soon have rattlesnakes aroun'.' How is this 'preference' misinterpreted by Tom?

(3) Jim's reaction to the idea of having a live rattlesnake with him is extremely humorous. What means has the novelist used here to make us laugh?

(4) In the paragraph beginning, 'Yes — easy enough. Every animal...' Tom is being very persuasive.
   (a) Explain how words, sentences and punctuation contribute to the overwhelming persuasive effect.
   (b) Which sentence ruins the effect? Why?

(5) What special reward does Tom hold out to Jim for being the first prisoner ever to keep a rattlesnake as a pet?

(6) '... ef you en Huck fetches a rattlesnake in heah for me to tame, I's gwyne to *leave*, dat's *shore*.' Do you see anything odd about this declaration by Jim?

(7) 'I never knowed b'fo', 't was so much bother and trouble to be a prisoner.' What can we deduce about Jim's character from this comment?

(8) Tom and Jim emerge for the reader as very different individuals. How has Mark Twain used language effectively to establish this difference?

(9) What do you think is the author's intention in this passage?

(10) Did you enjoy reading the passage? Why?

Thinking and Reasoning (4)

Facts and Opinions

In order to think critically, we need to be able to distinguish facts from opinions.
- **A fact** is a statement which is supported by the weight of available evidence.
  EXAMPLE: Kangaroos carry their young in pouches.
- **An opinion** is a statement which has some supporting evidence but in some respects is still uncertain.
  EXAMPLE: Kangaroos are a pest for farmers.

A person may believe an opinion strongly, but it remains an opinion until the collection of substantial evidence shows it to be a fact. An opinion may be right or wrong — there is insufficient evidence to decide. With the gathering of further evidence the opinion may be verified (then becoming a fact) or disproved.

In order to think critically we need to be able to distinguish facts from opinions. It is not that we put aside opinions as being unreliable once we have identified them. Rather, by distinguishing an opinion from a fact, we recognize that the statement needs checking. We may seek more supporting evidence; we may look at the 'credentials' of the person voicing the opinion; or we may simply hold it with a query alongside, in our mind.

Exercise 1

Separate facts from opinions in the following collection of statements.

(1) The life expectancy of professional trumpeters is shorter than that in most occupations.

(2) Fishing is relaxing.

(3) Teachers lose their sense of humour after a few years of service.

(4) Amnesty International exists to give support and help to prisoners of conscience.

(5) Schoenberg's music was never really appreciated until after his death.

(6) Australians drink more beer per head of population than any other nationality.

(7) Deafness is a more profound handicap than blindness.

(8) Every person has a right to basic literacy.

(9) Unemployment has risen dramatically in Australia in recent years.

(10) Overseas trade must be encouraged if we are to have a healthy economy.

(11) The cost of books is rising all the time.

(12) It takes many years of dedication to become a skilled musician.

Well-Known Facts versus Facts Needing Support

In the preceding exercise, did you at times *believe* a statement to be factual, but because you didn't *know* what the evidence indicated, you weren't *sure*? For example, it *is* true that professional trumpeters tend to die younger than people in most other occupations! Research has shown this to be so, but you may not have been aware of the research.

Some facts tend to be well known (we all *know* that grass is green!), while other facts (e.g. the life-span of trumpeters) need to be substantiated by evidence if they are to carry full weight in an argument. In presenting an argument — or evaluating one — it is important, then, to know at what point supporting evidence is needed. Don't assume that facts are always self-evident, and where possible don't hesitate to seek the available evidence whenever a 'factual' claim is presented.

Exercise 2

Evaluate the following facts and decide which ones are self-evident, and which ones still need supporting evidence.

(1) Arsenic is a deadly poison.

(2) Cotton is a cool, durable material.

(3) The presence of the death penalty in a legal system does not reduce the incidence of murder.

(4) Emotions tend to interfere with reasoned judgement.

(5) World communication networks have improved tremendously in the past ten years.

(6) Air fares are constantly rising.

(7) Poverty and slum conditions produce increased criminal activity.

(8) Soccer is the fastest-growing international sport.

(9) Smoking is a health hazard.

(10) Ned Kelly is Australia's best-known bushranger.

Discuss your answers around the class, explaining why you took your particular stance on each fact. Are you able to draw any conclusions about facts and the need for supporting evidence?

'Hard' Evidence Is Not Always Available

Lest we begin to think that facts are somehow 'better' than opinions, it is important to remember that many areas of life defy the easy (or even difficult!) collection of evidence. It is not easy to prove beyond a shadow of doubt that Beethoven's music is 'warmer' than Haydn's, or that sunsets are beautiful. Some areas require us to make judgements largely on the basis of our 'reasoned-out' *values* or personal *responses*, in the absence of hard *data*, and these judgements are not less important to us — and not just because the facts are hard to establish. After all, subjective judgements ('I prefer Haydn') are also valuable facts in their own right!

'Hard' evidence is difficult to collect in areas which, because of their vastness, are impossible accurately to research. Is there life on other planets, in other galaxies? It is often difficult to gather hard data in the sciences, let alone in religion, art or morality.

Exercise 3

Identify the statements below for which 'hard' data should be available, and those for which it probably will not be available (or is possibly not even desirable).

(1) The mining and use of uranium is producing increased risks for our world community.

(2) Ballet is the purest form of art.

(3) Lack of censorship is breaking down the moral fibre of our nation.

(4) Violence on television is producing violence in our children.

(5) Laughter is infectious.

(6) We are more sensitive to the needy of the world than people were in the time of the Roman Empire.

(7) Significant changes in the world's weather patterns have occurred in the last 20 years.

(8) A person of sixteen is too young to be married.

(9) Poetry is the most demanding and rewarding area of literature.

(10) Jogging has many significant benefits to offer to anyone who is contemplating taking it up.

Conclusion

Reasoning requires us to be able to distinguish opinions from established facts. But once we are able to make that distinction, we still cannot too lightly accept facts and dismiss 'mere opinions'. For many facts, we will want to see or hear the supporting evidence; while for many opinions, we will want to seek whatever evidence is available or (if none is available) make a judgement based on our own value-system.

Language Basics (4)

Making Sure of Agreement

The following rules will help you make sure that verbs and their subjects agree in the sentences you write.

Rule 1 ● If the subject is singular in number, the verb that goes with it must agree — i.e. must also be singular in number. If the subject is plural, the verb must also be plural.
  EXAMPLES: (a) The *programme* <u>was</u> simplicity itself.
  (b) Many *factors* <u>have</u> contributed to this apparent paradox.

Rule 2 ● A subject made up of two parts, both singular and joined by 'and', takes a plural verb.
  EXAMPLE: *Radio and television* <u>are</u> flourising.

Rule 3 ● Sometimes the subject comes *after* the verb, but they must still agree.
  EXAMPLE: Lying on the floorboards <u>was</u> the missing *script.*

Rule 4 ● If the subject is a group of words denoting a single thing — e.g. the title of a book or a film — then the accompanying verb needs to be singular.
  EXAMPLE: *'Programmes for the Eighties'* <u>is</u> on sale at newsagents.

Using the Rules

Correct the following sentences, all of which commit errors of agreement.

(1) 'TV Times' are widely read.

(2) Audio tape and the cassette is frequently used.

(3) Her display of frenzy, hysteria and panic were distasteful to observe.

(4) In economic terms the medium of radio have gone from strength to strength.

(5) 'Laughs with the Ronnies' are back on air.

(6) Compared with television costs, the costs of radio production is negligible.

(7) Laziness and discouragement is not a solution to this problem.

(8) The ratings takes place all next week.

Punctuation — More on capital letters

1. Words such as 'lake', 'channel', 'bay' (etc) are given capital letters only when they indicate a **particular place or feature**.
   EXAMPLES: (a) The Bay of Biscay has a radio station of its own.
   (b) He sailed slowly around the bay.

2. The words 'road' and 'street' (etc) are capitalized when they are part of an **actual name**.
   EXAMPLES: (a) All the car radios are blaring as the traffic crawls up Parramatta Road.
   (b) This is a rather unattractive road.

3. The points of the compass, when they indicate a **particular region**, are given capitals. When they indicate **direction** they are not capitalized.
   EXAMPLES: (a) Fly JAL to the exotic East.
   (b) Traffic, at the moment, is flowing north.

4. Use capitals for the names of **commercial products**.
   EXAMPLE: The Daihatsu van is ideal for television work.

Exercise

Capitalize the following sentences correctly.

(1) The english rock fans have welcomed the fact that a pirate radio ship is anchored out in the english channel.

(2) The west at least gives lip service to the idea of free speech in the media.

(3) Roseville road runs south right past the mount pleasant studio.

(4) The sanyo television set compares favourably with the rank-arena set.

(5) Hire a datsun and travel to lake george, near byron bay.

Unit Five

Comprehension (5)

Challenge at the Supermarket

If psychologists have found that women enjoy the constant trips to the supermarket, arguing that it is a recreation and a challenge, there are several things they have not considered. It might be a challenge — to try and purchase family requirements when faced with constantly rising prices and a fairly static income; but it is hardly a challenge which is recreational. Rather, it is likely to produce greater worry and tension — 'how to make ends meet' — and if this recreation is engaged upon with a couple of young children who pull things off shelves, pile up their mother's trolley with items she does not want (or cannot afford) so that she must spend extra time replacing them on the shelves, then it is not going to prove very relaxing. Many women claim that such trips to the supermarket, including getting there (especially without a car) and carting heavy groceries home, are so exhausting that they need to rest afterwards.

Going to the supermarket might be a *change* from domestic routines and a superficial relief from the isolation and loneliness of being cooped up in a house with small children but it is hardly a recreation or a challenge. Such shopping trips can actually exacerbate a woman's isolation for although she will *see* lots of other people, her actual contact with them is likely to be limited. Unless she happens to meet other women she knows, her only conversations will be with shop assistants and be circumscribed by the conventions of such casual contact. Many of the large suburban shopping complexes ... mount spectacular entertainments for shoppers, bringing well-known people from show business, sport etc. to 'meet the people'. These mass circuses may distract women shoppers from their personal problems but they are only momentary escapades, not real alternatives to the isolation of women in the suburbs from each other.

A further aspect of women spending money is exploited by advertisers. Quite often women will displace anxiety or depression by compulsive spending — the buying a new hat 'to cheer me up' syndrome — or by buying on impulse things they do not really need and maybe cannot afford. When this occurs, women's big spending is yet another measure of their oppression. Caught in a series of double-binds and conflicting desires about what she should do with her life, it is inevitable that many a woman will resort to that activity which is so assiduously encouraged in our market society — spending money. The advertisers are quick and cunning in their efforts to capitalize on a woman's anxieties and to woo money from her purse. Advertisements appeal to fears about being a good mother — 'your family needs product X' — and to anxieties about her appearance, her hair-style or colour, her body smells, her complexion, her clothes. They also appeal to a woman's anxieties about her family's status, encouraging her to conformity in her purchasing: certain types of furniture, or cooking utensils or other items will show *you* are a discerning woman.

Advertising which employs these techniques still holds the assumption that it is women who are primarily responsible for the management of their family's lifestyle, that they do most of the buying and they decide what is to be bought. This assumption permeates the sales pitch, becoming yet one more pressure on women who are either confused about their roles or are trying to change them in some way. To be constantly cajoled that your family *needs* this product will create self-doubts in a woman in either position.

Outwardly she may scoff at the advertisers' suggestions; inwardly her self-assurance is dented and the prescriptions and admonitions of the 'good mother' role will come flooding back into her confused consciousness. Often a woman who feels guilty about having a paid job will spend more, obediently complying with the advertisers' prescriptions in an effort to quell her self-doubts. She will compensate for her absence from full-time motherhood by plying her family with items it could not otherwise afford.

[from *Damned Whores and God's Police* by ANNE SUMMERS]

Check Your Understanding

(1) What are two of the writer's arguments against the idea that trips to the supermarket are recreational for women?

(2) Explain how shopping trips can actually exacerbate a woman's isolation.

(3) A 'coop' is a small pen for poultry. What is the meaning of the phrase 'cooped up'? What feelings does the word arouse in you for women at home with small children?

(4) What does the writer mean by, 'These mass circuses may distract women shoppers from their personal problems'?

(5) How does the advertiser play upon women's anxieties and fears?

(6) What is the writer's attitude to the advertisers?

(7) What is the meaning of, 'Outwardly she may scoff at the advertisers' suggestions'?

(8) Why could a woman feel 'guilty about having a paid job'?

(9) What do you think is the writer's purpose in this extract?

(10) Can you find evidence to suggest that the writer is a woman? Where?

(11) After reading this extract, do you feel sympathetic towards married women at home with children? Why?

(12) What is the meaning of the following words from the passage? (The back-of-the-book dictionary will assist you if you have any difficulties.)

Paragraph 1: static
Paragraph 2: superficial, escapades
Paragraph 3: syndrome, assiduously, discerning
Paragraph 4: permeates, cajole, admonitions

Working with Words (5)

Senior Spelling Demons	Confusing Pairs	The Media		Increase Your Word Power
absolutely	rein	controversy	correspondent	belligerent
channel	reign	exclusive	commentary	perennial
accept	gorilla	celebrity	documentary	demeanour
design	guerilla	forecast	spontaneous	fastidious
choose	canvas	impartiality	advertisement	vexation
distinguish	canvass	initiate	circulation	derisive
debt	formerly	journalist	columnist	solace
lovable	formally	precisely	personality	inclement
truly	ostensible	campaign	discretion	abstain
queue	ostentatious	description	exaggerate	ominous

Change the Words
Change to people

(a) debt ....

(b) design ....

(c) campaign ....

Change to verbs

(a) description ....

(b) exclusive ....

(c) derisive ....

(d) circulation ....

(e) personality ....

(f) commentary ....

Supply opposites by adding prefixes

(a) formally ....

(b) precisely ....

(c) discretion ....

(d) acceptable..

(e) contented..

Change to nouns

(a) exaggerate ....

(b) choose ....

(c) exclusive ....

(d) abstain ....

(e) derisive ....

(f) spontaneous ....

Change to adjectives

(a) controversy ....

(b) truly ....

(c) discretion ....

(d) distinguish ....

(e) accept ....

(f) circulation ....

Confusing Pairs

Write down the following sentences, filling each blank space with the correct word from the brackets.

(1) The .... forces halted the invaders' advance. [**gorilla**]

(2) At the end of his .... the king abdicated. [**rein/reign**]

(3) The mayor, ... an alderman on the council, ... welcomed the Prime Minister. [**formally/formerly**]

(4) Politicians often .... for votes. [**canvass/canvas**]

(5) The film star's clothing was .... [**ostensible/ostentatious**]

Increase Your Word Power

Replace the words or phrases in italics with appropriate words from the *Increase Your Word Power* list.

(1) The cricketer's *outward behaviour* irritated the spectators.

(2) The cook was *hard to please* about cleanliness.

(3) The priest gave the dying man *comfort*.

(4) The accident victim was *ready to fight*.

(5) Doctors advise that it is important to *refrain* from smoking.

(6) The talkative student was responsible for the teacher's *annoyance*.

(7) Some buildings seem to be *of an everlasting type*.

(8) The bank manager adopted a *mocking* attitude towards my application for a loan.

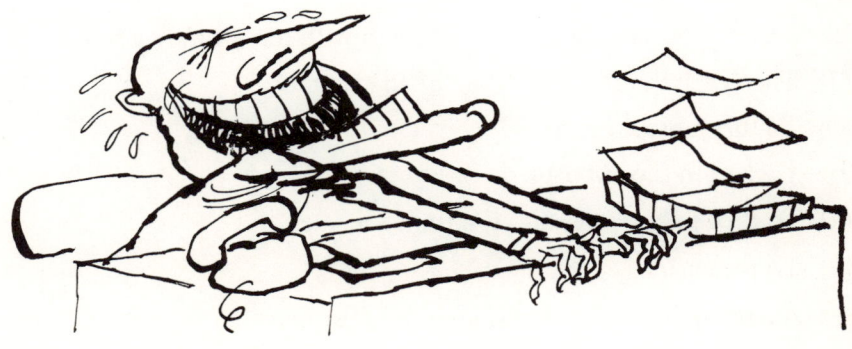

Missing Words

Correctly insert the words from the box into the spaces below.

documentary	ominous	celebrity	impartiality	exaggerate	derisive
abstain	commentary	columnist	belligerent	discretion	inclement

(1) .... stormclouds were an indication of .... weather.

(2) The television .... tried to ignore the .... comments of his critics.

(3) Although the reporter tried to show ...., the politician being interviewed was so .... that he threatened to hit the reporter.

(4) Sometimes a newspaper .... should use .... before making startling revelations.

(5) A newspaper journalist should .... from the urge to ....

(6) A television .... programme is almost always accompanied by a ....

Word Origins — 'Controversy'

A 'controversy' is a dispute or conflict of opinion. It comes from the Latin *contra* ('against') and *vertere/versus* ('to turn'). Thus, a controversy is a 'turning against'.

Here is a list of words all having some part of *vertere* ('to turn') in them.

convert	anniversary	advertise	adversary	extrovert
perverse	version	reverse	divert	invert	introvert

See whether you can match some of them with the meanings below.

(1) The yearly return of the date of an event.

(2) To turn upside down.

(3) Turned in the opposite direction.

(4) To turn public attention to things for sale.

(5) To turn aside.

(6) A person 'turned inwards' upon him- or herself.

Language in Action (5)

Ambiguity

A sentence that has two or more different meanings is said to be *ambiguous*. The word itself derives from the Latin *ambi* ('both ways') and *agere/actus* ('to act'). The incautious use of a word with a double meaning or the misplacing of a phrase or clause within a sentence can create doubt as to what meaning you really intend to communicate.

Sometimes a degree of unintentional humour is introduced through ambiguity, as many of the following sentences show.

Exercise

Rewrite the following sentences, eliminating the ambiguity in each one as you go.

(1) Competent lady, 31, with little dog, seeks post.

(2) I saw the thief enter the room through the keyhole.

(3) Blue Heeler for sale, will work cattle and stop to whistle.

(4) They were happy to find a number of small huts coming down the side of the mountain.

(5) Another Pacific country was sending two DC3s to carry a full military pipe-band and other soldiers and two submarines each with a crew of thirty.

(6) The bride was given away by her father in a full-length blue satin dress with flaring bodice.

(7) Auction: Lot 7 for Mr Proust who is leaving the locality (unless sold by private treaty).

(8) After adding herbs to the saucepan, sit on a hot plate and simmer till satisfied.

(9) The pilot had a narrow escape when a wingtip crashed through the cockpit narrowly missing his head. This had to be removed before he could be released.

(10) When he knocked on the door, the landlady came downstairs in a night-dress and opened it for him.

(11) TO RENT: small residence with two bedrooms, bathroom, kitchen and outside toilet, at present occupied by owner.

(12) A sheepdog was among the people barking at the Prime Minister.

(13) So he spake unto his sons saying, 'Saddle me the ass', and they saddled him.

(14) Position as daily help wanted by respectable woman (Sundays excepted).

(15) FOR SALE: new electric blanket. Owner leaving. Deep pink colour.

(16) At the Rialto theatre a small baby was needed for a scene in a play. A message was sent to Phyllis the theatre nurse: 'Please have a baby by nine o'clock tomorrow morning.'

(17) The tenants were forced to leave their houses through unsafe cracks in the walls.

The Language of Literature (5)

WOMAN TO MAN

The eyeless labourer in the night,
the selfless, shapeless seed I hold,
builds for its resurrection day—
silent and swift and deep from sight
foresees the unimagined light.

This is no child with a child's face;
this has no name to name it by;
yet you and I have known it well.
This is our hunter and our chase,
the third who lay in our embrace.

This is the strength that your arm knows,
the arc of flesh that is my breast,
the precise crystals of our eyes.
This is the blood's wild tree that grows
the intricate and folded rose.

This is the maker and the made;
this is the question and reply;
the blind head butting at the dark,
the blaze of light along the blade.
Oh hold me, for I am afraid.

JUDITH WRIGHT

Some Questions

(1) What is the poet's purpose in writing this poem?

(2) What is the tone of the poem?

(3) How well does the title suit the poem, and why?

(4) What feelings does the poet arouse in you?

(5) Did you notice any changes of mood? Find evidence to support your viewpoint.

(6) Why does the poem end with the words, 'Oh hold me, for I am afraid'?

Appreciation of a Poem

Throughout this poem Judith Wright sensuously lays bare her feelings concerning the seed within her womb. She takes the present, past and future and in turn presents her feelings towards each. In the first stanza she is exuberant in the present time, but she is eagerly looking forward to the seed's future 'resurrection day'. Indeed the poetry could be only that of a woman. In this poem Judith Wright conveys a sense of joy and pride. But we also see the influence of the force of creation upon her poetry. To describe her realization of fruition, Judith Wright turns to the earth for her symbols. She has become the earth and the seed in her womb has become the seed of the earth reaching forth to the light of day.

The poet gives the reader an incisive exploration of her feelings. In the second stanza she goes bckward in time to show her emotions, when the seed actually entered her womb. She is stressing the wonder and excitement of human love-making, but through her imagery she conveys the feeling that the child owes its essential characteristics to the union between man and woman. She has taken the single metaphor of hunting and has paradoxically related it to the seed. The inherent desire in human beings to procreate explains her use of 'hunter', and her use of the word 'chase' is resolved when we think of the seed as being the fruit of the love-making between man and woman. The oneness of her husband and herself is evoked in the words 'the third who lay in our embrace'.

In the third stanza Judith Wright stresses the fact that the embryo is the product of two creative forces. It can only result from the fusion of male and female. She uses the symbol of 'strength' to evince her husband's part in the production of the seed and she takes the symbol of the 'breast' to indicate the woman's role. The union of male and female is vividly brought out in the words 'precise crystals of our eyes'. The word 'precise' helps to convey the poet's wonder at the regenerative force of nature. Once again in the last two lines of the third stanza the poet resorts to the imagery of nature to help her display her sense of wonder at the miracle of creation. She takes the beautiful image of 'the intricate and folded rose' and looks forward to the future child folded within her womb.

In the last stanza Judith Wright confronts the reader with a paradox. The seed is both 'the maker' and 'the made'. The life cycle is continued. The question of living seems to have its answer in the 'reply' of the creation of the seed. The poet looks anxiously and fearfully ahead to the future. She evokes the child's blind struggle to release itself from the darkness of the womb to reach the light of day. The word 'butting' implies the struggling of the child to release itself from its mother, but it also indirectly makes the reader aware of the suffering which the mother receives in turn. In these two lines one can feel a sense of Judith Wright's anticipated release from pain as the child reaches the light. In the last line she reverts to her present feelings of her fear of the future.

Not only is this an intensely personal poem but it is a most unusual poem. Judith Wright gives the reader an insight into a woman's feelings for her unborn child, a description of the love relationship between husband and wife and the fears of a woman for the birth of her child.

Thinking and Reasoning (5)

Reasoning requires us not only to look at the evidence presented in support of a generalization or argument, but also to weigh up the *quality* of that evidence. In the next few sections on Thinking and Reasoning we will be looking at some of the kinds of evidence that are used to support arguments. In particular we will consider evidence:

- drawn from the use of analogies
- provided by 'experts'
- based on statistical information.

The Use of Analogies

An analogy is essentially a comparison of two things or situations.

(a) If an analogy is used simply *to illustrate something*, to make it clearer, it is usually quite acceptable.

> EXAMPLE: A university lecturer is explaining to trainee doctors the view that merely treating the symptoms of illness while not getting to the cause of the problem will not prevent the recurrence of the problem. To illustrate the point he says: 'If you have weeds growing in your lawn, the long-term answer to the problem is not simply to mow the lawn. Mowing the lawn *will* make the oservable weeds disappear, but because you have failed to deal with the roots of the weeds, they will grow again.'

(b) An analogy may also be used as a technique *to persuade*. Its use in this way relies on the fact that the two things being compared have some similarities, so that common conclusions can be drawn. However, when an analogy is used as evidence of the rightness of an argument, we need to recognize that it is poor evidence. Argument by comparison is a poor approach to proving something; the use of analogy does not 'prove' anything. Often when an analogy is used to persuade people about something, it makes use of an emotive bias of approval or disapproval in addition to its descriptive content. Used this way, an analogy is an attempt to get us 'thinking with our emotions'.

> EXAMPLE: 'Life is a body-contact sport. It is inevitable that some people should get hurt, so there's no sense in getting too upset about suffering throughout the world. And if we do get concerned, obviously our first concern should be for our own team-members. Let the other countries look after themselves.'

Exercise 1

(1) With what three great discoveries/inventions is the discovery of uranium compared in the cartoon at right?

(2) How does Pickering see the progress of man's use of each important discovery?

(3) What conclusions about the future of uranium does the cartoonist draw?

(4) Is this cartoon an example of the use of *descriptive* or of *persuasive* analogy?

(5) Granted that it has a place in the 'uranium debate', why would you nonetheless want to consider more material than just this cartoon in deciding your stance on the use of uranium?

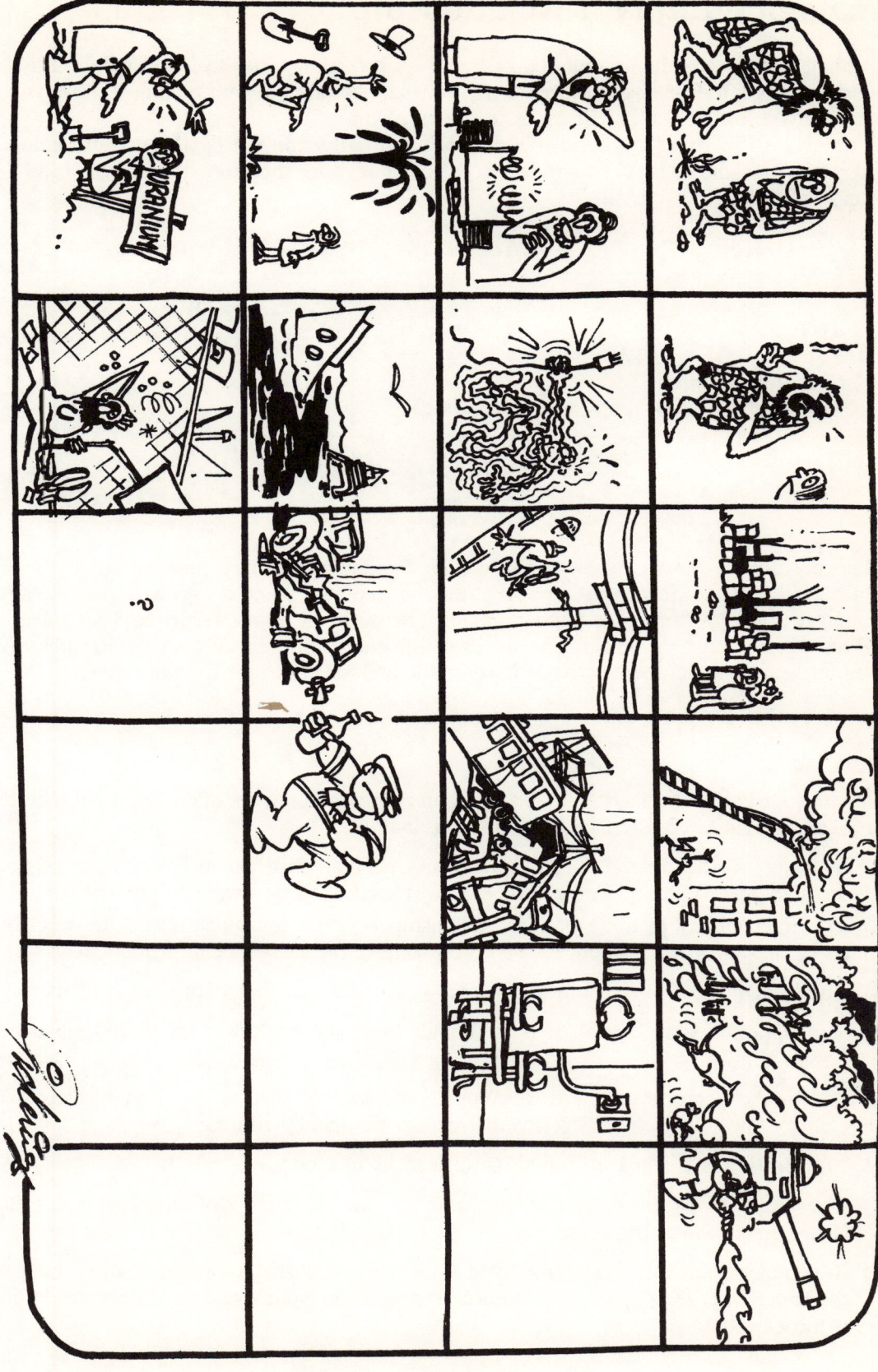

Analogies Imply a Relationship

'A young baby needs the stimulation of being spoken to in order to foster maximum growth and development. For the same reasons, you should talk to your young plants; you'll be amazed at the difference it will make to their growth.'

The above illustrates the kind of relationship usually implied by the use of analogies in argument. A leads to B; C is similar to A in some way; therefore the same action (A) in the case of C will produce B.

Object	Action	Result
1. A (young child)	TALK TO A	B (optimal development)
Relationship (Child and plant — both young, growing)		
2. C (young plant)	TALK TO C	B (optimal development)

The conclusion drawn by an analogy such as that above may turn out to be a correct one (there *is* some evidence to suggest that talking to plants promotes growth!) but the analogy in no way 'proves' this. It is a poor analogy because the relationship between plants and children is not a strong one. There are probably more differences than similarities, so that we cannot safely conclude that what is right for one will be right for the other.

Exercise 2

Using the child/plant diagram as an example, draw your own diagrams to illustrate the relationships being expressed in the following analogies.

(1) In order to acquire the skill of piano-playing one must practise. It is the same with the skill of relaxation. You must practise relaxation if you want to acquire it.

(2) To understand something of the relationship between the nucleus and the electrons of an atom, you might imagine planets following a prescribed orbit around their sun.

(3) The human mind is like blotting paper. It soaks up all that is presented to it.

(4) Schizophrenia is an illness. It is as though some germ has penetrated and poisoned the person's mind.

(5) Just as the doctor's task is to overcome the cause of disease, so the psychiatrist must identify and eradicate the 'germ' that causes the mental illness.

(6) The Bible is a roadmap given to us to lead us to God.

(7) After every rainstorm the sun shines again. So don't let life's storms defeat you. Remember, the sun will shine again.

(8) If you notice moisture coming from your skin, you are sweating; it must be hot. In the same way, if you notice moisture coming from your eyes, your eyes are sweating; it must be hot.

(9) Man is simply an animal, governed by his desire to avoid pain and to obtain as much pleasure as possible.

(10) Throw away ethics and morality in society and you have a boat with no rudder. The results for the boat and for society will be the same: shipwreck!

Conclusions Are Independent of the Analogy

Sometimes an analogy will be used to draw a conclusion with which we can agree. Other evidence or knowledge will enable us to make the judgement that the conclusion is correct. However, it is important to remind ourselves in such cases that it was *not* the analogy that proved the conclusion to be correct.

Exercise 3

Look back over the analogies used in Exercise 2 and evaluate each in terms of the following three issues.

1. Even though you recognize that the analogy did not *prove* the conclusion, was it helpful? What points of similarity are there between the things being compared.

2. Did the analogy have emotive overtones? Comment on any.

3. Regardless of the analogy, did you agree with the conclusion? Offer an explanation for your acceptance or rejection of the conclusion.

Exercise 4

'Living in a village can be uncomfortable if our neighbours are unthinking and careless with their dirt and garbage; living in the world will become impossible if our nuclear neighbours are unthinking and careless with their nuclear dirt and garbage. Unfortunately there is increasing evidence to indicate that they are, and will continue to be, if not actually irresponsible, at least fallible.'

[from *Uranium – Energy Source of the Future?*
by E. W. TITTERTON and F. P. ROBOTHAM]

(1) What two things are being compared in the analogy above?

(2) Is this essentially a persuasive or a descriptive analogy?

(3) Is there strong similarity or weak similarity between the things being compared?

(4) What emotive overtones (if any) does the analogy carry?

(5) Make a summarizing comment on the analogy used here.

Language Basics (5)

More on Agreement

Here are some further rules on subject–verb agreement.

Rule 1 ● Phrases beginning with 'of . . .' and following the subject have no effect on the agreement between verb and subject.
EXAMPLE: A <u>list</u> *of shopping items* <u>was</u> drawn up.

Rule 2 ● The verb is in the singular when two (or more) parts of the subject refer to the same person or thing.
EXAMPLE: A <u>housewife and mother</u> <u>finds</u> it hard to manage both roles.

Rule 3 ● 'With', 'as well as', 'and not', 'together with' join subjects, and in such cases the verb agrees with the original subject alone.
EXAMPLE: <u>My psychologist,</u> as well as several doctors, <u>is</u> in favour of more research on housewives' problems.

Using the Rules

Correct the following sentences for agreement.

(1) A trolley loaded with products are hard to trundle along the aisles of the supermarket.

(2) The constant pain and agony have reduced him to a shadow of his former self.

(3) Advertisers, as well as a large shopping complex, is quick to capitalize on a woman's anxieties.

(4) Some aspects of women spending money is exploited by advertisers.

(5) Sharp business practice and not commercials sometimes increase the shopper's anxiety.

(6) One of the large shopping complexes mount spectacular entertainment for shoppers.

(7) A part of the town precincts are made up of commercial enterprises.

(8) Retirement and sickness has contributed to the company's losses.

Punctuation – The exclamation mark

The exclamation mark is used after a word, phrase or sentence expressing emotion or command; and also for emphasis or irony.
EXAMPLES: (a) What a disgusting commercial!
(b) Attention!
(c) Well, if it isn't Miss Holier-than-thou!

Exercise A

By using the full stop, the question mark or the exclamation mark, distinguish exclamations from questions and statements.

(1) Householders are fussy shoppers

(2) Get out and stay out

(3) Will I fill out the form

(4) Some friend

(5) Stop that shoplifter

(6) Is it returnable

(7) What a hope

(8) Progress has passed us by

Exercise B

Change the following statements into exclamations using 'How' or 'What'.
EXAMPLE: Her complexion is perfect.
            What a perfect complexion she has!

(1) This is hard-sell advertising.

(2) Just being here makes me irritable.

(3) The whole thing was laughable.

(4) Going to the supermarket makes a change for her.

(5) She wears stylish clothes.

(6) They appeal to me.

(7) Their personal problems are pressing.

(8) Your purchase is tasteful.

Unit Six

Comprehension (6)

Jonathan Livingston Seagull

By sunup, Jonathan Gull was practising again. From five thousand feet the fishing boats were specks in the flat blue water, Breakfast Flock was a faint cloud of dust motes, circling.

He was alive, trembling ever so slightly with delight, proud that his fear was under control. Then without ceremony he hugged in his forewings, extended his short, angled wingtips, and plunged directly toward the sea. By the time he passed four thousand feet he had reached terminal velocity, the wind was a solid beating wall of sound against which he could move no faster. He was flying now straight down, at two hundred fourteen miles per hour. He swallowed, knowing that if his wings unfolded at that speed he'd be blown into a million tiny shreds of seagull. But the speed was power, and the speed was joy, and the speed was pure beauty.

He began his pullout at a thousand feet, wingtips thudding and blurring in that gigantic wind, the boat and the crowd of gulls tilting and growing meteor-fast, directly in his path.

He couldn't stop; he didn't know yet even how to turn at that speed.

Collision would be instant death.

And so he shut his eyes.

It happened that morning, then, just after sunrise, that Jonathan Livingston Seagull fired directly through the centre of Breakfast Flock, ticking off two hundred twelve miles per hour, eyes closed, in a great roaring shriek of wind and feathers. The Gull of Fortune smiled upon him this once, and no one was killed.

By the time he had pulled his beak straight up into the sky he was still scorching along at a hundred and sixty miles per hour. When he had slowed to twenty and stretched his wings again at last, the boat was a crumb on the sea, four thousand feet below.

His thought was triumph. Terminal velocity! A seagull at *two hundred fourteen miles per hour*! It was a breakthrough, the greatest single moment in the history of the Flock, and in that moment a new age opened for Jonathan Gull. Flying out to his lonely practice area, folding his wings for a dive from eight thousand feet, he set himself at once to discover how to turn.

[from *Jonathan Livingston Seagull* by RICHARD BACH]

Check Your Understanding

(1) 'Breakfast Flock was a faint cloud of dust motes, circling.' What are 'motes'?

(2) What evidence is there of Jonathan's physical delight at the beginning of this extract?

(3) Explain what is meant by 'terminal velocity'.

(4) Comment on the emotional effect of the two short one-sentence paragraphs in the middle of this extract.

(5) Comment on the force and appropriateness of the word 'fired' in 'fired directly through the centre of Breakfast Flock'.

(6) In what way does the element of luck figure in this incident?

(7) Explain why Jonathan has to slow to twenty miles per hour.

(8) How does the writer express Jonathan's feelings of triumph at his achievement?

(9) Apart from the fact that he aims to learn how to turn, what evidence is there at the end of the passage that Jonathan is still seeking to extend himself further?

(10) Identify one particular feature of style that you see as important in this extract. Give examples of this feature and comment on its effectiveness.

(11) How would you describe the character of Jonathan?

(12) How successful for you is Richard Bach, the author, in describing — and conveying the emotion of — this moment?

Working with Words (6)

Senior Spelling Demons	Confusing Pairs	People		Increase Your Word Power
biscuit	horde	successful	exhausted	deluge
barbecue	hoard	quarrelsome	dilemma	lethal
catalogue	straight	generous	influential	adept
antique	strait	intellectual	obstinate	chagrin
ancient	peace	cynical	eccentric	initiate
choose	piece	scandal	jealousy	lithe
scheme	contemptuous	prevail	fascination	sombre
schedule	contemptible	satisfaction	annoyance	ratify
sincerely	accede	efficiency	apology	nurture
pursue	exceed	adventurous	optimistic	implore

People

Consult the list for words that will complete the following.

(1) A person with strange habits or hobbies is said to be ....

(2) The opposite of 'pessimistic' is...........................

(3) A powerful person with all the right 'contacts' could well be termed ....

(4) One who is unbending in opinion is ....

(5) A situation requiring a choice between unpleasant alternatives is a ....

(6) This word stands for getting things done with a minimum of fuss: ....

(7) You can sometimes right a wrong with an ....

(8) The opposite of 'miserly' or 'tight-fisted' is ....

(9) A .... is likely to provoke malicious talk and gossip.

(10) Totally fatigued, or ....

(11) .... means believing the worst in people and mocking good motives.

(12) Someone who feels envious of, or even dislikes, those who are more fortunate is suffering from ....

(13) A synonym for captivation (or deep interest): ....

(14) One who is given to picking fights is a .... person.

(15) When one opinion rather than another gets the upper hand it is said to ....

(16) A synonym for 'irritation' is ....

(17) The antonym of this word is formed with 'dis-': ....

(18) Pertaining to the mind and mental activities: ....

(19) She led an .... life full of excitement and new experiences.

(20) Passing his exams was a source of great .... to him.

Confusing Pairs

Select the correct word.

(1) A [**horde**/**hoard**] of treasure.

(2) Bass [**Straight**/**Strait**] is safe for shipping.

(3) A choice [**piece**/**peace**] of real estate.

(4) What a [**contemptuous**/**contemptible**] thing to do!

(5) The Prime Minister will [**accede**/**exceed**] to your request.

Suffixes

Using suffixes, change each of the following words into the part of speech required.
EXAMPLE: **exhausted** (noun) *exhaustion*

(1) **generous** (noun) ....

(2) **antique** (adjective) ....

(3) **choose** (noun) ....

(4) **sincerely** (noun) ....

(5) **efficiency** (adjective) ....

(6) **straight** (verb) ....

(7) **pursue** (noun) ....

(8) **eccentric** (noun) ....

(9) **peace** (adjective) ....

(10) **contemptuous** (adverb) ....

(11) **exceed** (adjective) ....

(12) **satisfaction** (adverb) ....

(13) **scandal** (adjective) ....

(14) **jealousy** (adverb) ....

(15) **ratify** (noun) ....

(16) **obstinate** (noun) ....

Synonyms

Match up each word on the left with a synonym on the right.

initiate	confirm
scheme	skilled
sombre	deadly
adept	begin
schedule	disappointment
lethal	plan
chagrin	dark
deluge	plead
pursue	timetable
implore	agree
hoard	downpour
lithe	store
accede	supple
ratify	chase

Word Origins — 'Chauvinism'

Chauvin was one of Napoleon's soldiers. He was wounded seventeen times and retired on a paltry pension. Instead of being bitter, however, he remained unswervingly loyal to Napoleon and praised him so incessantly that in the end he was ridiculed by his comrades. Chauvinism today has come to mean exaggerated and often belligerent patriotism or loyalty — as, for example, to the male cause.

Language in Action (6)

Levels of Usage

There are three clearly distinguishable levels of usage in language. The first is what we call the **formal** level. Formal usage is serious in purpose. It is polished and thoughtful and has a dignity that separates it from other levels of usage. Very often it is directed at an educated audience.

The second level is the **informal** level. It is often referred to as colloquial language. This is basically the language of everyday conversation and familiar writing, not lower in quality and correctness than formal English but simply different because of situation and purpose. We will be examining ths informal use of language more closely in the next chapter.

The third level, which is highly informal, is known as **slang**, and is occasionally referred to as *vulgar* English. Everybody can recognize and use slang words, but people have trouble in defining exactly what slang is. Slang is a type of popular language, considered to be below the level of standard educated speech, in which new words are created or current words are used in a special way. What are the meanings of the following words when they are used as slang? — 'bird', 'chisel', 'cool', 'scab', 'nag', 'guts', 'wheels'.

Appropriateness

We need and use different types of language to suit different situations. Let us examine an analogy to explain this. We judge appropriateness by what is suitable to the occasion or the context in which we find ourselves. If we were setting out for a day at the beach in the hot sun, we would certainly not dress in a suit and tie. On the other hand, if we were attending a formal dinner party we would not arrive in a swimming costume, beach shirt and thongs. We dress for each particular situation and occasion. The same principle applies to our use of language. When we are talking informally to our friends we are relaxed and don't have to take care with every sentence we utter. Yet, if we are delivering a formal public address, our language needs to be polished and carefully prepared. Language varies according to the formality or informality of the situation.

Here are two passages, one (comprising two sections) in formal English and the other in slang. They both describe the betrayal of Christ by Judas. Carl Burke, a gaol chaplain in New York, found he could not get through to the hostile or indifferent youths from New York's toughest areas. He got them to retell the Bible stories in their own slang. Suddenly he found that they were interested in the stories. Read through the two passages and answer the questions.

The Betrayal by Judas

14 Then one of the twelve, who was called Judas Iscariot, went to the chief priests [15] and said, 'What will you give me if I deliver him to you?' And they paid him thirty pieces of silver. [16] And from that moment he sought an opportunity to betray him.

17 Now on the first day of Unleavened Bread the disciples came to Jesus, saying, 'Where will

you have us prepare for you to eat the pass-over?' [18] He said, 'Go into the city to such a one, and say to him, "The Teacher says, My time is at hand; I will keep the passover at your house with my disciples."' [19] And the disciples did as Jesus had directed them, and they prepared the passover.

20 When it was evening, he sat at table with the twelve disciples; [21] and as they were eating, he said, 'Truly, I say to you, one of you will betray me.' [22] And they were very sorrowful, and began to say to him one after another, 'Is it I, Lord?' [23] He answered, 'He who has dipped his hand in the dish with me, will betray me. [24] The Son of man goes as it is written of him, but woe to that man by whom the Son of man is betrayed! It would have been better for that man if he had not been born.' [25] Judas, who betrayed him, said, 'Is it I, Master?' He said to him, 'You have said so.'

47 While he was still speaking, Judas came, one of the twelve, and with him a great crowd with swords and clubs, from the chief priests and the elders of the people. [48] Now the betrayer had given them a sign, saying, 'The one I shall kiss is the man; seize him.' [49] And he came up to Jesus at once and said, 'Hail, Master!' And he kissed him. [50] Jesus said to him, 'Friend, why are you here?' Then they came up and laid hands on Jesus and seized him. [51] And behold, one of those who were with Jesus stretched out his hand and drew his sword, and struck the slave of the high priest, and cut off his ear. [52] Then Jesus said to him, 'Put your sword back into its place; for all who take the sword will perish by the sword. [53] Do you think that I cannot appeal to my Father, and he will at once send me more than twelve legions of angels? [54] But how then should the scriptures be fulfilled, that it must be so?' [55] At that hour Jesus said to the crowds, 'Have you come out as against a robber, with swords and clubs to capture me? Day after day I sat in the temple teaching, and you did not seize me. [56] But all this has taken place, that the scriptures of the prophets might be fulfilled.' Then all the disciples forsook him and fled.

[from The Bible (Revised Standard Version), *Matthew* 26: 14-25; 47-56]

A Stoolie in Jesus' Gang

Judas was a member of Jesus' gang,
  He was a stool pigeon.
    He figures he can get some money by turn-ing in Jesus
      To his enemies.

The stoolie goes over and makes a deal for thirty bucks
  And tells the other gang where he will be.

Later that night they come looking for Jesus
  With stoolie Judas leading the way.
    He came up to Jesus and said,
      'Hi, boss,' and gave him a kiss.

This made Jesus very sad
  And he said, 'Judas, why do you turn me in with a kiss?'
    Just then the rest of them grabbed Jesus,
      But Peter ain't about to let them get away with that
        And he pulls out his blade
          And, bingo, off comes a guy's ear.

Jesus don't go for that stuff
  And he tells Peter to put his blade away,
    And heals up the guy's ear and head.

They put the cuffs on Jesus and takes him away.
  He got taken to the house of a character called Annas.
    And this started a long trial.

Later the stoolie started wishing that he hadn't done what he done
  And he tried to give back the money,
    But they wouldn't take it, no matter how much he tried
      To get them to do it.

The more he thunk of what he did
  The madder he gets at himself.
    He can't get it outa his mind.

There's no other way, so he gets a rope
  And hangs himself.

This is more than feeling sorry for himself —
  It's what the head shrinkers call guilt, whatever that is.

[from *God is for real, man* by CARL BURKE]

Questions

(1) For what kind of reader do you think the first passage would be suitable?

(2) What criticism could you make of the language of the first passage?

(3) Why do you think the second passage was so successful with the prisoners?

(4) Write down three examples of slang from the second passage and explain the meanings.

(5) Do you think the second passage would be suitable in a normal church service? Explain your viewpoint.

Formal English

Formal English has been defined as 'the language used by a reputable writer or speaker when he is addressing an educated audience and writing or speaking in a straightforward and serious tone, in his own person'. Look at the following example of formal English. It is a letter from King George VI to Winston Churchill, the British prime minister during World War II. In this letter the King is requesting that Churchill not be aboard a battleship to watch the bombardment of the Normandy coast immediately before the D-Day landing of 6 June 1944.

Buckingham Palace,
June 2, 1944.

My Dear Winston,

I want to make one more appeal to you not to go to sea on D Day. Please consider my own position. I am a younger man than you, I am a sailor, and as King I am the head of all these services. There is nothing I would like better than to go to sea, but I have agreed to stay at home; is it fair that you should then do exactly what I should have liked to do myself? You said yesterday afternoon that it would be a fine thing for the King to lead his troops into battle, as in old days; if the King cannot do this, it does not seem to me right that his Prime Minister should take his place.

Then there is your own position. You will see very little, you will run a considerable risk, you will be inaccessible at a critical time, when vital decisions might have to be taken, and however unobtrusive you may be your mere presence on board is bound to be a very heavy additional responsibility to the Admiral and Captain. As I said in my previous letter, your being there would add immeasurably to my anxieties, and your going without consulting your colleagues in the Cabinet would put them in a very difficult position, which they would justifiably resent.

I ask you most earnestly to consider the whole position again, and not to let your personal wishes, which I very well understand, lead you to depart from your own high standard of duty to the State.

Believe me,
Your very sincere friend,
GEORGE R.I.

Questions

(1) In what ways is the tone of this letter serious?

(2) Do you consider this to be a friendly letter? Why?

(3) What evidence can you find to suggest that the King has thought a good deal about the contents of his letter?

(4) What evidence can you find in the language used to suggest that this letter was written by an educated person?

(5) Do you think this letter would have succeeded in its purpose? Explain your viewpoint.

The Language of Literature (6)

Coming to Terms with Drama

- A dramatist uses **characterization** to tell us about his/her characters in a number of ways:

1. We learn a good deal about a character from what he/she says about himself/herself and others.
2. We also form an opinion about a character by the way he/she reacts to other characters and to the problems (etc) which he/she encounters.
3. Another important means we use to evaluate a character is carefully to consider the things that other characters in the play say about the character.
4. Sometimes the playwright gives specific advice in the stage directions on how he/she believes some of the characters should look, act, dress and behave. Whilst many in the audience would be unfamiliar with the stage directions of the script, it would be the task of the director to ensure that these are brought to life in the scene being enacted.

Just from looking at this scene from *The Club* by David Williamson, what comments would you make about the character of Geoff (on your right) and Laurie (on your left)?

- **Climax** is the point in the play at which the peak of physical or emotional tension is reached.
- **Conflict** is the clash of ideas, personalities or actions of the characters.

As you look at this action clip from *The Club*, explain how you know that there is some kind of conflict between the two characters.

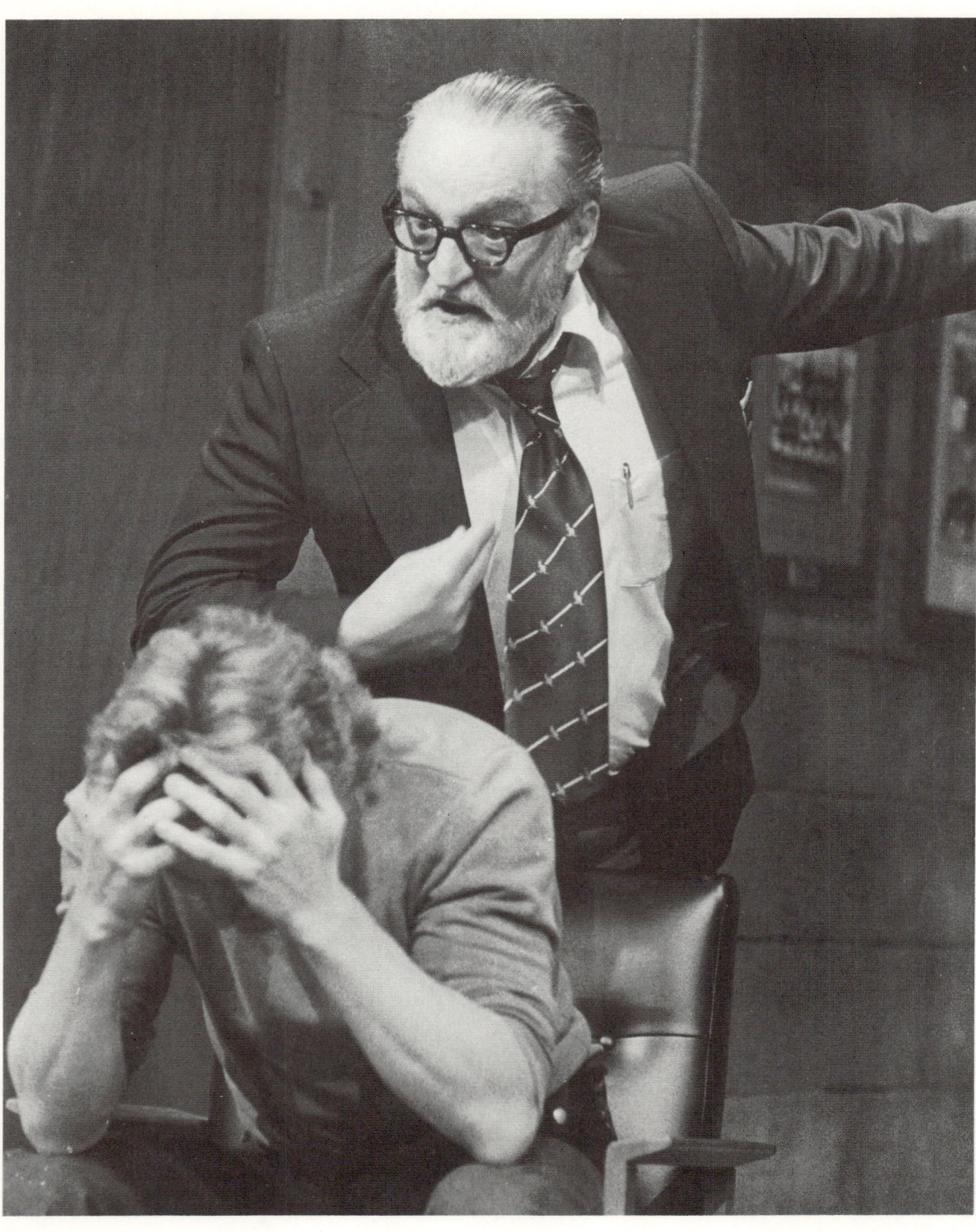

- **Dialogue** is the conversation carried on by the characters.
- **Plot** is the story of the play. It is 'what the play is about'.
- **Setting** is the location or background of the play. It is where the play takes place.

Look at this scene carefully. What comments would you make about the setting of *The Club*?

- **Structure** is the underlying pattern of development of the play. The following simple diagram will give you some idea of the structure of a play.

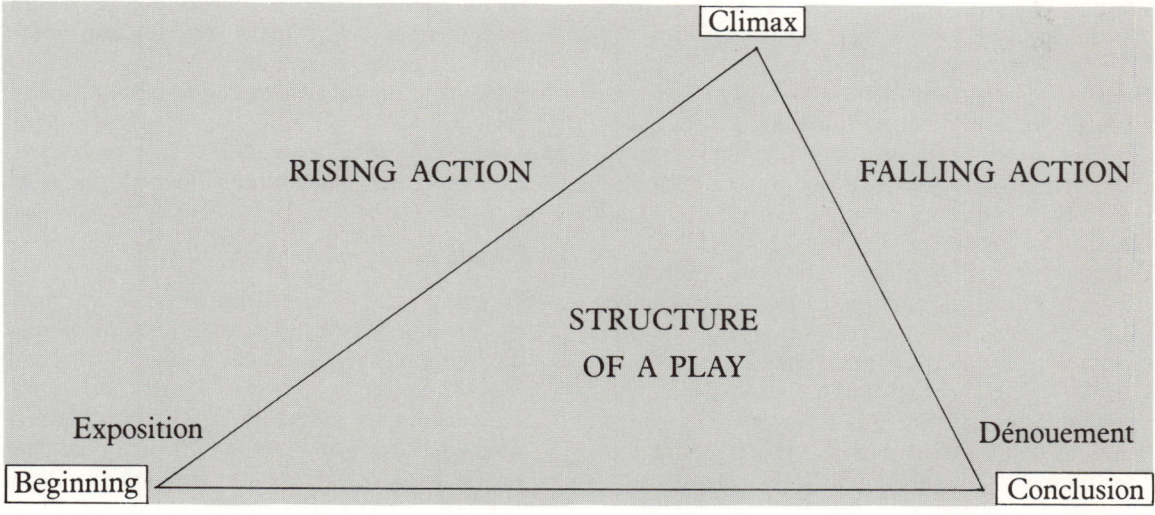

- **Suspense** is the building up of tension and uncertainty. The audience is in a state of doubt or expectancy as to what will finally happen.
- **Theme** is the central idea or main problem of the play.

In the following dialogue, the club star, Geoff — 'the fabulous, flashy import, who doesn't give a continental about the Club' — reveals his true colours to Laurie, the fatherly old coach who is threatened with dismissal. Geoff also reveals an ugly underside of the Selection Committee.

A Lively Exchange

Laurie: You've read the morning papers, I suppose?

Geoff: Yep.

Laurie: The Committee are meeting in just over an hour to decide whether they're going to accept my resignation. I think they're going to ask me to reconsider it but it's hardly worth my while if you're going to keep defying me.

Geoff: So what are we supposed to do? Kiss and make up?

Laurie: I don't want you to defy me in front of the players again.

Geoff: I don't want to be told to do push-ups again.

Laurie: If you break discipline you do push-ups. Everyone does.

Geoff: I don't.

Laurie: Nobody else objects to push-ups.

Geoff: That's because most of them have got ear-to-ear bone.

Laurie: I see. You've done a few subjects at University so you're out of our class.

Geoff: If you like doing push-ups I must be.

Laurie: All right. Point taken. You don't like push-ups, but it goes deeper than that, doesn't it? Why are you playing so badly?

Geoff: I'm doing my best.

Laurie: No you're not. You played two good games at the start of the year, you went to pieces in your third game and you've got progressively worse ever since.

Geoff: I've lost form.

Laurie: It's more than that. You're not even trying. Is it just that you object to me personally or is there some other reason?

Geoff: I've lost form. That's all.

Laurie: Look, I know there's some degree of antagonism from the other players. You came to the Club with a big reputation and a lot of money so there's bound to be, but it's not going to help matters if you lay down and stop trying.

Geoff: You're reading too much into it. I've lost form.

Laurie: It's more than that. Last week you stood down on the forward line staring into the crowd for over a minute. The ball came and you let it go right past you. Look, level with me, Geoff. That's more than being out of form. What's going on?

Geoff: All right. If you really want to know, what's going on is that I'm sick to death of football and I couldn't care less if I never played another game in my life. It's all a lot of macho-competitive bullshit. You chase a lump of pigskin around a muddy ground as if your bloody life depended on it and when you get it you kick it to buggery and go chasing it again. Football shits me.

Laurie: I wish you'd let us know your attitude to the game before we paid ninety thousand dollars for you.

Geoff: If you think you can buy me like a lump of meat then you'd better think again.

Laurie: You took our money with your eyes open, Geoff. Don't you think you owe us something?

Geoff: If you're stupid enough to offer me that sort of money I'll take it, but all you've bought is my presence out on an oval for two hours every Saturday afternoon.

Laurie: We thought we were buying a lot more than that.

Geoff: Took your money? It was practically thrown at me. You weren't there at that final sign-up session?

(**Geoff** *shakes his head ruefully.*)

It was a joke. There were three of my guys on one side of the table and Gerry, Jock and Ted on the other. Jock was looking at me, and I'm not joking, as if I was a giant pork chop. He was almost salivating. I felt sure that any moment he'd bring out a little hammer and test whether my reflexes are as good as they're cracked up to be. I couldn't believe that those three goons were for real. By the time we'd got ourselves through the pleasantries I was getting pretty crapped off and I decided to make myself a bit difficult, so when they shoved the form in front of me to sign, I read it through four times, put down the pen, shook my head and said I wanted more money. I didn't really expect to get any more — I just wanted to establish myself as something more than a tailor's dummy — but it was marvellous. All hell broke loose. Your guys called my guys cheats, Jock thumped our President on the snout, and Gerry sat there stirring his coffee with a retractable biro. I was just about to burst out laughing when I looked across and there was Ted Parker sitting in the middle of all this pandemonium, his face as white as a sheet, scribbling frantically in his cheque book. 'Ten thousand,' he yelled. 'I'll go an extra ten thousand, but that's my limit.' Everyone had a ball.

[from *The Club* by DAVID WILLIAMSON]

Some Questions

(1) Doing push-ups is an accepted punishment for the infringement of club rules — e.g. late arrival for training. Why does Geoff refuse to accept such punishment?

(2) How does Laurie use sarcasm and an accusation of snobbery in an attempt to bring Geoff to his senses?

(3) In answer to Laurie's questions about the reason for his bad performance, Geoff keeps on insisting that he has simply 'lost form'. How does Laurie induce Geoff, finally, to give the real reasons?

(4) What are Geoff's heartfelt objections to the game?

(5) Instead of loyalty, Geoff is prepared to offer only one thing. What is this?

(6) How did the three members of the final sign-up session offend Geoff's dignity as a human being?

(7) What means does Geoff use to condemn the sign-up session?

(8) David Williamson's plays are noted for their faithful reproduction of the vernacular — that is, the ordinary everyday speech of the street, the police station, the footie club. Notice Geoff's 'Yep' in the second line. Comment on the playwright's use of other words and expressions to achieve a vernacular effect.

(9) Comment on the change in the quality of Geoff's speech that occurs when he becomes upset and angry.

(10) Geoff's vilification of football is highly subjective. Do you agree with it?

(11) Comment on Laurie's tone towards Geoff throughout this passage. What can you infer from this tone about his success (or otherwise) as a coach.

(12) Conflict — the clash of characters, wills, ideas, events — is the lifeblood of drama. How is it brought out in this extract?

Thinking and Reasoning (6)

Appealing to Experts and Other Important People

A technique frequently used to persuade people of the rightness of a particular point of view is to include the supporting statement of an 'expert' or a famous person. At its best, this can be a powerful way of adding strength to an argument — if the person appealed to really is an expert in the particular area under discussion. It can even have some strength when the person, though perhaps not expert in the field, is believed to be reliable. At its worst, it can be a blatant attempt to appeal to our emotions — or to exploit our gullibility — by using one of society's idols or heroes to support a particular claim.

How Expert Is the 'Expert'?

The first consideration for anyone thinking critically is to weigh up the credentials of the expert being used. How expert *is* the 'expert'? Is this a field he/she has special knowledge about?

Exercise 1

(1) Cheyne Horan is one of Australia's 'super-surfers'. What effect is his status as a surfer intended to have on our attitude to Rip Curl wetsuits?

(2) Explain how wetsuits might be within Cheyne Horan's field of expertise.

(3) What is added to the expert's recommendation by this particular picture of Cheyne?

(4) What is added to the expert's recommendation by the emotive words 'stoked' and 'ultimate'?

(5) Does the conjecture that Cheyne was probably paid for this advertisement have any effect upon its impact for you? Explain.

Exercise 2

Consider the following fields of controversy and rate each of the three experts offered according to their relevance to the issue.

Field of Controversy	Experts
(1) The advisability of shorter working-hours	the Federal Treasurer; a trade-union leader; an economist
(2) Need for changes in the education system	a senior school student; an employer; a school principal
(3) Censorship of sex and violence on TV	a concerned parent; a sociologist; a minister of religion
(4) Better preparation for bereavement and death	a doctor; a minister of religion; one who has recently experienced a bereavement
(5) Racism in Australia	a politician; an Aboriginal community leader; a social worker in inner-city areas
(6) Guidance in selecting friends	parents; peer group; yourself
(7) Religious commitment or otherwise	a minister; an atheist; parents
(8) Diet	a health 'freak'; an accredited dietitian; editor of a popular women's magazine

How Biased Is the 'Expert'?

The second consideration for anyone thinking critically is to weigh up the bias of the expert whose supporting testimony is being used. Is this person prejudiced in some way? Is he being paid to say this? Often this question of bias is hard to find a clear answer to, but whenever we *can* establish prejudiced testimony we need to discount its value to some extent.

Exercise 3

(1) What is there to suggest that 'Amalgamated Sneakers' may be biased in their view-point?

(2) What experts might you consult to find out if jogging really is good for you?

Some Difficulties

You may already have discovered that there is often considerable difficulty in deciding who is 'expert' in some fields. For example, there is much debate throughout the world on nuclear safety. Who is an expert on nuclear safety? Is it a *nuclear scientist*? He should know about the science of nuclear physics but is he competent to judge what is 'safe' for the world? Is it a *worker* in a nuclear power station? He has some first-hand knowledge of a reactor and its attendant risks. Is it a *doctor*? A *politician*? Perhaps a top *national-security official*? Often, it is immensely difficult to decide who the 'supreme' expert is. In such cases we should recognize that many different people have some expertise to offer; to the best of our ability, we should try to be aware of our own biases; finally, we can take each contribution into account and thus 'judge' the issue and decide for ourselves.

Language Basics (6)

Agreement Again

Here is another set of rules that will help you to communicate correctly in the sentences you write.

Rule 1 ● Make sure that the verb 'to be' agrees with the subject and not the complement.
EXAMPLE: Their <u>flights</u> from the rock <u>are</u> part of the instinctive urge to take wing.

Rule 2 ● A compound subject joined by 'either . . . or', 'neither . . . nor', or 'not only . . . but also' takes a verb that agrees in number with the nearer subject.
EXAMPLE: Neither <u>the gull</u> nor <u>the sailors</u> <u>were</u> aware of the approaching storm.

Rule 3 ● If two or more parts of a subject joined by 'either . . . or' or 'neither . . . nor' are singular, then the verb is also singular.
EXAMPLE: Neither <u>Jonathan</u> nor <u>the other gull</u> <u>goes</u> into an uncontrollable dive.

Rule 4 ● The following nouns take a plural verb:

gloves	shears	jeans	tweezers	thanks	pincers
scissors	proceeds	trousers	statistics	premises	

Exceptions: (a) When 'pair' is used with words such as some of the above (e.g. 'a pair of trousers'), it conveys the idea of a single thing and a singular verb is required.
(b) 'News' takes a singular verb.

EXAMPLES: (a) Scissors <u>were</u> needed to cut the string.
A pair of shears <u>was</u> used to cut through the wire.
(b) No news <u>is</u> good news.

Using the Rules

Correct the following sentences.

(1) Either the terminal velocity or the solid wall of sound were enough to destroy his judgement.

(2) The wings of a bird is an intricate part of its skeletal structure.

(3) A pair of tweezers were used to remove the oil-soaked feathers.

(4) New premises is needed to house the shipwreck victims.

(5) Not only the feet but also the bill of the seagull are perfectly adapted to an aquatic existence.

(6) News of the shipwreck are still coming through.

(7) Fishing boats mobilized by the port authority was soon to the rescue.

(8) Neither the rudder nor the oars was in working order.

Punctuation — The comma

Commas are used:
- to mark a natural pause in a sentence.
  EXAMPLE: The boat was a crumb on the sea, four thousand feet below.

- after a phrase beginning a sentence.
  EXAMPLE: By sunup, Jonathan Gull was practising again.

- to mark off an explanatory expression.
  EXAMPLE: Jonathan, a gull with a mission, flew fast to his destination.

Exercise

Insert commas, where necessary, into the following sentences.

(1) He swallowed knowing that if his wings unfolded at that speed he'd be blown into a million tiny shreds of seagull.

(2) When they hear of it he thought they'll be wild with joy.

(3) The sailor rushed to the side of the ship megaphone to his lips.

(4) A single wingtip feather he found moved a fraction of an inch.

(5) Diving down from one thousand feet Jonathan began his pullout.

(6) It was a breakthrough the greatest single moment in the history of the flock.

Unit Seven

Comprehension (7)

Social Life in the Insect World

We are near the end of August. The male Mantis, a slender and elegant lover, judges the time to be propitious. He makes eyes at his powerful companion; he turns his head towards her; he bows his neck and raises his thorax. His little pointed face almost seems to wear an expression. For a long time he stands thus motionless, in contemplation of the desired one. The latter, as though indifferent, does not stir. Yet the lover has seized upon a sign of consent: a sign of which I do not know the secret. He approaches: suddenly he erects his wings, which are shaken with a convulsive tremor.

This is his declaration. He throws himself timidly on the back of his corpulent companion; he clings to her desperately, and steadies himself. The prelude to the embrace is generally lengthy, and the embrace will sometimes last for five or six hours.

Nothing worthy of notice occurs during this time. Finally the two separate, but they are soon to be made one flesh in a much more intimate fashion. If the poor lover is loved by his mistress as the giver of fertility, she also loves him as the choicest of game. During the day, or at latest on the morrow, he is seized by his companion, who first gnaws through the back of his neck, according to use and wont, and then methodically devours him, mouthful by mouthful, leaving only the wings. Here we have no case of jealousy, but simply a depraved taste.

I had the curiosity to wonder how a second male would be received by a newly fecundated female. The result of my inquiry was scandalous. The Mantis in only too many cases is never sated with embraces and conjugal feasts. After a rest, of variable duration, whether the eggs have been laid or not, a second male is welcomed and devoured like the first. A third succeeds him, does his duty, and affords yet another meal. A fourth suffers a like fate. In the course of two weeks I have seen the same Mantis treat seven husbands in this fashion. She admitted all to her embraces, and all paid for the nuptial ecstasy with their lives.

[from *Social Life in the Insect World* by J. H. FABRE]

Check Your Understanding

(1) What is the meaning of, 'The male Mantis . . . judges the time to be propitious'?

(2) How does the female Mantis react to the male Mantis's 'making eyes' at her?

(3) What noticeable difference is there in the physical appearance of the male and female Mantis?

(4) What do you think was the writer's purpose in this passage?

(5) What explanation does the writer give for the female's killing of the male Mantis?

(6) What evidence can you find to show that the writer allows his own feelings to be revealed?

(7) What evidence can you find to suggest that the writer is a dedicated naturalist?

(8) What do the following words mean: (a) prelude (b) tremor (c) sated (d) nuptial?

(9) What does the writer mean by 'conjugal feasts'?

(10) Did you sympathize with the male Mantis? Why?

(11) What comments would you make about the style of this writer? Would you expect a scientists, biologist or naturalist to write like this? Why?

(12) What is the writer's tone in this passage?

IF MANTIS IS THE FOOD OF LOVE....

Working with Words (7)

Senior Spelling Demons	Confusing Pairs	On the Move	Sport	Increase Your Word Power
original	past	pedestrian	participate	boycott
distribute	passed	velocity	tenacity	veracity
premature	rout	automatic	incentive	exonerate
weird	route	registration	vigorous	assail
exhibit	ingenious	vehicle	competitive	avaricious
exceedingly	ingenuous	certificate	forfeit	levity
calendar	principal	maintenance	athlete	prowess
weight	principle	concentration	professional	resilience
burglar	liable	mechanical	recreation	extricate
patience	libel	collision	achievement	pallid

Change the Words

Change into people

(a) competitive..

(b) assail..

(c) participate ....

(d) exhibit ....

(e) mechanical ....

(f) distribute..

Change into adjectives

(a) athlete..

(b) libel ....

(c) tenacity..

(d) recreation ....

(e) resilience ....

(f) veracity..

Change into nouns

(a) original...

(b) vigorous..

(c) liable...

(d) ingenious..

(e) avaricious ....

(f) automatic...

Change into verbs

(a) weight..

(b) maintenance ....

(c) collision..

(d) concentration....................................

(e) competitive..

(f) original...

Change into adverbs

(a) original...

(b) automatic..

(c) patience..

Increase Your Word Power

Replace the words or phrases in heavy type with words from the *Increase Your Word Power* column.

(1) The British government decided to **shut off all business dealings with** Russia.

(2) The fly managed to **free** itself from the spider's web.

(3) While recovering from influenza, some people have a **pale** complexion.

(4) King Midas was extremely **greedy for money.**

(5) Thanks to the new evidence, the teenager was **proved blameless.**

(6) With her words the teacher began to **attack** the lazy student.

(7) The judge doubted the **truth** of the criminal's words.

(8) The Australian and New Zealand soldiers showed great **valour** at Gallipoli.

Confusing Pairs

Complete these sentences by inserting the correct words (from the brackets) into the blank spaces.

(1) The .... witness failed to appear in court. [**principle/principal**]

(2) If one is proved guilty of negligent driving, one is .... to face a severe fine. [**libel/liable**]

(3) The speedboat .... over the tow-rope as it sped .... the swimmer. [**past/ passed**]

(4) For a mere pittance, the .... inventor sold his .... labour-saving device. [**ingenuous/ingenious**]

(5) The .... of the army took place on the .... through the treacherous mountain pass. [**rout/route**]

Match the Meanings

Match the words in the left-hand column with their meanings in the right-hand column.

velocity	frank, open
ingenuous	frivolity
premature	stimulus, motivation
forfeit	persistence, stubbornness
rout	display
exhibit	swiftness
tenacity	overwhelming defeat
ingenious	too early
incentive	penalty, loss of right
levity	clever

Word Origins

'Boycott'

Notice the word 'boycott' in your word-list. It comes from the surname of an Irishman, Captain C. C. Boycott, who managed the estates of an absentee Irish landlord. Boycott demanded such high rents for the land that the tenants threatened to kill him and, more importantly (from our point of view), refused to have any contact or dealings with him. Thus, 'boycott' is now used to describe any refusal to deal or associate with a person, company, government, etc.

'Tenacious'

This word comes from the Latin verb *tenere* ('to hold'). Someone who is 'tenacious' holds on firmly. All the following words come from *tenere*: tenant, retain, retentive, retinue, tentacles, tenure, tenet, contain, pertinent. See whether you can use some of them to complete the following sentences.

(1) A person who occupies (holds) land under a landlord is a ....

(2) An octopus holds onto things with its ....

(3) The student had a .... mind.

(4) A .... is a belief or doctrine held as a truth by some group or person.

(5) The king had a large ....

(6) The mayor's .... was for five years.

Language in Action (7)

Colloquial Language

Colloquial language is familiar, informal language — the language of relaxed, friendly speech and writing. Friends meet and exchange greetings:
    'How're you doing, Pete?'
    'Not bad, mate. How's yourself?'
    'Good, real good. What're you been up to?'
And so on.
    Formal language would be inappropriate. These are friends and their speech is relaxed, making use of common and familiar words and phrases.
    Here, then, are the features of colloquial language. It:

- is at an *informal* level of speech or writing;

- makes use of widely understood, idiomatic words and phrases — e.g. 'How're you doing?', 'been up to' — which are usually identified as *colloquialisms;*

- often features the use of *contractions* rather than the more formal complete words or phrases — e.g. 'How're' instead of 'How are';

- may, at times, *break strict grammatical correctness* in conforming to popular use — e.g. 'What're' instead of 'What have', or 'real good' instead of 'really well'.

A Mosquito Yarn

Anyway, as I was saying before you so rudely interrupted, the mosquitoes are big in the Territory. Their stings brought out lumps on Truthful Jones as big as tennis balls. He tried everything to get a bit of sleep; DDT, poison gas, and a sawn-off shot-gun, but they didn't turn a hair. So, one night, he thought of a bright idea: instead of going to bed, he took his mattress and blankets and a hammer and got into a big iron tank that was empty on account of the dry season.

Why the hammer?

Well, he knew the mossies would find him and attack with their pro — what's-their-names — and try to cut a hole in the tank. And he was right. They attacked one at a time at first, and every time a proboscis stuck through he bent it with a hammer. A shrewd old head was Truthful.

Must have been.

You can say that again. But then the rest of the mossies had a conference and decided to attack in dive-bomber formation. And *zoom!* — a row of proboscises stuck through shaped liked a 'V'. And old Truthful bent them over with his hammer. Well, the mossies brought up reinforcements and Truthful heard them talking outside the tank . . .

Just a minute, do you expect me . . .

No, I don't expect you to believe that Northern Territory mosquitoes can speak English but, you see, Truthful had picked up a smattering of their particular lingo, an aboriginal dialect, needless to say. And he heard them planning to form their proboscises into a hacksaw to cut a hole in the tank. And *zoom!* they attacked in a line. But Truthful was too quick for them. He bent each proboscis in turn with his hammer, like playing a tune on a xylophone. And pretty soon every mosquito in the area was caught by the nose in the walls of the tank.

I believe you — but millions wouldn't.

You can ask old Truthful Jones. He didn't get his nickname for nothing. Anyway, he was very weary seeing as he hadn't slept for six months. So he soon fell sound asleep. And when he woke up the tank was on the banks of the Yarra River in Melbourne two thousand miles away. Truthful Jones never went back to the Territory after that.

[from *The Yarns of Billy Borker* by FRANK HARDY]

Exercise 1

(1) What is 'the Territory'? Who are the people most likely to call it 'the Territory'?

(2) What is the meaning of the colloquialism 'didn't turn a hair'?

(3) Suggest a reason for the use of '*on account of* the dry season' instead of '*because of* the dry season'.

(4) What is the meaning of 'a smattering of their particular lingo'?

(5) Comment on any features of the reply, 'Must have been'.

(6) What effect is the speaker trying to achieve by using the expression 'I believe you — but millions wouldn't'?

(7) What would be a grammatically more correct rendering of 'he was very weary seeing as he hadn't slept for six months'?

(8) Offer a possible explanation for the invention of the colloquial word 'mossies'. Would this term be acceptable in a biologist's research paper? Support your answer.

(9) What effect is achieved by the use of colloquial speech in this extract? For example, what does it do to the atmosphere of the extract?

Colloquial Language — Good or Bad?

Questions about whether the use of colloquial language is good or bad miss the point. There are no 'right' or 'wrong' levels of language that exclude all others. The goodness or badness of language can be evaluated only in the light of the purpose of the language and the situation in which it is used. If the colloquial level of use is appropriate to the situation and purpose, then it can be justified. However, if it is out of character with the situation and the purpose, we are justified in being critical of its use.

'SIR.. YOU HAVE A HEAD LIKE A ROBBER'S DOG!'

Exercise 2
Comment on the appropriateness or inappropriateness of the following colloquial expressions in the given situations.

Expression	Situation
(1) 'Hmm. You've got the dog's disease.'	A doctor examining a patient.
(2) 'Strike a light! How are you?'	A person responding upon being addressed by the queen.
(3) 'I'm sitting.'	A person playing cards with friends.
(4) 'Get out there, and go for the doctor.'	Cricket captain to next batsman.
(5) 'C'mon! You're draggin' the chain.'	Leader of a hiking party to a member.
(6) 'Oh, pull your head in.'	Speaker in a debate, referring to a member of the opposition team.
(7) 'He couldn't fight his way out of a paper bag.'	Boxer being interviewed about his next opponent.
(8) 'Milkos all over the country are battling to make a go of it.'	Politician, addressing parliament on economic issues.
(9) 'He's as game as Ned Kelly.'	Football coach describing a team member.
(10) 'She'll be apples.'	Headmaster addressing school assembly.

Exercise 3 — 'Shooting through'

Look over the following extract taken from G. A. Wilkes's *A Dictionary of Australian Colloquialisms.*

> **shoot through** As for 'go through' q.v.
>
> **1951** Seaforth Mackenzie *Dead Men Rising* 37: 'I'm shooting through — my woman's sick and I've waited longer than I should have.'
>
> **1957** Randolph Stow *The Bystander* 191: 'Just shoot through, son, and leave us to settle this.'
>
> **1962** John Morrison *Twenty-Three* 181: 'And — let us have it in plain Australian — while he was taking the call you shot through.'
>
> **1970** Richard Beilby *No Medals for Aphrodite* 233: 'You can shoot through on your own if you like, but I'm going to get her to Athens somehow.'
>
> **see Bondi tram**

Notice how, in this particular dictionary, the expression is initially defined ('As for "go through" q.v.'). By referring back to 'go through' in the dictionary, we find this definition:

> To abscond, make a swift departure,
> esp. to avoid some obligation.

Then, a number of examples of the use of the expression in Australian literature are cited. In each case, the year the book was published is given, then the author's name, the book title, and the page number.

Questions

(1) Give your own definition of the colloquial expression 'shoot through'.

(2) Use the dictionary reference to enable you to cite an example of the use of the expression in a reasonably recent Australian book.

(3) In what kind of a situation would the use of the expression 'shoot through' be acceptable?

(4) Give an example of a situation in which the use of 'shoot through' could not be considered appropriate.

(5) What meaning is added when the expression is extended to become 'shoot through like a Bondi tram'?

(6) Offer an explanation for the creation of the expression 'shoot through like a Bondi tram'.

(7) What does the colloquial expression 'have a shot at' mean? Use it in a sentence.

(8) What does the colloquial expression 'That's the shot!' mean? Give an example of it in use.

(9) What does a person do when he 'shoots off his mouth'?

The Language of Literature (7)

The Poetry of War

About twenty-five years before the birth of Christ, the Roman poet Horatius Flaccus (otherwise known as Horace) had written in a book of his poetry: *'Dulce et decorum est pro patria mori.'* ('It is sweet and fitting to die for one's country.') This viewpoint of the Romans was also held by the English during World War I. Wilfred Owen takes this statement of ideals and mockingly applies it to the horrors of the 1914–18 war.

DULCE ET DECORUM EST

Bent double, like old beggars under sacks,
Knock-kneed, coughing like hags, we cursed through sludge,
Till on the haunting flares we turned our backs,
And towards our distant rest began to trudge.
Men marched asleep. Many had lost their boots,
But limped on, blood-shod. All went lame, all blind;
Drunk with fatigue; deaf even to the hoots
Of gas-shells dropping softly behind.

Gas! Gas! Quick, boys! – An ecstasy of fumbling,
Fitting the clumsy helmets just in time,
But someone still was yelling out and stumbling
And floundering like a man in fire or lime—
Dim through the misty panes and thick green light,
As under a green sea, I saw him drowning.
In all my dreams before my helpless sight
He plunges at me, guttering, choking, drowning.

If in some smothering dreams, you too could pace
Behind the wagon that we flung him in,
And watch the white eyes writhing in his face,
His hanging face, like a devil's sick of sin;
If you could hear, at every jolt, the blood
Come gargling from the froth-corrupted lungs,
Bitter as the cud
Of vile, incurable sores on innocent tongues,—
My friend, you would not tell with such high zest
To children ardent for some desperate glory,
The old Lie: Dulce et decorum est
Pro patria mori.

WILFRED OWEN

Check Your Understanding

(1) Do you think the title of the poem is suitable? Why?

(2) Owen himself was killed in 1918 in the trenches. What evidence in the poem can you find to suggest that it was written from first-hand experience?

(3) What do you understand by 'blood-shod'?

(4) What was the physical condition of the soldiers as revealed in the first stanza?

(5) Why were the soldiers at first 'deaf to the hoots / Of gas-shells dropping softly behind'?

(6) What is meant by 'ecstasy of fumbling'?

(7) What is the 'green sea' the poet is describing?

(8) Why does the poet refer to the soldier without his gas-mask as 'drowning'?

(9) Why does the poet say 'my helpless sight'?

(10) Why does Owen entreat: 'If . . . you too could pace / Behind the wagon that we flung him in, . . . '?

(11) How does the poet react to the suffering of the gassed soldier?

(12) Why is 'Dulce et decorum est / Pro patria mori' the 'old lie'?

(13) What is your reaction to war after reading this poem?

(14) Throughout the poem, what has the poet sought to show the reader about war?

Thinking and Reasoning (7)

The Use of Statistics

Statistics are frequently quoted as evidence to support a claim that is being made. On the surface, they usually appear to be valid — they are important evidence for our mind-computer to process.

However, there are several ways in which we need critically to examine any statistics quoted in support of a particular viewpoint. Three 'R' words will serve to remind you of questions that should be asked.

1. How RELIABLE is the *source* of these statistics?

If the figures are quoted by a team-member in a debate, there is a good chance that they may be 'made up' or 'fiddled'. Certainly they need further checking! On the other hand, if the statistics are offered by a reputable opinion-poll group, or the Commonwealth Statistician, or a respected textbook, we can have considerably *more* confidence in the source.

2. How REPRESENTATIVE is the *sample* from which the statistics have been drawn?

Since it is too huge a task to question every person in Australia, or to analyse every car accident (etc), we usually find that statisticians draw their conclusions from a *sample* rather than from the whole population. Such samples need to *represent*, as accurately as possible, the picture that we would obtain if we were indeed to check with the whole population. To be truly representative, samples generally should be:

(i) **large enough** to reflect the whole population. The larger the sample, the more confidently can we accept conclusions drawn from it. It would be risky to draw conclusions about the academic standards of a large high school, for example, by looking at the exam results of just ten students. On the other hand, we might feel quite confident of conclusions drawn from a sample of a hundred students.

(ii) **random.** By 'random' we mean that the people or objects used as the sample have been chosen as though by chance — i.e. the sample is not 'stacked' to yield a certain conclusion. For example, choosing a thousand people from the wealthier areas of a large city, in order to assess the average income of the people of the city, would result in distorted conclusions being reached. The sample was not random. People in poorer areas were not given any chance of being represented in the sample.

3. How RELEVANT are the statistics to the *conclusions*?

Sometimes statistics are misused to impress us or confuse us — so that on further analysis they may well turn out to be irrelevant or, at the most, to have a tenuous relationship to the conclusions which are reached. For example, would statistics quoted about the increasing number of car accidents in Australia be a strong argument if used as support for further government spending on public transport?

The supermarket special is often just a hoax

SUPERMARKET specials are often a hoax and some shoppers are forced to pay inflated prices for old stock, according to a survey by one of Australia's top consumer groups.

The group also slams manufacturers for concentrating on "giant, family and economy" sized packages, which are of little use to pensioners, the unemployed and single people.

The hard-hitting report, compiled by the Australian Consumers Association and released in the June edition of its magazine Choice, shows:

● That a survey of 66 supermarkets in Australian capital cities proved shoppers should be prepared to change brands and shop around for the best bargains.

● By forgetting brand names and buying on price, it is easy to save up to $175 a year on food and household bills and up to 20 per cent on weekly supermarket bills.

● The dearest supermarket surveyed was in Perth and the cheapest supermarkets were in Sydney, particularly in the western suburbs.

● Beef and veal prices have risen by 45.5 per cent in the 12 months to February this year; lamb and mutton prices

have gone up 21.3 per cent; pork by 19 per cent and other meats by 28.6 per cent. The prices of fish during the same period rose by 19.7 per cent and poultry by 5.6 per cent.

● Support for criticism of the processed food industry by the Prices Justification Tribunal, about the way in which manufacturers set prices on store "specials".

The PJT has already reported that the cost of price reductions on supermarket "specials" is often recouped by making other store items dearer.

The association says

that its survey disclosed that its checkers often found that an item marked as a "special" in one shop was no cheaper than the price in other shops.

"Sometimes it was even more," the report says.

"Our checkers found that some items bore two or even three price stickers. This means that groceries have been 'over-ticketed' as price rises have occurred."

It says that while the PJT had found that large retailers claimed to be selling processed foods at pre-price-rise charges, consumers were often paying the new price for grocery items that the supermarket had in stock.

The Choice report also says that while bulk-buying has some economical advantages, there are drawbacks in the trend to bigger packages — particularly for important, disadvantaged groups in the community, old age pensioners, the unemployed and single people.

"In England it is still

possible to buy small containers of milk, tea, butter and other grocery items that can be consumed by one person before they go bad or lose their freshness," the report adds.

"Australia, in joining the trend towards bulk selling over the past 20 years, has ignored the buying patterns of these groups."

Choice also was surprised to find that a major part of the survey showed Sydney's supermarkets, overall, appeared to be the cheapest for consumers who consistently bought brand name products.

The average price for 19 everyday brand-name items in Sydney was $15.63. Brisbane followed with $15.66, Adelaide with $16.30, Canberra $16.62, Melbourne $16.69, Perth $17.05 and Hobart $17.35.

This conflicts with the latest Consumer Price Index figures which show that Sydney food prices rose higher than those in most other capital cities over the past 12 months.

Exercise 1

(1) Who has compiled the statistics quoted in this article? How would you rate the reliability of the source of these statistics?

(2) How many supermarkets were surveyed? Do you think that this is a large enough sample?

(3) What is there about the supermarkets chosen to suggest that there was some attempt to make the survey a representative one?

(4) What conclusions are drawn from the survey? Do these follow from the statistical evidence?

Graphs

Sometimes statistical information is presented in graph form. Always look carefully at the heading of a graph, and also at the labels given to each axis, and make sure you understand them, before going on to study the graph itself.

Exercise 2

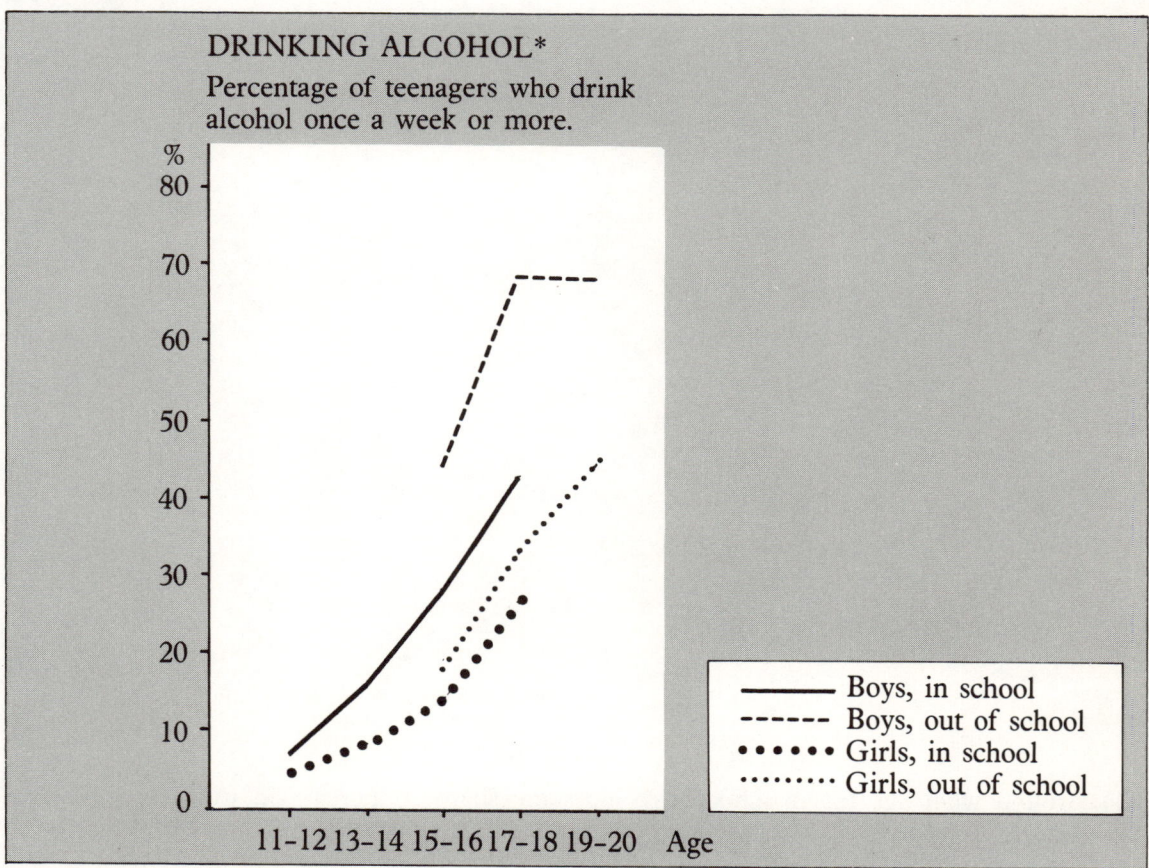

DRINKING ALCOHOL*
Percentage of teenagers who drink
alcohol once a week or more.

——— Boys, in school
- - - - Boys, out of school
•••••• Girls, in school
·········· Girls, out of school

*Based on data from *12 to 20: Studies of City Youth* by W. F. Connell *et al.*, Hicks Smith & Sons Pty Ltd, 1975.

(1) Which of the four groups has the highest percentage of drinkers?

(2) For which of the four groups does consumption show the sharpest increase? Around what age?

(3) Who has the higher percentage of weekly drinkers — 17–18-year-old out-of-school girls or 15–16-year-old in-school boys?

(4) At around what age does the percentage of weekly drinkers level off for out-of-school boys?

(5) Who has the higher percentage of weekly drinkers — 15–16-year-old out-of-school boys or 19–20-year-old out-of-school girls?

(6) 'There are more *non*-drinking boys and girls in schools than there are drinkers.' True or false?

(7) 'Most boys who have just left school do not drink alcohol once a week.' True or false?

(8) Which of the four groups shows the slowest rate of increase in consumption? Around what age?

Exercise 3

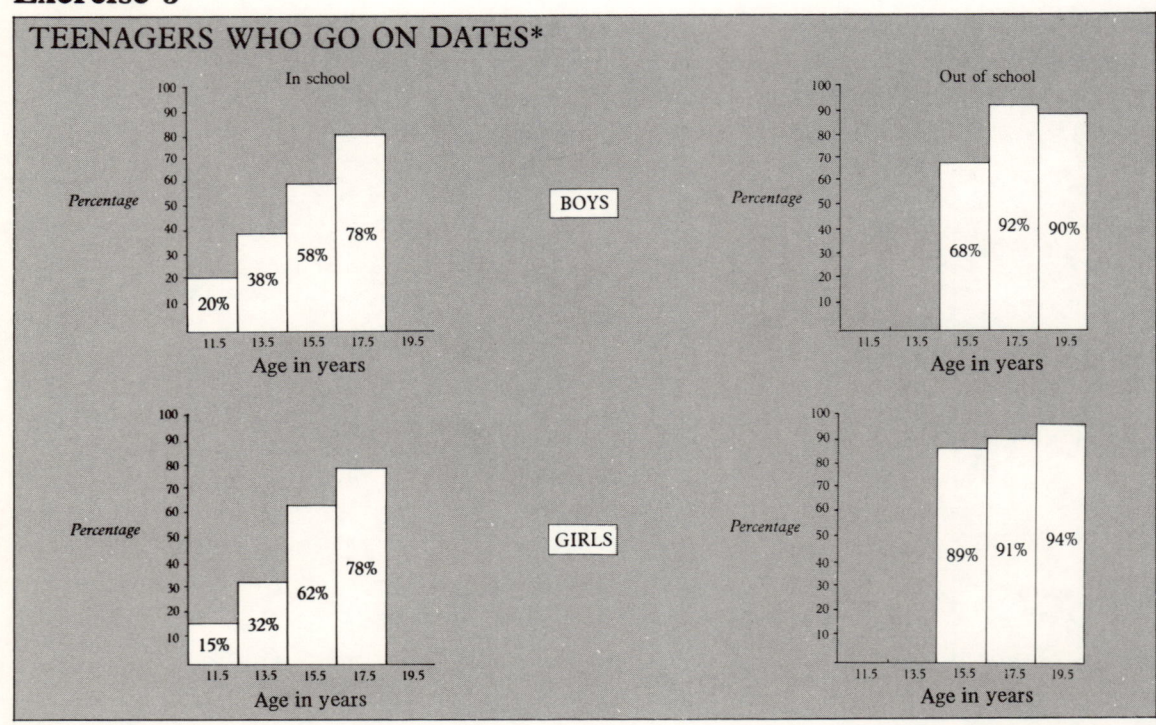

*Based on data from *12 to 20: Studies of City Youth* by W. F. Connell *et al.*, Hicks Smith & Sons Pty Ltd, 1975.

(1) Around what age for in-school girls does the sharpest increase in numbers who date occur?

(2) What is the most obvious factor about percentages of dating for out-of-school girls between the ages of 15.5 and 19.5?

(3) Does a higher percentage of boys or of girls date at earlier ages?

(4) Does a higher percentage of boys or of girls date around age 15.5?

(5) At what age does the percentage of in-school boys and girls come closest to being the same?

(6) At what age does the highest dating percentage occur? Is it for boys or girls? In-school or out-of-school?

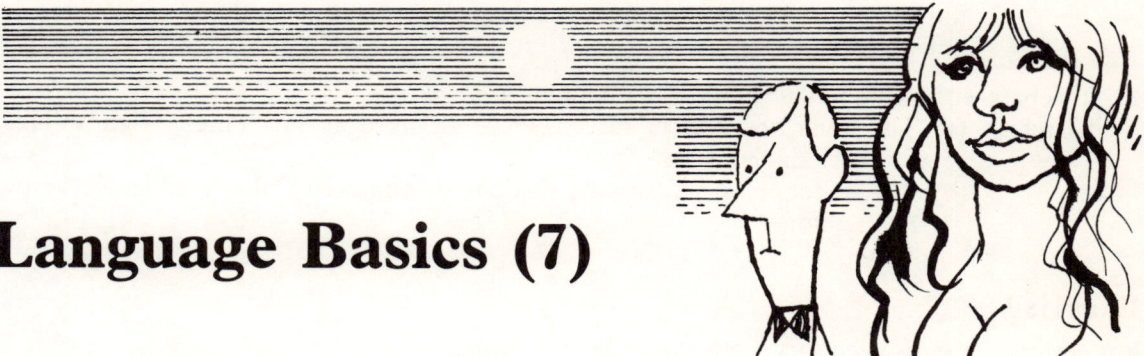

Language Basics (7)

Be Consistent

Shifting from one tense or person to another in a piece of writing is often confusing. Follow these rules on consistency:

Rule 1 • Maintain the same tense throughout a piece of writing.
     EXAMPLE: We <u>are</u> near the end of August. The male Mantis <u>judges</u> the time to be propitious.

Rule 2 • Maintain the same person or point-of-view throughout a piece of writing.
     EXAMPLE: <u>I</u> thought the little pointed face of the Mantis seemed to wear an expression, although <u>I</u> couldn't tell exactly what it meant.

Using the Rules
Use the rules to correct the following sentences.

(1) As you watched the female Mantis, one simply could not be sure how she would react.

(2) If the poor lover is loved by his mistress as the giver of fertility, she also loved him as the choicest of game.

(3) She admits all to her embraces and all paid for the nuptial ecstasy with their lives.

(4) We observed the insects carefully and one was aware of the ferocity of their existences.

(5) After I saw the shocking cannibalism that always terminated the relationship of male and female insects, one never knew whether to be awed or simply indifferent.

(6) We hastened to the viewing cage but the insects are not there.

(7) She will mate with more lovers in the future than she is doing in the past.

(8) He bows his neck and then raised his throax.

Punctuation — Commas again

Commas are used:

1. To separate names, adjectives, actions (etc), when listed as a series or a sequence.

   EXAMPLE: The ant, the spider, the wasp and the scorpion are sometimes aggressive.

   [*Note:* 'And' placed before the last name in a list usually takes the place of a comma, although some writers favour the extra comma ('... the wasp, and the scorpion ...'), especially since ambiguity could sometimes result from its omission.]

2. To separate the component parts of an address.

   EXAMPLES: (a) The great observer of insect behaviour lived at The Pines, High Village, Suffolk, England.

   (b) The insect colony was in the shrubbery behind 16 Duke Avenue, Reckelby, Palmerston.

Exercise

Put commas, where necessary, into the following sentences.

(1) J. H. Fabre author of 'The Wonders of Instinct' finished the last word in the manuscript in January 1917.

(2) Crawling flying breeding and fighting are the elements of most insect existences.

(3) Vandenberg the great entomologist was born in 1890 and spent most of his life in Amsterdam Holland.

(4) The Mantis's jaws were long curved powerful and deadly.

(5) Snow storms in May 1914 a bad year for weather made insects hard to locate.

(6) The entomologist tracked the Mantis to the grass verge lifted the net brought it down swiftly trapped the insect and transferred it to a travelling cage.

Unit Eight

Comprehension (8)

Blood on the Shamrock

His name was Sean but, of course, everybody called him Paddy at the riverside warehouse where he worked. Soft-spoken, helpful, unobtrusive, he was well-liked by his workmates. Frequently they poked fun at him when he produced the inevitable four rounds of cheese sandwiches from the dented biscuit tin he brought to work each day in a polythene carrier bag.

One day — for the first time in two years — Sean failed to turn up for work. His biscuit tin was blown to smithereens an hour after he left the carrier bag in a shop doorway on a main London street. Two people were seriously injured.

Sean is typical of the IRA urban guerrilla. He can hide far more easily than his counterpart in the jungle. He does not have to worry about special camouflage, or a twig snapping beneath his feet. He is not forced to use little-known tracks or to cut his way through dense bush, and he never wears a uniform.

The urban guerrilla can be any man in any street, on any bus or any train. He can plant a bomb on his way to work and then, when it explodes, killing and maiming, he can join in the anger expressed by his workmates.

Commonplace is his camouflage, and because of this he is a terrifying threat to democracy.

The bomb is his weapon of negotiation. He believes that it will make this nation capitulate on his terms.

Sean was born and raised in Belfast of Catholic-Republican parents. As a child, he took scant notice of the folklore tales of the old-time IRA, recounted by his father and grandfather. It was enough that he hurled stones at the British soldiers who patrolled the streets. This was a game he liked.

Only when he started to drink in the Republican bars did his attitude begin to change. Older men talked to him of the glory to be won in the cause of a united Ireland. He heard tales of martyrdom, heroism, danger, and self-sacrifice. All for Ireland. The hated British must be forced to leave, and the old men shook their heads sadly. It was to the young that they must look; and Sean, his patriotic fervour fed with romanticism and liquor, 'volunteered' to serve the Provisional IRA.

A week later he was collected by car, blindfolded, and driven to a house where he was interrogated by three men, one of whom was to become his 'battalion commander'. At first he was entrusted only with small jobs, fetching and carrying messages and supplies for the revolutionary hierarchy. He was given a 'cover' job with an IRA-funded construction company, and his superiors, now convinced of his devotion to the cause, told him he was to be sent across the border for special training at a 'military college'. At a remote farm in Monaghan, he joined a class to learn the basics of bomb-making. In the fields he practised with pistols and rifles, many of which, he noticed, were American- and Russian-made.

Back in Belfast, he was summoned to battalion HQ and told he had been selected for a 'mission' in England. Sean was given two hundred pounds and instructed to find a flat in the King's Cross area of London. He was warned against mixing regularly with other members of the Irish community — 'we don't want you falling about in a Kilburn pub' — and cautioned to keep away from women. He must get a job, keep his political opinions to himself, and integrate with the English.

He was given a telephone number to memorise (it was a telephone box in Camden Town, though he did not know it then), and told to ring it every

Friday promptly a eight p.m., when any orders for him would be issued.

For months he was brusquely told by his anonymous contact: 'No orders.' But one Friday the voice instructed: 'Be at home on Sunday afternoon. You will have a visitor.'

The courier brought eight sticks of gelignite, detonators, batteries, three cheap clocks fitted with interceptor contacts, and wire.

Sean used three sticks of gelignite in his first bomb. His target was a main-line railway station, and he was ordered to telephone a warning to the Press Association, using the Provisional IRA identification code. Police cleared the station, and no one was hurt.

During the next eighteen months he was twice again visited by the courier, and manufactured five more bombs. Only one failed to explode. The last fitted snugly into his lethal biscuit tin.

He never went back to work. He was recalled to Belfast, to teach others how to make bombs. Now he was a 'hero' who had maimed innocent victims, a man to inspire other gullible, out-of-work, depressed youngsters with fantasies of misguided patriotism.

[from *Bomb Squad* by BOB HUNTLEY]

Check Your Understanding

(1) What were some of the attributes of Sean that helped him to be an effective IRA urban guerrilla?

(2) Account for the fact that workmates frequently 'poked fun' at Sean.

(3) Explain why his 'dented biscuit tin' is later described as a 'lethal biscuit tin'.

(4) In what ways is the task of the urban guerrilla easier than that of the jungle guerrilla?

(5) What is the greatest asset of an urban guerrilla?

(6) A 'terrifying threat to democracy'. Is there any reason why democracy is particularly threatened by terrorism?

(7) 'The bomb is his weapon of negotiation.' Explain this in your own words.

(8) Explain why 'volunteered' is in inverted commas in the passage.

(9) Which are some of the countries that appear to supply the IRA with arms?

(10) 'Military college' would be an example of which literary device as it is used to describe Sean's training farm: (a) metaphor (b) euphemism (c) satire?

(11) What were some of the traps that an IRA guerrilla could fall into when he had a job to do?

(12) Explain the meaning of each of the following words as used in this passage. Consult the back-of-book dictionary where necessary.
(a) scant (b) recounted (c) fervour (d) brusquely (e) gullible

(13) Suggest why Sean would have been instructed to issue a warning with his first bomb.

(14) Explain how the last sentence reveals the writer's attitude to the bombings by the IRA.

(15) What is the tone of the writing in this extract?

Working with Words (8)

Senior Spelling Demons	Confusing Pairs	People		Increase Your Word Power
anxiety	lose	mischievous	conscientious	malignant
associate	loose	courteous	peculiarity	tenacious
leisure	cloth	suspicious	irritable	irrevocable
familiar	clothe	oblivious	competent	aspire
foreign	perspective	vivacious	infatuation	proclaim
despair	prospective	pessimistic	ambitious	ultimate
recipe	urban	arrogant	gregarious	demoralized
separate	urbane	dissimilar	hypocrisy	inflexible
secretary	perpetrate	contemptible	confidential	fatality
ordinary	perpetuate	dissatisfied	curious	repugnant

Word Forms

Complete the table by inserting the correct form of the word in each case.

NOUN	ADJECTIVE	VERB	ADVERB
anxiety			
	familiar		
			mischievously
		separate	
	suspicious		
			competently
	irritable		

Increase Your Word Power

Select words from the *Increase Your Word Power* list to complete these sentences.

(1) He was a man of .... will, for he would never change his mind once it was made up. Indecision was .... to him.

(2) You are a young lady with plenty of ambition and this firm trusts that you will .... to the .... position, that of Managing Director.

(3) The departmental employees became .... by the constant stream of complaints that kept pouring in.

(4) Today's road-accident victim is the sixth .... on that stretch of highway.

(5) According to the specialist, the present strain of cholera is highly ....

(6) The Principal said that he was happy to be able to .... a half day's holiday.

(7) Broadcasting systems must recognize that once their words go over the air they are ....

(8) You can only call this plant .... since it will climb and cling to brick or any other kind of wall.

Confusing Pairs

Select a word from the *Confusing Pairs* list to begin each of the following.

(1) .... means cultured, witty, polished.

(2) To .... is to mislay.

(3) .... has to do with the probable or expected future. It can also apply to someone who has just joined an organization (for example, a club) and hopes in time to become a member.

(4) To .... is to commit, or cause to happen, something undesirable.

(5) .... is not firm, not tight.

(6) .... means of, or belonging to, a city.

(7) To .... is to dress.

(8) To have this is to possess 'vision' — an ability to take into account other points of view. It can also refer to three-dimensional representation in art.

(9) .... is material from which garments (etc) are made.

(10) To .... is to prolong indefinitely, preserve from oblivion.

People

Form a person from each of these words.

EXAMPLE: **foreign** *foreigner*

(1) **pessimistic** ....
(2) **aspire** ....
(3) **suspicious** ....
(4) **hypocrisy** ....
(5) **confidential** ....

(6) **perpetrate** ....
(7) **lose** ....
(8) **participate** ....
(9) **oppose** ....
(10) **practice** ....

Origins — 'Pulling the wool . . .'

The expression **'to pull the wool over his eyes'** has a very logical explanation. It dates back to the time when all gentlemen wore long wigs similar to the ones worn today by judges. A rather childish practical joke was to tilt a man's wig over his eyes so that he couldn't see, and from this came today's meaning of the expression: to deceive or hoodwink a person. (Before it acquired its modern meaning, to 'wink' meant to close the eyes: so 'hoodwinking' was closing the eyes with a hood, so that you could not see.)

Language in Action (8)

Slang — and Colloquial Language

From roughly the middle of the 19th century, 'slang' has been the accepted term for 'illegitimate' colloquial speech. It is an even more informal level of language than colloquial language. Slang differs from colloquial language in two particular ways.

(i) Slang expressions are usually not as widely understood or used as are colloquial expressions.

(ii) Slang is more ephemeral than colloquial language. It tends to be 'in' for a few years, then lost from frequent usage. New generations usually are unsure of, or do not understand the meaning of, slang expressions of the preceding generation. Consider some slang expressions of the 1960s: to 'dig' something; to be 'ultra-cool'; to have a 'gas' time. In contrast, colloquial expressions are familiar for perhaps hundreds of years.

However, despite these variations, it is important to realize that differences between colloquial language and slang, like the differences between formal and colloquial language, are not clear-cut. They frequently overlap.

Why Slang?

Most students of language have agreed on three basic purposes behind the creation of slang expressions:

(i) the desire to achieve a more lively effect through language;

(ii) the desire to achieve a greater degree of intimacy through language;

(iii) the desire to be different and to express one's personality through language.

While the issue of 'goodness' or 'badness' is again something that no-one can generalize about, it is important to realize that the use of slang may be marked by good or bad features.

Good Features

The use of slang is to be commended when:

(i) it is appropriate to the situation and purpose;

(ii) it consists of concrete terms, vivid metaphors and generally lively phrases;

(iii) by its emotional force, it is stronger than more conventional usage;

(iv) because of its immediacy, it possesses a greater store of associations than do conventional expressions.

Bad Features

Slang can be criticized when:

(i) the usage is inappropriate to the purpose and situation (for example, students should normally avoid using slang expressions in writing a formal essay);

(ii) it employs over-used, threadbare, lifeless expressions;

(iii) it uses expressions that have become vague and imprecise, marking a laziness (or inability) on the part of the user to choose more precise language.

Exercise 1

Read through the following passage and then answer the questions.

STREET-TALK

'After leaving the cage he busted suds for a while, got into a lot of ink, went through his share of jefferson airplanes and finally got into mething around.'

Translation: After leaving high school, he worked as a dishwasher, started drinking cheap wine, used matches split down the middle to hold remnants of marihuana cigarettes and finally began to use amphetamines like methedrine.

(1) What criticisms can you make of the street-talk slang? Why do you think a translation was necessary?

(2) What value would street-talk slang have?

(3) This passage comes from a newspaper. Can you suggest why the paper bothered to publish the street-talk version rather than just the translation?

Here's an example of slang that you might find a little easier to understand.

Tramp 1: I applies for the job. First thing 'e doesn't like me face-lace. Reckons I should 'a shaved. Never gave me a go, 'e didn't.

Tramp 2: Did yer do yer block?

Tramp 1: No, beefing don't get yer anywhere. I jes' says 'Boss, if yer won't take me on, will yer gimme some grub? Honest I'll beat it, no worries if I can get some chow. I'm jest about done in.'

Tramp 2: He wouldn't have cared.

Tramp 1: No. Here's me thinking 'I'll have to croak before he shows 'is 'eart'. So I quits chewing the rag and checks out. No wonder I'm feelin' so butcher's.

Exercise 2

Rewrite the above exchange, eliminating all the slang expressions and replacing them with a more formal style of language.

Exercise 3

Think of as many slang expressions as you can for:

(1) money (e.g. *loot*)

(2) excellent

(3) 'Go away!'

(4) nonsense

(5) girl

AH! A '62 HUNTER VALLEY CLARET! AN EXCELLENT VINTAGE.... TOO MUCH NONSENSE TALKED ABOUT WINE.. TO WINE BUFFS I SAY 'GO AWAY'! MONEY CAN'T BUY THE DELIGHT OF DRINKING THIS FINE WINE ... AS ROBUST AND FRUITFUL AS A GIRL IN SUMMER.... I'LL JUST KNOCK THE NECK OFF!

The Language of Literature (8)

A Critical Poem

In 'Standardization', A. D. Hope has set out to condemn those who complain about the way standardization has intruded on our lives. The crux of his argument is the premise that Mother Nature is the world's greatest standardizer. In the first four stanzas of his poem Hope attacks some of those who condemn aspects of modern society — the journalist, the aesthete, the theosophist and the modern-day Nature poet.

STANDARDIZATION

When, darkly brooding on this Modern Age,
The journalist with his marketable woes
Fills up once more the inevitable page
Of fatuous, flatulent, Sunday-paper prose;

Whenever the green aesthete starts to whoop
With horror at the house not made with hands
And when from vacuum cleaners and tinned soup
Another pure theosophist demands

Rebirth in other, less industrial stars
Where huge towns thrust up in synthetic stone
And films and sleek miraculous motor cars
And celluloid and rubber are unknown;

When from his vegetable Sunday School
Emerges with the neatly maudlin phrase
Still one more Nature poet, to rant or drool
About the 'Standardization of the Race';

I see, stooping among her orchard trees,
The old, sound Earth, gathering her windfalls in,
Broad in the hams and stiffening at the knees,
Pause, and I see her grave malicious grin.

For there is no manufacturer competes
With her in the mass production of shapes and things.
Over and over she gathers and repeats
The cast of a face, a million butterfly wings.

She does not tire of the pattern of a rose.
Her oldest tricks still catch us with surprise.
She cannot recall how long ago she chose
The streamlined hulls of fish, the snail's long eyes,

Love, which still pours into its ancient mould
The lashing seed that grows to a man again,
From whom by the same processes unfold
Unending generations of living men.

She has standardized his ultimate needs and pains.
Lost tribes in a lost language mutter in
His dreams: his science is tethered to their brains,
His guilt merely repeats Original Sin.

And beauty standing motionless before
Her mirror sees behind her, mile on mile,
A long queue in an unknown corridor,
Anonymous faces plastered with her smile.

A. D. HOPE

Looking into the poem

(1) What does the phrase 'darkly brooding' suggest about the journalist's attitude towards our society?

(2) Why does the poet refer to the journalist's woes as 'marketable'?

(3) What is the poet's attitude to the journalist and his writing? From your own experience, do you agree with the poet's point of view? (*N.B.* 'fatuous' = silly; 'flatulent' = inflated.)

(4) An aesthete professes to be sensitive to beautiful things. Why does the aesthete 'whoop with horror at the house not made with hands'?

(5) What does the widespread use of vacuum cleaners and tinned soup suggest about our way of life?

(6) Theosophists can be said to believe in mystical experience of the Absolute (or, of 'God'). Why is the theosophist depicted as wishing to escape from our modern industrialized society?

(7) What do you think is meant by 'synthetic stone'? Explain how 'synthetic stone' contributes to standardization in our lives.

(8) What words suggest that the poet is in favour of motorcars? Do you believe that they help standardize our lives? Why?

(9) Why might the theosophist be opposed to celluloid and rubber?

(10) What is your own attitude to the views of (a) the aesthete, and (b) the theosophist?

(11) What words of the poet suggest that he is opposed to the Nature poet?

(12) What kind of poetry would a Nature poet tend to write?

(13) What change in approach do you notice in the fifth stanza?

(14) How does the poet show that no manufacturer can compete with the old sound Earth?

(15) 'The streamlined hulls' is an unusual phrase to apply to fish. What does the poet achieve by his use of this expression?

(16) What invention do 'the snail's long eyes' remind you of?

(17) How does the poet argue that even Love is standardized?

(18) What do you understand by the term 'Original Sin'? Explain how the poet works this concept into his argument.

(19) How does the poet maintain that beauty is standardized?

(20) When you read, 'Anonymous faces plastered with her smile', what picture comes to your mind?

(21) What does the poet hope to achieve by showing that nature is the greatest standardizer the world has ever known?

(22) Do you disagree with any of the poet's arguments? Explain your viewpoints.

Thinking and Reasoning (8)

Cause and Effect

In an earlier section we looked at analogies, noting that they are frequently used to point out a relationship between different things. Sometimes, as we noted, there are more differences than similarities between the two things used in the comparison.

Cause-and-effect statements are another attempt to show relationships between things. However, as with analogies, we need to evaluate them carefully for accuracy if we are to be thinking critically.

Exercise 1

Comment on the accuracy, as you see it, of these cause-and-effect statements.

(1) The number of suicides is rising every year in Australia. It must be the result of increased stress.

(2) Unchecked government spending will inevitably lead to increased inflation.

(3) Only 14 out of every 1000 people in Bulgaria suffer from heart complaints — a very low percentage in comparison with Australia. Since Bulgarians have high-oatmeal diets, this must be the reason.

(4) All these nuclear tests have messed up our weather. That's why we're having so many droughts and floods.

(5) A systematic study program will always lead to better school results.

Single and Multiple Causality

The truth is that many things which occur in our world are the result not of a single cause, but of a number of causes. For example, a child may have become a delinquent because he/she:

(i) was beaten by parents;

(ii) mixed with a peer group made up of delinquents;

(iii) had parents who never showed much interest, or never spent much time, with their children;

(iv) found that delinquency brought some excitement into an otherwise dreary life.

This is a picture of **multiple causality** – a number of factors all interacting to produce the final result. Often doctors and social scientists hold to this approach in what has been called the 'poker-machine' model. A person may not contract a certain illness if only one factor turns up in the 'window', but if all three (or more) turn up at once then it is almost certain that the illness will be contracted. If a person has, for example, a genetic predisposition to cancer, *and* is under considerable stress, *and* the body is being affected by carcinogenic substances such as nicotine, and so on, then the windows of the 'poker-machine' are full or starting to fill. Because of the interaction of multiple causes, cancer is becoming increasingly likely.

The point here is that sometimes a statement attributing something to a single cause will, upon examination, turn out to be naive.

Exercise 2

Which of the following single-cause statements do you find to be fairly convincing? For which would you propose a 'poker-machine' model of causality?

(1) Increased divorce rates are the result of our more permissive standards in society.

(2) Fuel prices keep rising because of increased charges by the oil-producing countries of the world.

(3) Exercise produces physical fitness.

(4) Regular pay-rises for politicians have led people to be cynical about government wage-policies.

(5) Reduced government spending on education will result in poorer educational facilities.

(6) Unemployment lies behind the increase in violence that we can see in society.

(7) Our human desire to get rich quickly explains the increase in the number of gambling projects in recent years.

(8) Clothing fashions, from one year to another, follow the whims of fashion designers.

Exercise 3

Following a 'poker-machine' model of causality, list as many causal factors as you can for each of the following.

(1) Increased number of deaths in sport.

(2) The excellent safety-record of most airline companies.

(3) The fall in demand for new cars in recent years.

(4) Public disenchantment with doctors/teachers/politicians. [*Choose any one!*]

(5) The maintenance of discriminatory attitudes towards men and women in our society.

(6) Australia's (relative) high standing in most areas of sport.

(7) Greater longevity (length of life) in most Western countries than in most Third World countries.

(8) Increasingly permissive attitudes to sex in our society.

Language Basics (8)

Direct and Indirect Speech

- **Direct speech** is the *quoting* of the words actually spoken.
- **Indirect speech** is the *reporting* of the words spoken.

    EXAMPLES: (a) He said, 'My name is Sean but everybody calls me Paddy.'
                  (the actual words spoken are directly quoted)
            (b) He said that his name was Sean but that everybody called him Paddy.
                  (what Sean said is reported — that is, given indirectly)

Exercise A

Change the following sentences from *direct* to *indirect* speech.

(1) 'The bomb is my weapon of negotiation,' he grimly replied.

(2) The voice instructed: 'You must be at home on Sunday afternoon because you will be having a visitor.'

(3) 'I believe,' he said, 'the bomb is going to make Ireland free.'

(4) 'My loyalty to the Cause shows me that iolence is acceptable,' he stated.

(5) 'At what time and in what place did you say I had to plant the explosive?' he enquired.

Exercise B

Change the following sentences from *indirect* to *direct* speech.

(1) They told us that Sean was typical of the IRA urban guerrilla.

(2) He instructed the courier to prepare the explosive which would blow up the car.

(3) They asked Paddy at what time he had left.

(4) Sean told the reporter that that was the house which he had helped to destroy.

(5) He was informed that he was a 'hero' and would have to set an 'example'.

Punctuation — Commas yet again

Use commas:

1. To separate the names of people addressed or spoken to.
EXAMPLE: It's up to you, Paddy, to plant this bomb.

2. After 'yes' or 'no' when they begin a sentence that answers a question.
EXAMPLE: Is that Paddy? No, it's the police.

Exercise

Punctuate these sentences by inserting commas where necessary.

(1) Sean it's a telephone call for you.

(2) He heard tales of martyrdom heroism danger and self sacrifice.

(3) I'm a Police Inspector my young man and I intend to see that you are punished.

(4) Are you Paddy Liffey? Yes that's my name.

Unit Nine

Comprehension (9)

Pity does damn-all for the paraplegic

Next year is one of those UN Years. Like International Women's Year and the International Year of the Child. This time it's the International Year of the Disabled Person — and I heard you stifling that yawn.

I'm in the middle of touring Australia talking to paras and quads (i.e. plegics) trying to learn the difference between disablement, impairment and handicap. I've met with people who were born mentally retarded, with others who were mutilated in car or industrial accidents, with a truly beautiful girl who'll spend the rest of her life in a chair because she failed to die in a suicide pact. And over and over again I'm being told the same thing — 'We don't want your pity or your charity. We want our *rights*. We have the right to social equality, to sexuality, to dignity. We're tired of institutions, of the sort of paternalism that treats us as children or, even worse, as grotesque pets. We want access to jobs, to closed buildings and closed minds.'

I'm on the ninth floor of a building in Adelaide, and a young paraplegic, whose massive shoulders dominate a bent and wasted body, insists that I climb into a second wheelchair. Beside him, a quadriplegic in a motorised chair gives me my orders. Without assistance, I am to leave the office, take the lift and get myself out into the street. I must then go around the block and buy a can of lemonade at the milk bar.

Feeling absurd and conspicuous (the sensation of being stared at by 'straights', 'ordinaries', 'verticals' and 'uprights' is, inevitably, an unavoidable aspect of the disabled person's experience), I turn myself around and head for the lift. Here I find that the signal button is a few inches too high. I stretch until, cheating a bit, I reach it. Soon, with a 'ding', the lift arrives and I have the terrifying experience of trying to manipulate myself

inside while those great rubber teeth in their steel gums keep closing on the wheels and my fingers.

Downstairs, after much to-ing and fro-ing, I manage to heave myself through the clenching jaws to face the next difficulty. There are heavy glass doors before me and, beyond them, a flight of stairs. To break out of H division at Pentridge would be easier. So I turn and wheel myself down the corridor towards the fire escape. At least here the architect has provided access, of a sort; provided you can push open a two-tonne door (Christ, why doesn't it *slide!*) and untangle your wheels from a thick door mat, you can get into the car park. Here giant juggernauts are trying to get out, or manoeuvring to get in and your angry cries are pointless. After all, even if a driver can hear you, he can't see you.

Now, dodging delivery trucks, I wheel myself up a side lane towards Victoria Square. Already my arms and shoulders are aching and the migraine I'd beaten into submission with a wide selection of Adelaide's most potent medications is, once again, unfurling its tentacles. In an unfunny parody of a Keystone comedy, a truck driver comes to a sudden halt, thus allowing me to elude his giant Dunlops.

Out in the street I find myself able to mount the kerb, thanks to one of the few specially designed kerbs you find anywhere in Adelaide — or in any city of Australia, come to that. But the next problem you find is ... the footpath itself. While it *looks* flat, it's cambered to allow water to run off into the gutters. So *you* begin to run off into the gutter. (It takes all my strength to steer the chair away. It's as though the chair had developed a club wheel, like a malfunctioning trolley in a supermarket, the sort that seems determined to tip you into the freezer cabinet after ricocheting off the Heinz soup display.) Ignoring the pitying stares from the passers-by (one of whom murmurs 'I didn't know that Adams chap was a cripple — explains a lot about his articles') I risk a right turn to seek out the milk bar in my Mission Impossible. But this involves tackling two more kerbs, one down, one up. A few inches high, they might as well be Matterhorns. After teetering at the edge, I decide to cheat — and much to the astonishment of some ladies at a bus stop, who suspect they're witnessing a Lourdes-type miracle, I clamber out of the chair and do some lifting.

The first milk bar is totally inaccessible because of the small step and an impassable collection of display stands. But further on there's a sandwich bar that I can just about manage. But once inside I find I can't reach the lemonade in the vertical fridge — and that I can't get any help because I'm invisible to those behind the counter. Counter? From my angle, it looks more like the Great Wall of China.

The night before, I'd sat at a meeting with 18 disabled people. There was the shy epileptic, the blind solicitor, the paraplegic barrister, the deaf lady who runs the local Humanist Society and so on. Plus a small, compellingly beautiful black girl sitting in her wheelchair. From memory she was the last, and the quietest, to speak. 'I'm tired of being catalogued,' she said. 'First as a woman, then as an Aboriginal, then as someone in a chair.'

She told of her recent experience in a milk bar, after struggling to get a can of lemonade. With some difficulty she'd removed the tab (modern packaging makes most cans and all those hotel sachets of butter, jam and coffee as invulnerable as the Reserve Bank's safe). She'd taken a couple of sips and rested, can in her lap. Whereupon a matron rushed up to her with a cry, 'Oh, you poor child,' and shoved 20 cents in the slot. 'Which ruined my bloody lemonade,' said the girl, provoking an eruption of laughter from around the table.

There's not much left to say after that anecdote. It sums it all up — the difficulties in coping with the simplest problems in a world designed for uprights, straights, verticals, etc. — problems compounded by the appalling prejudices that lead to a destruction of a disabled person's dignity through that lethal, condescending emotion of pity.

In Melbourne, a young woman with more degrees than I've had hot breakfasts, tells another anecdote provoking a similar explosion of laughter from the disabled people in the room: 'I'm at Boston airport, being wheeled around by a friend. And I'm *desperate* for a pee. But I can't get my chair into any of the loos. I'm getting desperate and I'm getting angry. So I find myself an airport official and his response sums it up — the way, that is, we're *always* treated as children. You see, he starts apologising not to me, but to the girl wheeling my chair. He looks right *over* me, as if I wasn't there. So I yell up at him: "Don't apologise to her — I'm the one that wants the bloody piddle!" '

If you find the thought of the International Year of the Disabled Person boring, just think about this. Every Australian who lives to the age of 70 will be disabled in one way or another. It'll be too late to get angry then, if you can't open the butter or go into a building or negotiate a loo. So forget about pity and compassion and charity. Enlightened self-interest suggests we do something about physical access right now.

So, as well as saving the dolphin, the whale, the kangaroo, the Barrier Reef and God knows what else from urgent threat, let's save the disabled person from humiliation. Even if you don't get multiple sclerosis or have a spinal injury in a car accident, disablement is as inevitable as death and taxes.

[by PHILLIP ADAMS
in *The Bulletin*, 15 July 1980]

Check Your Understanding

(1) What message does Adams find that he is receiving from disabled people all over the country? (One sentence.)

(2) Find four slang terms in this article for people who have no physical impairment.

(3) Explain the meaning of these words in the context of the passage: (a) elude (b) teetering (c) juggernaut (d) potent (e) inaccessible (f) lethal (g) cambered (h) invulnerable.

(4) Explain why a quadriplegic would need a motorized wheelchair while a paraplegic can operate one without a motor.

(5) Explain how Adams feels as he starts his 'Mission Impossible'. Do you think this is a common experience for people in wheelchairs?

(6) What kind of door *can* be operated by a paraplegic?

(7) How does the writer make the lift seem human?

(8) Adams's migraine begins to reappear. Comment on the image, 'unfurling it's tentacles'.

(9) Explain the meaning of: (a) 'teetering at the edge', and (b) 'ladies at a bus stop, who suspect they're witnessing a Lourdes-type miracle'.

(10) Explain how modern packaging makes things 'as invulnerable as the Reserve Bank's safe' for disabled people.

(11) A woman 'with more degrees than I've had hot breakfasts'. Comment on this use of language.

(12) What personality qualities do you see in the woman who tells about the incident at Boston airport?

(13) Explain why 'disablement is as inevitable as death and taxes'.

(14) Why, according to the writer, is pity such a destructive emotion?

(15) What do you think was the writer's purpose in writing this article?

(16) What can *we* do, as normal able-bodied citizens, to assist the disabled?

(17) Has your attitude towards disabled people changed as a result of this article? Explain any changes.

Working with Words (9)

Senior Spelling Demons	Confusing Pairs	Actions and Reactions		Increase Your Word Power
pierce	disease	annihilate	ovation	assimilation
citizen	decease	enumerate	acrimony	exigency
siege	alliance	generosity	reciprocate	coherent
juice	allegiance	initiate	exploit	avert
bachelor	respectable	concede	justifiable	contemptuous
existence	respectful	concession	convene	contrite
ancestor	assent	affirm	incessant	inception
survivor	ascent	perception	expedite	premonition
spectator	eligible	immunity	abdicate	prerogative
capacity	illegible	intermittent	monotony	impervious

Change the Words

Change into nouns

(a) expedite...

(b) affirm..

(c) avert...

(d) annihilate...

(e) contrite...

(f) abdicate...

Change into verbs

(a) survivor...

(b) perception..

(c) immunity..

(d) assimilation..

(e) justification..

(f) ascent..

Change into adjectives

(a) existence..

(b) generosity..

(c) acrimony..

(d) ancestor...

(e) perception..

(f) monotony...

Change into adverbs

(a) respectful..

(b) respectable..

(c) justifiable..

Add prefixes to form opposites

(a) respectful..

(b) fortunate...

(c) coherent..

(d) eligible..

(e) responsible..

(f) movable...

Find-a-Word

Replace the words in heavy type with list-words.

(1) The soldiers pledged their **loyalty** to the king.

(2) The old woman had a **forewarning** of her death.

(3) The teacher had to change schools because of an **emergency.**

(4) The defeated team revealed their **bitterness** at the end of the game.

(5) The large department-store tried to **ward off** bankruptcy.

(6) Never **repay** evil with evil.

(7) He had an injection to give him **protection** from smallpox.

(8) The champion tennis player wished to **state positively** that she was retiring from the game.

(9) The director decided to **assemble** the shareholders of the company.

(10) It is the prime minister's **special privilege** to decide when the elections will be held.

Confusing Pairs

Match up the correct word from each pair with its meaning opposite.

Pairs	Meanings
disease/decease	death
alliance/allegiance	union by treaty
respectable/respectful	showing respect
assent/ascent	agreement
eligible/illegible	impossible to read

Missing Words

Correctly insert the words from the box into the spaces below.

coherent	impervious	abdicate	inception	avert	ovation
incessant	exploit	disease	justifiable	annihilate	immunity

(1) Because he had been unable to .... the disaster, the king decided to ....

(2) The singer received a standing .... from the audience.

(3) The noise was ....

(4) Since its .... the new advertising campaign had proved financially ....

(5) Propaganda aims to .... the emotions of masses.

(6) There was very little .... from the dreaded .... which threatened to .... whole towns.

(7) The headmaster was .... to all the demands of the students.

(8) He gave a .... account of the disaster.

Antonyms

Write down words from the list which are opposite in meaning to those that follow. The first letters have been given to help you.

(1) **unrepenting** c............................
(2) **descent** a............................
(3) **completion** i............................
(4) **continuous** i............................
(5) **respectful** c............................

(6) **dissent** a............................
(7) **victim** s............................
(8) **obstruct** e............................
(9) **life** d............................
(10) **meanness** g............................

Word Origins

Using the information given in the first part of each of the following, work out the meanings of the words specified in the second.

(1) The Greek word *monos* means 'one' or 'alone'. What is the meaning of **monotony**?

(2) The Latin word *similis* means 'like' ('similar'). Explain the meaning of **assimilation**.

(3) *Acer* is Latin for 'sharp' or 'fierce'. What is the meaning of **acrimony**?

(4) The Latin word *nihil* means 'nothing'. Explain the meaning of **annihilate**.

(5) *Cedo* is Latin for 'I yield'. What is a **concession**?

(6) *Specto* in Latin means 'I look at'. What does a **spectator** do?

Language in Action (9)

What Is Jargon?

Jargon is technical language developed and used by people who participate in a specialized field. Every occupation or special field of interest, from rocketry to rock collecting, hang-gliding to hydroponics, has its specialized vocabulary. These functional varieties of language are fully understood only by the initiated — those who know their way about that particular field.

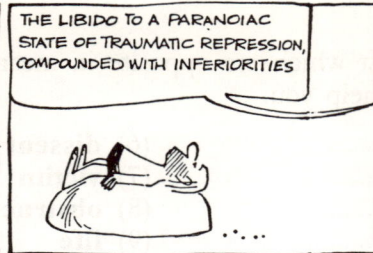

Exercise 1

(1) From what profession do the jargon words in this cartoon derive?

(2) How appropriate would it be to use such jargon with 'the man in the street'?

(3) Can you identify any jargon word used in the cartoon which has come into common use? How is it used by most people?

The Uses of Jargon

It seems true, in general, that things are invented or brought into being in response to a need. This is certainly true of jargon.

The invention of specialized vocabulary in specialized fields has come about because of:

(i) the need to communicate about things and ideas which cannot be accurately described using ordinary colloquial, or even formal, language — or, in other cases, the need to communicate in one word (or few words) what would otherwise require many words of descriptive, everyday language. This use of jargon seems to be justified.

(ii) the desire to hide knowledge from the 'uninitiated' (those not qualified in a particular field). Jargon words, in this instance, are intended to mystify and to sound impressive. When used this way they *hinder* communication rather than facilitating it. Such use, whether in commerce, law, medicine, or a field of science, deserves critical exposure.

VERSATILE ANALOG MULTIMETER

An electronic analog multimeter which provides 62 measuring ranges, including current up to 10A and resistance to 30M, has been launched by Philips Test & Measuring Instruments. The new meter, the PM 2505, features a built-in audible continuity tester and automatic potency indication, and has an input impedance of 10M.

Exercise 2

(1) Identify five jargon words in the passage just quoted.

(2) What purpose is served by the use of jargon here?

(3) Would it be possible to rewrite this extract without the use of jargon? Explain your answer.

JARGON GENERATING

An innovative manipulable device to assist you in generating and disseminating meaningful education jargon for important instructional communications on any occasion:

- public presentations
- research reports
- program evaluations
- professional articles
- staff conferences
- slide programs
- parent meetings
- project proposals
- memos

ASSEMBLY

Cut out Wheel #2 and Wheel #3. Punch out the centers of all three wheels and join the wheels with a paper fastener through the center.

USE

Simply spin the wheels in either direction and stop at any word combination that suits you. There are 1.000 possible phrases

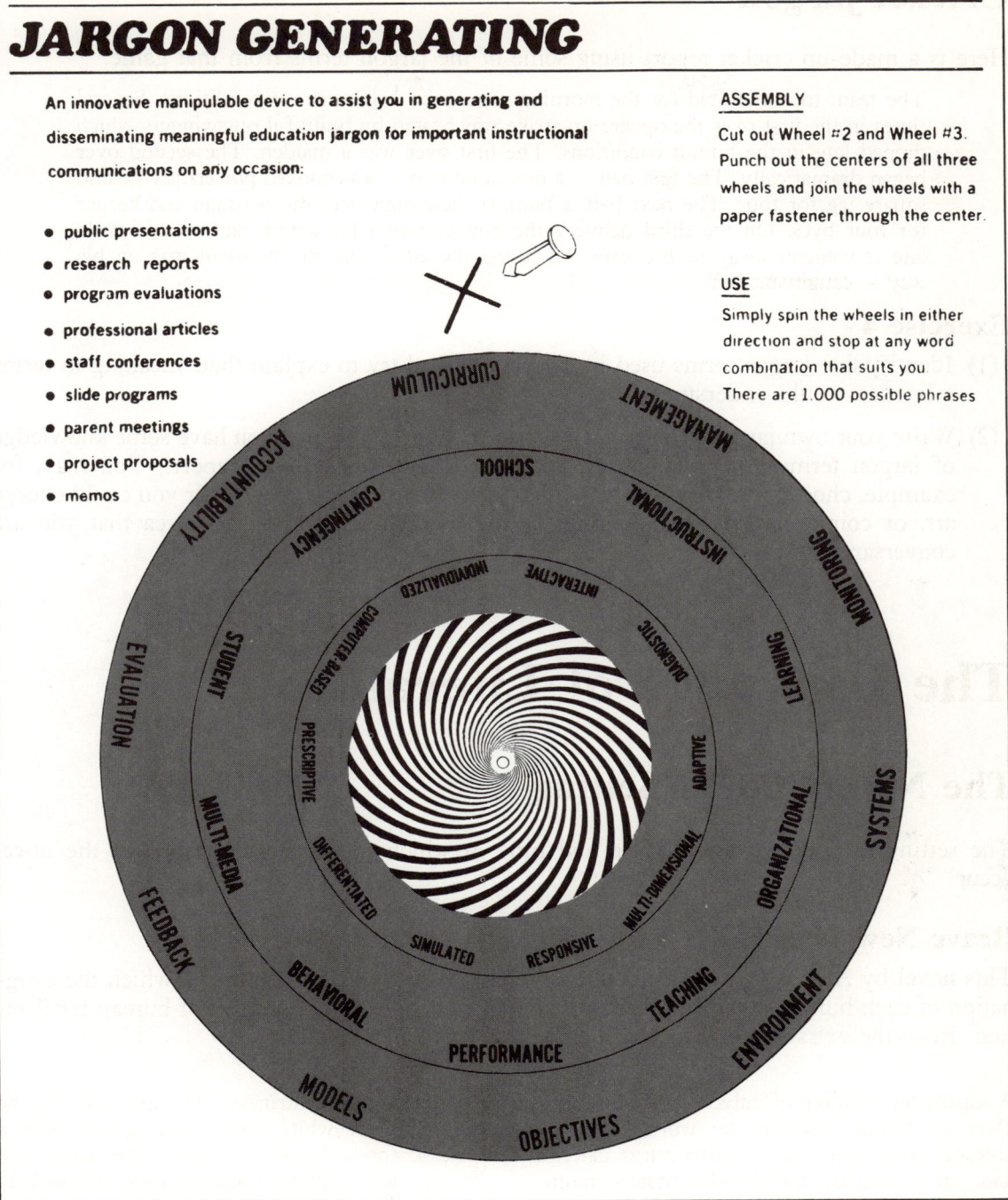

Exercise 3

Study the send-up of education jargon (the 'jargon wheel', above).

(1) Make up five education-jargon phrases using one word from each of the concentric wheels — e.g. 'simulated behavioural objectives'.

(2) What does the 'text' accompanying the wheel imply the purpose behind education jargon of this type to be?

Cricket Jargon

Here is a made-up cricket report using some of the jargon terms from that game.

> The team took the field for the morning session, in bright, sunlit conditions. Several times in the first over the opener on strike was beaten by beautiful outswingers which dipped late in the humid conditions. The first over was a maiden. The second over began dramatically. The first ball — a rank long hop — was hooked powerfully behind square leg for four. The next ball, a bumper, flew high over the batsman and keeper for four byes. On the third delivery the bowler found his length and, with a little late movement away to the slips, he found the edge, and the batsman was on his way — caught behind.

Exercise 4

(1) Identify five jargon terms used in the passage and try to explain their meaning in terms a layman would understand.

(2) Write your own jargon report on any sport or subject in which you have some knowledge of jargon terms. (Try to make it about as long as the cricket report.) You may, for example, choose another sport which has jargon terms (e.g. surfing). Or you could choose art, or coin-collecting, or spinning, or the mechanical field — *any* area that you are conversant with.

The Language of Literature (9)

The Novel and its Setting

The setting of a novel is the place and time in which the events described in the novel occur.

Brave New World

This novel by Aldous Huxley is about an incredible but realizable future in which the assignation of each human being to a certain social class begins at the moment of human fertilization. Read the extract and then consider the questions that follow.

A squat grey building of only thirty-four stories. Over the main entrance the words, CENTRAL LONDON HATCHERY AND CONDITIONING CENTRE, and, in a shield, the World State's motto, COMMUNITY, IDENTITY, STABILITY.

The enormous room on the ground floor faced towards the north. Cold for all the summer beyond the panes, for all the tropical heat of the room itself, a harsh thin light glared through the windows, hungrily seeking some draped lay figure, some pallid shape of academic goose-flesh, but finding only the glass and nickel and bleakly shining porcelain of a laboratory. Wintriness responded to wintriness. The overalls of the workers were white, their hands gloved with a pale corpse-coloured rubber. The light was frozen, dead, a ghost. Only from the yellow barrels of the microscopes did it borrow a certain rich and living substance, lying along the polished tubes like butter, streak after luscious streak in long recession down the work tables.

'And this,' said the Director opening the door, 'is the Fertilizing Room.'

[from *Brave New World* by ALDOUS HUXLEY]

Questions

(1) 'Over the main entrance . . . ' What do we learn about the political organization of this new world of the future?

(2) How is the reader's curiosity aroused in the first paragraph?

(3) What aspect of nature is given dominance in the setting of this passage?

(4) How is this aspect of nature given a living quality?

(5) 'Wintriness responded to wintriness.' How has this happened?

(6) What colour pervades the setting?

(7) Explain what kind of contrast is made towards the end of the second paragraph.

(8) In view of what has gone before, is the Director's statement in any way surprising or unexpected?

(9) What kind of feeling does Huxley want his readers to experience in this description of setting that begins his novel?

(10) Comment on the ways Huxley uses vocabulary to achieve the desired response from the reader.

The Heart of Darkness

The primal heart of the forest, relating in a sombre but recognizable way to the dark, chaotic heart of the twentieth century, is the omnipresent setting of Joseph Conrad's novel.

'Going up that river was like travelling back to the earliest beginnings of the world, when vegetation rioted on the earth and the big trees were kings. An empty stream, a great silence, an impenetrable forest. The air was warm, thick, heavy, sluggish. There was no joy in the brilliance of sunshine. The long stretches of the waterway ran on, deserted, into the gloom of overshadowed distances. On silvery sandbanks hippos and alligators sunned themselves side by side. The broadening waters flowed through a mob of wooded islands; you lost your way on that river as you would in a desert, and butted all day long against shoals, trying to find the channel, till you thought yourself bewitched and cut off for ever from everything you had known once — somewhere — far away — in another existence perhaps. There were moments when one's past came back to one, as it will sometimes when you have not a moment to spare to yourself; but it came in the shape of an unrestful and noisy dream, remembered with wonder amongst the overwhelming realities of this strange world of plants, and water, and silence. And this stillness of life did not in the least resemble a peace. It

was the stillness of an implacable force brooding over an inscrutable intention. . . . '

[from *The Heart of Darkness* by JOSEPH CONRAD]

Questions

(1) What comparison is presented in the opening sentence?

(2) How does this sentence also suggest that the forest is inimical to humankind?

(3) *Atmosphere,* the feeling that pervades a place, is an integral part of setting. An author will carefully choose particular words and phrases to create a certain atmosphere. What kind of atmosphere has Conrad succeeded in creating in this passage?

(4) Comment on Conrad's choice of words and phrases which create this atmosphere.

(5) The impact of nature is overwhelming. How is this shown in the passage?

(6) What is particularly apt about the long, rambling sentence beginning, 'The broadening waters . . . '?

(7) What is the distinction that is made between 'stillness' and 'peace'?

(8) Show how the last sentence seems to sum up and explain the rest of the description.

Nineteen Eighty-Four

Winston Smith is the main character in George Orwell's chilling vision of the repressive future. In the world of 1984 — the world of Big Brother — life is squalid and full of fear.

Part of the setting is Victory Mansions — one of the huge but sordid apartment complexes reserved for Party members. Mrs Parsons, one of Winston's neighbours, asks him to unblock a kitchen sink. He enters the Parsons' flat. . . .

The Parsons' flat was bigger than Winston's, and dingy in a different way. Everything had a battered, trampled-on look, as though the place had just been visited by some large violent animal. Games impedimenta — hockey-sticks, boxing-gloves, a burst football, a pair of sweaty shorts turned inside out — lay all over the floor, and on the table there was a litter of dirty dishes and dog-eared exercise-books. On the walls were scarlet banners of the Youth League and the Spies, and a full-sized poster of Big Brother.

There was the usual boiled-cabbage smell, common to the whole building, but it was shot through by a sharper reek of sweat, which — one knew this at the first sniff, though it was hard to say how — was the sweat of some person not present at the moment. In another room someone with a comb and a piece of toilet paper was trying to keep tune with the military music which was still issuing from the telescreen.

[from *Nineteen Eighty-Four* by GEORGE ORWELL]

Questions

(1) As Orwell passes from general impression to particular details in introducing the setting, how is the reader's imagination engaged?

(2) What is the overall impact of the listing of the items of 'games impedimenta'?

(3) What kind of atmosphere do the adjectives attached to the items help to convey?

(4) The sense of smell is particularly evoked in this description of setting. What skilful use of words and phrases achieves this?

(5) What smell is common to the whole building?

(6) In this description of the flat, what evidence can you find of the omnipresence of the enormously powerful and repressive regime of 1984? This evidence hints at certain activities condoned by the regime. What are they?

Thinking and Reasoning (9)

Correlation

Many people, and most newspapers, confuse **causality** and **correlation** from time to time. A correlation is a statistical statement referring to the *degree of relationship* between two things, but it does not mean that one *causes* the other. Technically, a correlation is a statement about how closely the occurrences between two things fall along a single straight line. The degree to which this happens is expressed as a figure between -1.00 and +1.00.

EXAMPLES   (1)   (2)   (3)

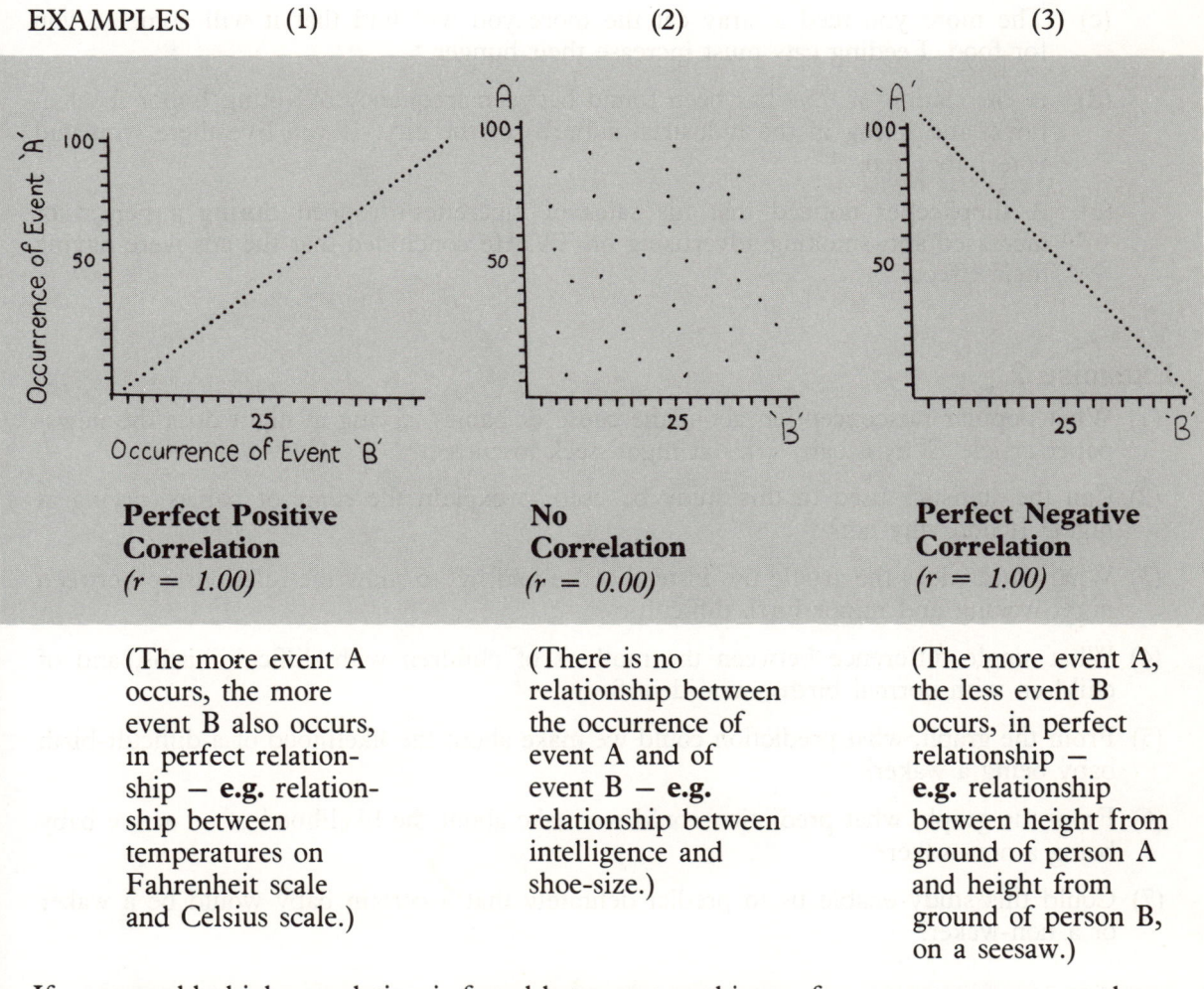

Perfect Positive Correlation
(r = 1.00)

No Correlation
(r = 0.00)

Perfect Negative Correlation
(r = 1.00)

(The more event A occurs, the more event B also occurs, in perfect relationship — **e.g.** relationship between temperatures on Fahrenheit scale and Celsius scale.)

(There is no relationship between the occurrence of event A and of event B — **e.g.** relationship between intelligence and shoe-size.)

(The more event A, the less event B occurs, in perfect relationship — **e.g.** relationship between height from ground of person A and height from ground of person B, on a seesaw.)

If a reasonably high correlation is found between two things, after many measures or observations have been made, we are able to make predictions about the likelihood of one thing occurring if the other occurs, *but we cannot claim that one causes the other!* To illustrate this: there is a high correlation between people suffering heart attacks on a single day in Sydney and the melting of tar on the roads. Should we conclude that one causes the other? Does the melting tar give off a poisonous gas, or something? Not likely. These two events correlate, but in this case both (we know) are caused by a third distinct factor — high temperature.

Exercise 1

(1) A teacher found that 5 boys and 10 girls sat in the front half of his class, while 10 boys and only 3 girls sat in the back half. Is there a correlation between sex and seating preference? Would it be positive or negative?

(2) Comment on the conclusions drawn in the following statements.

(a)   There is a high degree of correlation between the extended blackout in the city and the increased number of babies born nine months later. Blackouts must cause babies!

(b)   There is a higher correlation between motivation and results than between intelligence and results in Australian universities. Therefore a measure of a university student's motivation would be a better predictor of success than an IQ score.

(c)   The more you feed a stray cat the more you will find that it will come to you for food. Feeding cats must increase their hunger.

(d)   A correlation of 0.89 has been found between frequency of voting Labor in elections, and living in the industrial suburbs of the city. If *you* live there, you will vote Labor too.

(e)   A shopkeeper noticed that his sales of cigarettes dropped during a period of increased anti-smoking advertising on TV. He concluded that the ads were having their effect.

Exercise 2

(1) What popular misconception about the cause of babies' crying at night does the newspaper article 'Why a baby cries at night' seek to correct?

(2) Can the statistics used in this study be used to explain the *cause* of babies' crying at night? If not, why not?

(3) What words does the article use instead of 'caused by' to show the relationship between night-waking and minor birth difficulties?

(4) What single difference between the mothers of children with difficult births, and of children with normal births, was identified?

(5) From the graph, what prediction could we make about the likelihood of a difficult-birth baby being a waker?

(6) From the graph, what prediction could we make about the likelihood of an active baby being a non-waker?

(7) Could this study enable us to predict definitely that a certain baby would be a waker or a non-waker?

Why a baby cries at night

from a special correspondent

ONE OF the most common complaints that mothers make about their young children is that they wake regularly at night.

Such children — about one in five of all babies — are exhausting, and their persistent waking, often accompanied by incessant crying, can be a serious problem.

In a number of popular manuals on how to bring up babies, Dr Spock and others suggest that night-waking can be avoided by leaving the child to cry or by other such rigid procedures. This is wrong. Parental mishandling does not cause night-waking and parents should not feel that they are to blame if their baby wakes at night.

A study carried out at the Institute of Child Health in London shows that night-waking is linked to a number of minor obstetric difficulties surrounding the birth of the child, and that parental handling is irrelevant.

Dr N. Blurton Jones, a pediatrician at the institute, worked with three colleagues. They compared the medical histories of a group of night-waking children (at 15, 21, 27, 33 and 39 months) with another group who slept normally.

The pediatricians also observed the mother and child for several hours to see if the mothers of the wakers behaved any differently from the mothers of non-wakers.

The chart shows the most important differences. A far higher proportion of wakers had histories of "sub-optimal" births — that is, their births were more likely to be associated with a number of small difficulties.

For example, they were late, they were delivered by forceps, or perhaps there was a relatively long while between birth and the first cry.

Wakers were also more likely to have higher "active baby score" — this is an index, based on whether the child cried a lot in its first weeks, slept little during the day at this time and woke at night almost from the start.

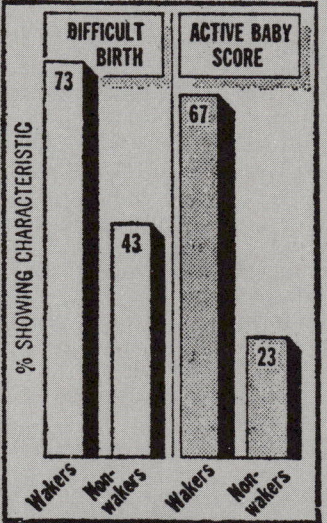

The correlation of difficult birth and high activity with night-waking babies.

The chart is important, because it shows that a mother's reaction to her child's crying plays no real part in creating night-waking. The night-wakers had always been night-wakers from the start; moreover, they slept less during the day than did the non-wakers.

And there was no evidence that night-waking was "created" later on as a result of how a mother treated her baby.

This was underlined by another finding in the study which showed that there was no real difference between the behaviour of mothers of night-wakers and mothers of non-wakers. The only difference found was between the mothers of babies who had had difficult births and mothers of children with normal births.

Not all babies with difficult births became night-wakers. But whether they did or not, Dr Blurton Jones and his colleagues, who report their study in a journal, Development Medicine and Child Neurology, found that mothers reacted much more quickly to their cries than the mothers of children with more normal births.

There was no question of this "creating" children who were likely to cry a lot and hence, perhaps, cry more often at night on waking. Rather, says Dr Blurton Jones, it seems to reflect a different character in the crying of these children, perhaps as a result of the events surrounding their birth, and the mothers seem to know that this crying will not be stopped by leaving the baby alone.

The study also suggests that night-waking could be predicted at birth and such help as is available begin right away. This, best of all, would arm the mother against people who try to tell her that she herself is to blame.

Language Basics (9)

Pronouns

Here are some rules that will help you avoid confusion when using pronouns.

Rule 1 ● Use a **singular pronoun** to refer to a **singular noun.**
       EXAMPLE: My <u>wheelchair</u> is good only on even surfaces. <u>It</u> is an early model.

Rule 2 ● Use a **plural pronoun** to refer to a **plural noun.**
       EXAMPLE: <u>Paraplegics</u> are concerned about safety. <u>They</u> intend to let the government know about their fears.

Rule 3 ● An **emphatic pronoun** should not be used as the subject of a verb.
       EXAMPLE: The social worker and <u>I</u> agreed on the seriousness of the case. (*not* The social worker and <u>myself</u> . . . .)

Rule 4 ● The **order** of personal pronouns in a sentence should be: **third** person, **second** person, **first** person.
       EXAMPLE: <u>He</u>, <u>you</u> and <u>I</u> will ask permission to try out the new facilities.

Exercise

Correct the pronouns in the following sentences.

(1) The letter has been typed. Now they can be duplicated.

(2) The journalist has asked for an interview with some of the sheltered-workshop people so I, Sheila and you will see him.

(3) The architect and yourself have already shown us the plans.

(4) The kerbs are too high for wheelchairs. It needs lowering.

(5) As far as the provision of shopping ramps for the disabled is concerned, the mayor and myself feel that the time has come for action.

(6) This wheelchair is very safe. They are now widely used.

(7) The heavy glass door is before me. They are the revolving kind.

(8) Phillip Adams and herself are experienced journalists.

(9) The committee has given Geoff, I and you some brochures.

(10) Feeling absurd and conspicuous, myself tried to prise the chair out of the gutter.

Punctuation – Quotation marks

1. Quotation marks are used to enclose the words *actually* spoken.

    EXAMPLES: (a) 'Let me help you across the road,' said the policeman.
    (The quotation marks enclose only the words actually spoken.)

    (b) I said, 'Let me help you across the road.'
    (The first word inside the quotation marks begins with a capital letter.)

2. Commas and full stops are used with quotation marks as follows.

    EXAMPLES: (a) When the words actually spoken are placed thus:

    > I said, '............ .'
    > He said, '............ .'
    > She said, '............ .'

    the comma is placed *outside* the quotation marks in each case, and the full stop is placed *inside* the quotation marks in each case.

    (b) When the words actually spoken are placed thus:

    > '.......... ,' I said.
    > '.......... ,' he said.
    > '.......... ,' she said.

    the comma is placed *inside* the quotation marks in each case.

Exercise

Correct the following for quotation marks and associated punctuation.

(1) be careful of that gutter he warned.

(2) He sat a long time just looking at me before he said I can manage

(3) I'll have a milkshake I said thinking all the time that the counter looked as high as the Great Wall of China.

(4) He shook his head I can manage thank you.

(5) allow me she said full of politeness.

(6) I said I'm beginning to think this chair has square wheels

Unit Ten

Comprehension (10)

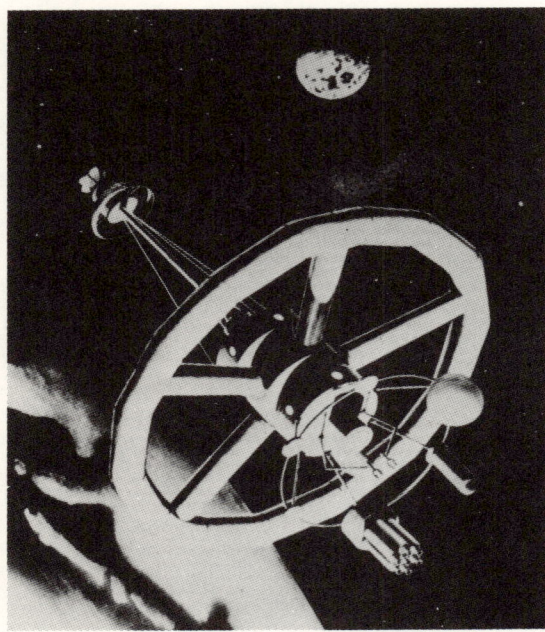

Profiles of the Future

As communications improve, so the need for transportation will decrease. Our grandchildren will scarcely believe that millions once spent hours of every day fighting their way into city offices — where, as often as not, they did nothing that could not have been achieved over telecommunication links.

For global phone and vision services, enabling men to confer with each other anywhere on the planet, are only a beginning. Even now we have data-handling systems linking together factories and offices miles apart, controlling nation-wide industrial empires. Electronics is already permitting the decentralization which rising rents and transport costs — not to mention the threat of the mushroom cloud — encourage more strongly every year.

The business of the future may be run by executives who are scarcely ever in each other's physical presence. It will not even have an address or a central office — only the equivalent of a telephone number. For its files and records will be space rented in the memory units of computers that could be located anywhere on Earth: the information stored in them could be read off on high-speed printers whenever any of the firm's officers needed it.

The time may come when half the world's business will be transacted through vast memory banks beneath the Arizona desert, the Mongolian Steppes, the Labrador muskeg or wherever land is cheap and useless for any other purpose. For all spots on Earth, of course, would be equally accessible to the beams of the relay satellites: to sweep from Pole to Pole would mean merely turning the directional antennae through seventeen degrees.

And so the captains of industry of the twenty-first century may live where they please, running their affairs through computer keyboards and information-handling machines in their homes. Only on rare occasions would there be any need for more of the personal touch than could be obtained via wide-screen full-colour TV. The business lunch of the future could be conducted perfectly well with the two halves of the table 10 000 miles apart; all that would be missing would be the handshakes and exchange of cigars.

Administrative and executive skills are not the only ones which would thus become independent of geography. Distance has already been abolished for the three basic senses of sight, hearing and touch — the latter thanks to the development of remote-handling devices in the atomic energy field. *Any* activity which depends on these senses can, therefore, be carried out over radio circuits. The time will certainly come when surgeons will be able to operate a world away from their patients, and every hospital will be able to call on the services of the best specialists, wherever they may be. . . .

An application of satellites which has already been considered in some detail by the astronautical engineers is what has been called the Orbital Post Office, which will probably make air-mail obsolete in the quite near future. Modern facsimile systems can automatically transmit and reproduce the equivalent of an entire book in less than a minute. By using these techniques, a single satellite could handle the whole of today's trans-atlantic correspondence.

A few years from now, when you wish to send an urgent message, you will purchase a standard letter-form on which you will write or type whatever you have to say. At the local office the form will be fed into a machine which scans the marks on the paper and converts them into electrical signals. These will be radioed up to the nearest relay satellite; routed in the appropriate direction round the Earth, and picked up at the destination, where they are reproduced on a blank form identical with the one you inscribed. The transmission itself would take a fraction of a second; the door-to-door delivery would extend this time to several hours, but eventually letters should never take more than a day between any two points on the Earth. There are, of course, problems of privacy, which might be solved by robot handling at all stages of the operation. However, even the old-style human postmen have been known to read the mail . . . .

Perhaps a decade beyond the Orbital Post Office lies something even more startling — the Orbital Newspaper. This will be made possible by more sophisticated descendants of the reproducing and facsimile machines now found in most up-to-date offices. One of these, working in conjunction with the TV set, will be able on demand to make a permanent record of the picture flashed on the screen. Thus when you want your daily paper, you will switch to the appropriate channel, press the right button — and collect the latest edition as it emerges from the slot. It may be merely a one-page news-sheet; the editorials will be available on another channel — sports, book reviews, drama, advertising, on others. We will select what we need, and ignore the rest, thus saving whole forests for posterity. The Orbital newspaper will have little more than the name in common with the newspaper of today.

Nor will the matter end here. Over the same circuits we will be able to conjure up, from central libraries and information banks, copies of any document we desire, from Magna Carta to the current Earth-Moon passenger schedules. Even books may one day be 'distributed' in this manner, though their format will have to be changed drastically to make this possible.

All publishers would do well to contemplate these really staggering prospects. Most affected will be newspapers and pocket-books; practically untouched by the coming revolution will be art volumes and quality magazines, which involve

not only fine printing but elaborate manufacturing processes. The dailies may well tremble; the glossy monthlies have little to fear.

How mankind will cope with the avalanche of information and entertainment about to descend upon it from the skies, only the future can show. Once again Science, with its usual cheerful irresponsibility, has left another squalling infant on civilization's doorstep. It may grow up to be as big a problem-child as the one born amid the clicking Geiger counters beneath the Chicago University squash-court, back in 1942.

For will there be time to do any work at all on a planet saturated from Pole to Pole with fine entertainment, first-class music, brilliant discussions, superbly executed athletics, and every conceivable type of information service? Even now, it is claimed, our children spend a sixth of their waking lives glued to the cathode-ray tube. We are becoming a race of watchers, not of doers. The miraculous powers that are yet to come may well prove more than our self-discipline can withstand.

If this is so, then the epitaph of our race should read, in fleeting, fluorescent letters: 'Whom the Gods would destroy, they first give TV.'

[from *Profiles of the Future* by ARTHUR C. CLARKE]

Check Your Understanding

(1) What kinds of things is the author thinking of when he uses the phrase 'telecommunication links'?

(2) What do you understand by the word 'decentralization'? What, according to the writer, are two advantages of decentralization?

(3) Explain the meanings of: (a) 'physical presence' (b) 'captains of industry'.

(4) What point is the author making when he describes the business lunches of the future?

(5) What do you understand by the term 'facsimile system'?

(6) What is one important advantage that the Orbital Post Office will possess over air-mail? What is one possible disadvantage it may have?

(7) What is the meaning of 'saving whole forests for posterity'?

(8) Why do you think the writer uses the expression 'avalanche of information' rather than 'mass of information'?

(9) What do you understand by the 'usual cheerful irresponsibility' of Science? Can you think of any examples of this irresponsibility?

(10) 'Squalling infant' is an unusual expression. Can you explain its meaning?

(11) Why do you think the writer uses the term 'cathode-ray tube' rather than 'television'?

(12) What does the writer mean by 'our self-discipline'?

(13) What point is the writer making in the last sentence of the passage?

(14) Did you gain any impression of the writer as a person from his language and ideas? Explain your viewpoint.

(15) What do you think is the writer's intention in this passage?

(16) Explain the meanings of these expressions: (a) 'conjure up'
(b) 'sophisticated descendants of the reproducing and facsimile machines'
(c) 'epitaph of our race'.

Working with Words (10)

Senior Spelling Demons	Confusing Pairs	Environment	Space Travel	Increase Your Word Power
allocate	yolk	devastation	altitude	incongruous
fulfil	yoke	sanctuary	physicist	insomnia
interfere	riotous	conservation	satellite	graphic
agility	righteous	atmosphere	astronaut	inane
necessary	vacation	industrial	gravity	inanimate
essential	vocation	catastrophe	nuclear	monologue
tongue	appreciable	contamination	isolation	maudlin
abandon	appreciative	excessive	astronomy	indefatigable
ability	populace	malnutrition	universe	indict
amateur	populous	pollution	system	nostalgia

Change the Words

Change into people

(a) astronomy ....

(b) conservation ....

(c) insomnia ....

Change into nouns

(a) necessary ....

(b) interfere ....

(c) fulfil ....

(d) appreciative ....

(e) allocate ....

(f) incongruous ....

Change into verbs

(a) conservation ....

(b) gravity ....

(c) isolation ....

(d) vacation ....

(e) populous ....

(f) excessive ....

Change into adjectives

(a) agility ....

(b) nostalgia ....

(c) universe ....

(d) ability ....

(e) atmosphere ....

(f) catastrophe ....

Change into adverbs

(a) graphic ....

(b) system ....

(c) necessary ....

Write plurals for

(a) satellite ....

(b) sanctuary ....

(c) radius ....

Increase Your Word Power

Replace the words or phrases in heavy type with words from the word lists.

(1) She was **tireless** in her efforts to help the poor.

(2) Wearing a swimming-costume to the cinema would be **out of place.**

(3) The police intend to **charge** the bank robber.

(4) The immature student made some **silly** statement.

(5) The refugee was suffering from **a lack of food.**

(6) The state government has established a **place of refuge** for koalas.

(7) The tired office worker was suffering from **sleeplessness.**

(8) Older people sometimes betray **a longing for the past** when reminiscing.

(9) The actor delivered a **long speech.**

(10) Minerals are regarded as being **without life.**

Match Up

For each word in the left-hand column, select *two* from the group in the right-hand column which are similar to it in meaning.

List-Words	Possible Meanings
isolation	gaiety, interference, seclusion, solitude
catastrophe	prosperity, disaster, hatred, ruin
agility	nimbleness, fatigue, impulsiveness, readiness
graphic	intermittent, realistic, inanimate, lifelike

Confusing Pairs

Correctly match one word from each of the confusing pairs with its meaning opposite.

(1) yolk/yoke	the yellow part of an egg
(2) riotous/righteous	virtuous
(3) vocation/vacation	career or occupation
(4) appreciable/appreciative	capable of being estimated
(5) populous/populace	the common people

THE POPULACE OF COMMON PEOPLE IS VERY POPULOUS

Missing Words

Correctly insert the words from the box into the following sentences.

devastation	populace	nuclear	vocation	appreciable
indict	monologue	yoke	indefatigable	

(1) The rabble-rouser knew how to sway the ....

(2) The student decided to make teaching her ....

(3) The mayor delivered a long, boring ....

(4) The magistrate was prepared to .... the escapee.

(5) The prime minister was .... in his efforts to attack poverty.

(6) There was .... growth in the number of new cars on the road.

(7) The conquerors imposed an oppressive .... on the defeated nations.

(8) .... war is certain to bring widespread ....

Word Origins – 'Get the sack'

In the early days of the Industrial Revolution in England, skilled tradesmen and mechanics had to supply their own tools. If they were dismissed, their employer usually gave them a sack in which to take their tools away — hence the expression 'to get the sack' when someone is fired. The Australian bushman, wishing to sack his employees with the minimum of ill-will, traditionally uses the expression, 'It's a good day for travelling'.

Language in Action (10)

Denotation and Connotation

Denotation

Every word has two kinds of meaning for the reader or hearer. The first of these is the **denotation** of the word, the specific object/quality/feeling/aspect/action (etc) that is indicated by the word.

- The denotation of **'dog'** is 'quadruped of many breeds, wild and domesticated' *(Concise Oxford)*.

- The denotation of **'slow'** is 'not quick, deficient in speed, taking a long time to traverse a distance or do a thing' *(Concise Oxford)*.

Connotation

But every word also contains personal significance and associations for each individual. A person brought up from childhood with a friendly Collie dog will possibly have the specific connotation of *a friendly Collie* when hearing the word 'dog'. A postman may have feelings of dislike towards the word 'dog'; for him it connotes a barking (and maybe biting) frightening animal — perhaps a small one.

An elderly lady will have connotations for 'slow' different from those of a young man who has just taken up speedway racing. Theoretically the number of different connotations a word may have is unlimited.

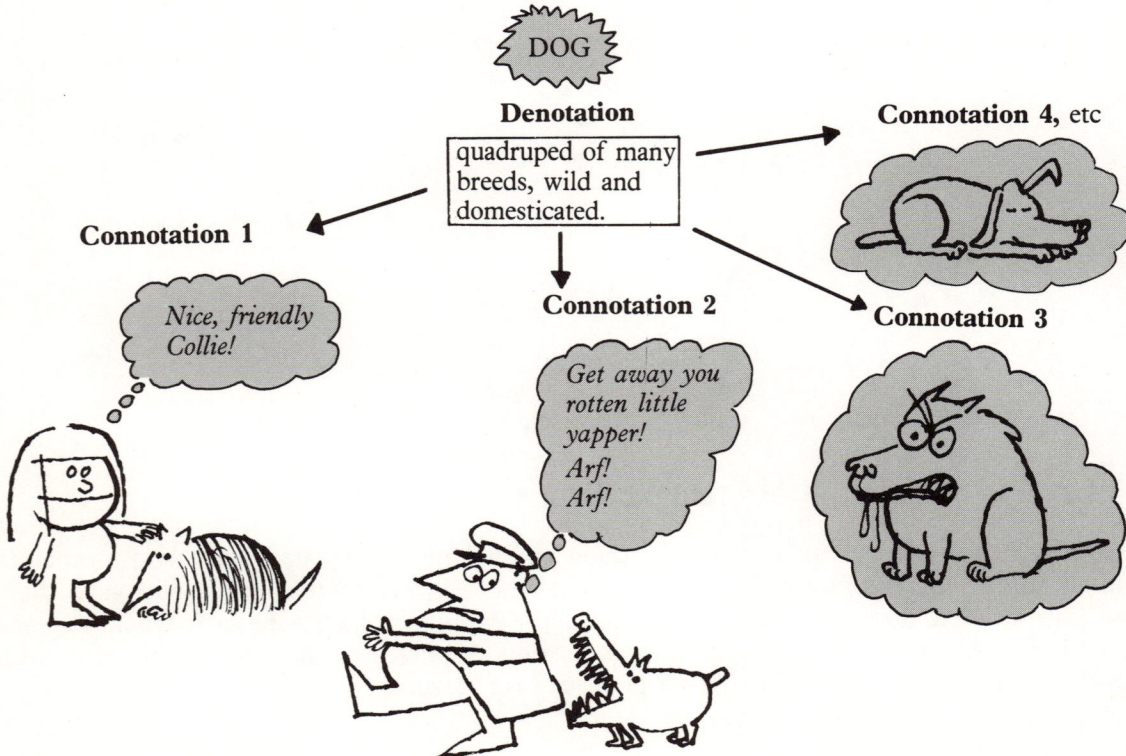

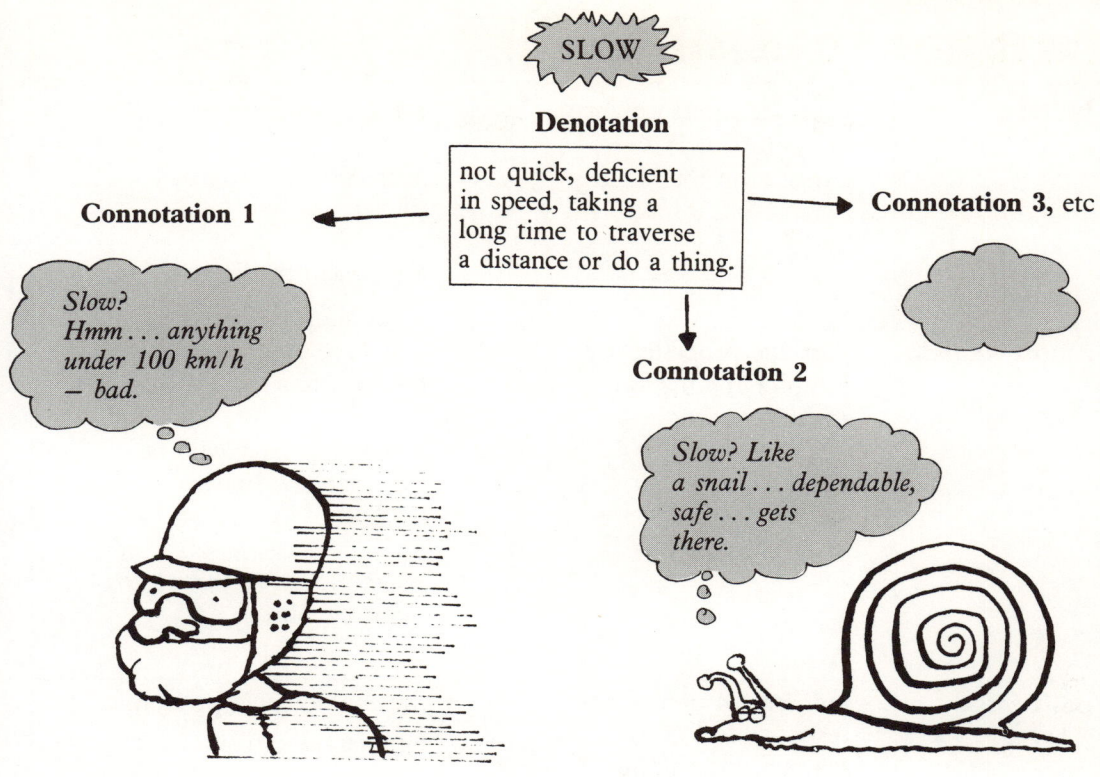

The connotation of a word, then, can be thought of as the *private meaning* that a word has for the individual who hears or reads it, or as the *implied value* that the word carries in the context.

Exercise 1

Each word listed below and overleaf has its denotation written beside it. Consider the various people listed in the third column and suggest additional connotations that they might see in the word in each case.

WORD	DENOTATION	PEOPLE
(1) **sea**	expanse of salt water covering most of Earth's surface and enclosing its continents and islands	a sailor an inland dweller who has never seen the sea a non-swimmer
(2) **algebra**	investigation of the properties of numbers by means of general principles	a physicist a student who is not good at maths

WORD	DENOTATION	PEOPLE
(3) **ballet**	combined performance of professional dancers on the stage	a ballet student a professional football player a classical musician
(4) **motor vehicle**	carriage propelled by a motor for use on ordinary roads	a status-conscious businessman a young person who has just received his/her licence an employee at the Motor Registry office
(5) **policeman**	member of civil force responsible for maintaining public order	the mother of a policeman an average citizen a criminal
(6) **snake**	serpent	a herpetologist an ordinary housewife
(7) **food**	victuals, nourishment, provisions	yourself a well-fed, overweight person a starving man
(8) **schoolteacher**	person responsible for giving instruction to students at a school	a person who was expelled from school a keen student a pre-school child
(9) **violin**	musical instrument with four strings of treble pitch played with a bow	a reluctant violin pupil the next-door neighbours a doting mother
(10) **heroin**	a sedative drug prepared from morphine	a policeman a drug addict an addict's parent

Connotation — A Personal Experience

Often, emotive words are used by speakers and writers because they are aware that these words carry connotations of 'goodness' or 'badness' apart from their objective meaning, and these connotations are widely accepted.

But even though the connotation of a word may be generally understood, it is still subject to personal differences. For example, the word 'Communist' generally carries a connotation of disapproval in our society, but then the strength of this disapproval will vary from person to person, and for some people the word will even connote positive rather than negative attributes. The connotations which a word has for us are personal.

Exercise 2

Following is a list of words. In each case write down what the word denotes, and also the personal connotation that the word holds for you. To get at this connotation, you will need to monitor the feelings it creates within you due to personal association. Use disjointed phrases to help you unmask the connotations. (The first one is done for you as an example.)

LIST OF WORDS	DENOTATION	CONNOTATION
(to) bath	to subject to washing in a bath	not a particularly nice way to wash — a bit of a waste of time — I love showers!
plane		
coffee		
Rugby League		
meat pie		
opera		
haircut		
Christian		
(to) study		
bushwalking		
snow		

The Language of Literature (10)

BERT SCHULTZ

Bert Schultz on his West Coast farm
Eases backwards through the doorway of his truck,
And the cabin grows around him, the wheel
Finds comfort in a padded stomach rut.
Bert Schultz in motion is a monstrous forward shoot
Because he crushes the accelerator like a toadstool
Under his six-pound boot.

Bert Schultz on his West Coast farm
Wears braces like railway tracks
That start from button boulders,
Junction in the middle of his back
And climb over the mountains of his shoulders.

Bert Schultz in his West Coast town
Has a fence-post arm to buttress up the bar,
Spins a thimble schooner in the stale-smelling ebb,
Talks about sheep and the way prices are.

The glass hidden in his ham-bone fist,
An hour later he still talks farm,
While the flies tip and veer
In the tangle of the wire sprouting on his arm.

Bert Schultz down a West Coast street
Makes me certain Eyre Peninsula
Has taken to its legs,
And is walking round the place on tree-stump feet;
Makes me feel the steel of yaccas,[1]
And the supple punch of mallee,[2]
And the thirsty tug of eighteen-gallon kegs.

Bert Schultz knows something of tractor oils and sumps,
Sheep dogs and petrol pumps
And an occasional punch to the chin,
But when he laughs like a shaking mountain,
Or gullies his face badly with a grin,
He opens suddenly and lets you in.

COLIN THIELE

---

1 *yaccas:* small, hardy trees.
2 *mallee:* strong, shrubby eucalypts.

Check Your Understanding

(1) The word 'rut' is usually applied to roads and tracks. What does its use here suggest about Bert's stomach?

(2) Explain the relationship between Bert and his truck.

(3) Explain what you think the poet is trying to achieve by comparing the accelerator of the truck to a toadstool.

(4) What is the poet trying to suggest about Bert when he compares Bert's braces to 'railway tracks'? What other words in the second stanza continue this simile?

(5) Bert's size is emphasized throughout the poem. Jot down two phrases you have not yet mentioned which show that Bert is a large man.

(6) A 'schooner' is a large glass of beer. Why does the poet refer to Bert's schooner as a 'thimble schooner'?

(7) How can Bert have a 'fence-post arm'?

(8) What qualities of Bert make the poet certain that 'Eyre Peninsula has taken to its legs'?

(9) Explain what the poet means by 'the tangle of wire sprouting on his arm'.

(10) What does 'an occasional punch to the chin' suggest about Bert's character?

(11) What picture do you have of Bert when the poet writes that 'he laughs like a shaking mountain'?

(12) What does, 'He opens suddenly and lets you in' suggest about Bert's nature?

(13) Jot down various lines from the poem that depict Bert at work and at play.

(14) What examples of exaggeration can you find in the poem?

(15) What kind of picture of Bert was the poet trying to convey to his reader? Did he succeed? Why?

(16) Did you enjoy the poem? Why or why not?

(17) Colin Thiele has said of this poem: 'I was born and brought up on a wheat-farm and I spent ten years of my grown-up life on Eyre Peninsula (called the West Coast in SA). I came to know many of the farmers there very well. Bert Schultz could easily have been one of them – but in actual fact when I wrote the poem I had several men in mind and built up a kind of combined picture.'

Do you agree with the poet when he claims that Bert Schultz 'could easily have been one of them'? Why?

Thinking and Reasoning (10)

In this section we would like you to try out your reasoning powers on a few tasks that require you to think critically.

Evaluating Analogies

Make reasonably wide-ranging comments on the uses of analogy in the two passages that follow.

A

In some ways life is like the Dodgem Cars at the show. We meet another person, smile, and bump, and away we go again. How are you? Bump. Not bad, mate. Bump. Goodday. Bump, bump. Hi. Fine. Real beaut. Great. Bump, bump. And so, everywhere, lost and lonely people search for someone who will be a friend, someone who will really care. And instead, they run into Dodgem Cars. Bump, bump, bump.

B

Mr Speaker, the learned member from .... accuses me of following a Socialist line, of being a Communist. How long must we put up with labels instead of arguments in this Parliament? His words are a tired old tune, played on a barrel organ. When you have no arguments, nothing worth saying, just kick the Communist can again. It's worked before; it will work again! At least that's what the learned Organ-grinder opposite thinks.

'A RED UNDER EVERY BED GETTING INSIDE YOUR HEAD'

Now puzzle through these!

(1) Use your reasoning ability to solve the puzzle opposite, after reading the boxed instructions below. It can be solved most quickly by using a systematic approach, rather than by guessing. Describe the systematic approach after you have worked it out, and solved the puzzle.

THE INTERPRETERS

Have you ever had to work your way through a maze of interpreters at an international conference? If so, you will have had useful practice for overcoming the language difficulty at the Great World Conference, whose vital importance may be measured by these portraits of the interpreters engaged for it.

The Swedish and Indonesian delegates wish to talk to each other, but among the sixteen interpreters, not one speaks both Swedish and Indonesian. The only way round this problem is to form a chain of interpreters. For example, an English-French interpreter could talk to a French-Italian interpreter who in turn could speak to an Italian-Spanish interpreter and so on. . . . Each interpreter, however, must have a booth of his own, and there are only four booths available.

Which four interpreters will you place in the booths so that the Swedish and Indonesian delegates can talk to each other? The interpreters both speak and understand the languages listed next to their respective numbers.

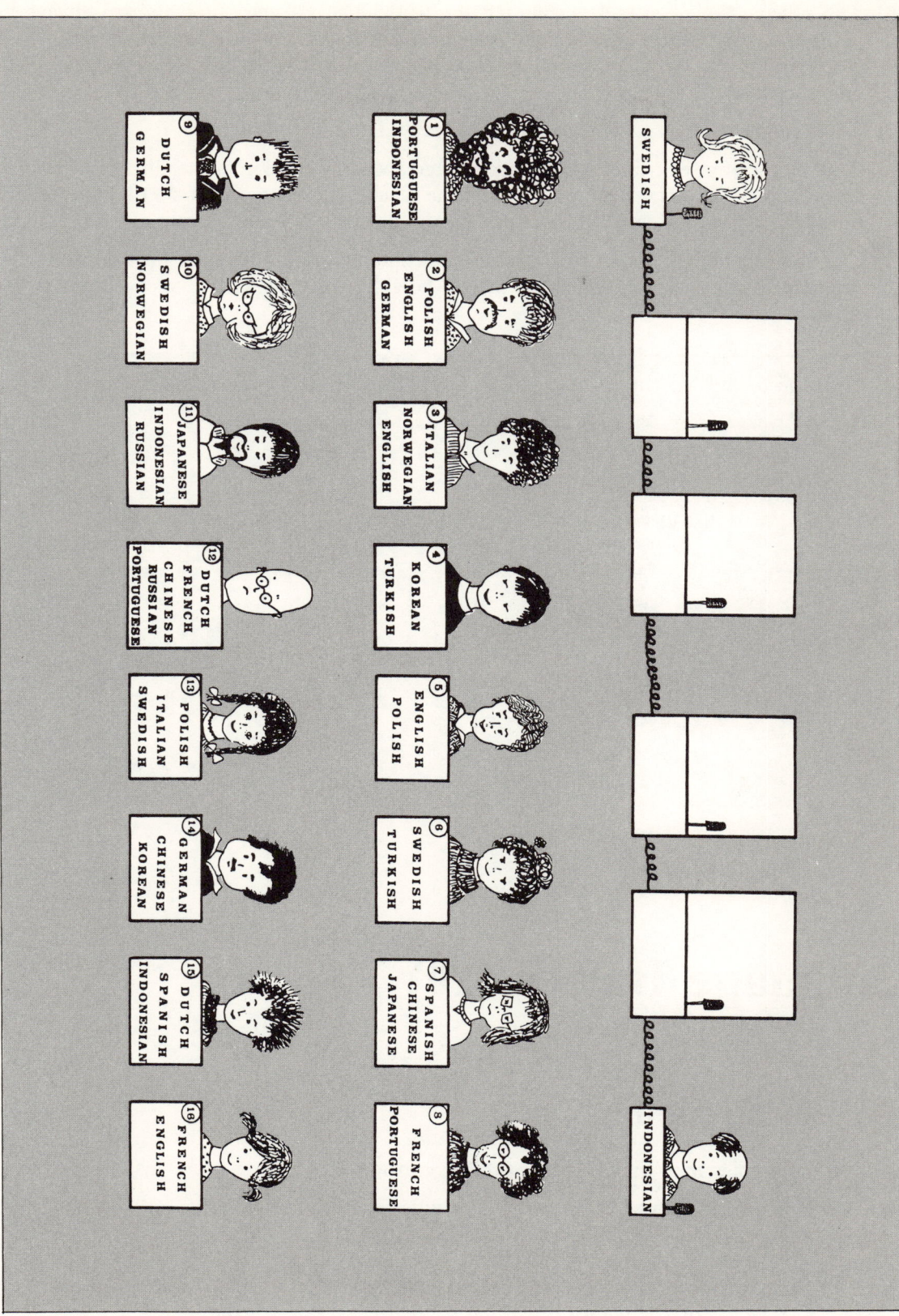

(2) The villagers of Grimmel always tell the truth. The villagers of Brummel always lie. While walking near their villages you meet a villager, but are uncertain whether he is a Grimmelian or a Brummelian. How can you establish which he is by asking just one question?

(3) What single word is spelt incorrectly in every dictionary?

(4) A plane flies out of Melbourne at an average speed of 500 km/h, heading for Brisbane. An hour later a plane flies out of Brisbane at an average speed of 600 km/h, heading for Melbourne. Which plane is closer to Melbourne when they meet?

(5) Can you put both 5 litres of milk from one container, and 4 litres of milk from another container, into a larger container and still be able to see which is which? Explain your answer.

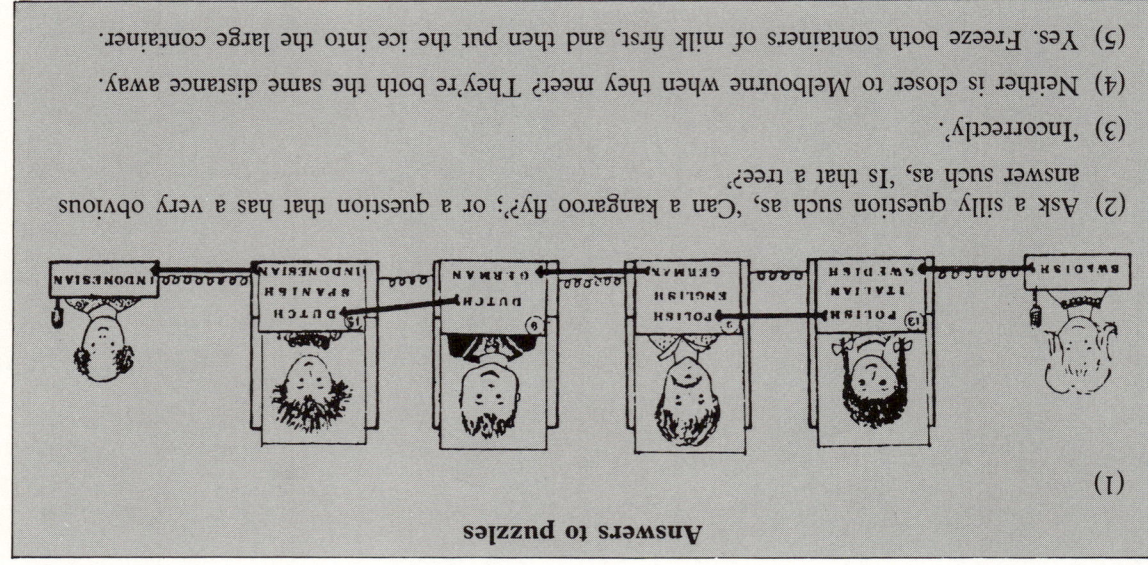

Answers to puzzles

(1)

(2) Ask a silly question such as, 'Can a kangaroo fly?'; or a question that has a very obvious answer such as, 'Is that a tree?'

(3) 'Incorrectly'.

(4) Neither is closer to Melbourne when they meet? They're both the same distance away.

(5) Yes. Freeze both containers of milk first, and then put the ice into the large container.

Language Basics (10)

More on Pronouns

Here are more rules that will help you avoid confusion when using pronouns.

Rule 1 • **You** takes a plural verb even if it stands for only one person.
   EXAMPLE: <u>You</u>, Helmut, <u>are</u> a dweller in the 21st century.

Rule 2 • Pronouns that follow prepositions are placed in the objective case.
   EXAMPLE: Interplanetary travel has a great attraction <u>for me</u> [*not* 'I'].

Rule 3 ● The following take singular verbs:

everybody	**each**
everyone	**anybody**
no-one	**anyone**
nobody	

EXAMPLE: <u>Everybody</u> <u>was</u> present at the satellite launching.

Exercise

Correct the following sentences.

(1) A message for she has been displayed by the computer.

(2) Each of the scientists are a specialist.

(3) Was you able to take your interplanetary call, Garth?

(4) Nobody were surprised by the failure of the space programme.

(5) A robot does all the work for he in half the time.

(6) You have all the necessary input for the Univac programme hasn't you, Donna?

(7) Instructions for free fall have been handed to we.

(8) At present, anybody are eligible to book a seat on the first public moon flight.

(9) Communication satellites flew over they.

(10) There's a seat for everyone who have a ticket.

Punctuation — More on quotation marks

Here are more rules on the correct ways to use quotation marks.

1. Commas and full stops are used with quotation marks as follows.

(a) When the words actually spoken are arranged thus:

(b) Or thus:

'.............,' —————, '............ .'

'.............,' ————— . '............ .'

EXAMPLES: (a) 'I want to use a tape,' said the engineer, 'so that I can replay it.'
(b) 'He's late again,' said the instructor. 'It isn't the first time.'

2. Always enclose within the quotation marks the question mark or exclamation mark associated with the words actually spoken.
EXAMPLES: (a) 'Are you ready to receive an instantaneous message from Mars?'
(b) 'Blast off!'

3. Use quotation marks for titles of books, films, records, etc.
> EXAMPLE: Arthur C. Clarke's 'Profiles of the Future' is really a book of scientific predictions.

> NOTE: <u>Underlining of titles</u> is preferred by many to using quotation marks.

Exercise

Correctly punctuate the following sentences.

(1) What course do we set asked the navigator I want to go there directly.

(2) Look out UFO

(3) Satellites will replace power grids said the lecturer because they have proved their worth.

(4) The most popular science-fiction films of the period were 2001: A Space Odyssey and Star Wars.

(5) The captain asked have we a list of successful launches

(6) Keep clear of the tail-jets shouted the trooper.

Unit Eleven

Comprehension (11)

Death of Ronald Ryan

The life that was Ronald Ryan's was taken from him yesterday.

He died silently. His face white but impassive. His thin lips together, but not clenched.

You get weird mental impressions. His face was strangely like a small child who had composed himself into calm bravery just before the doctor gives a needle.

Only once did this change. The hangman readying the knot jolted his head with the rope. Ryan turned his head slightly towards him. That was all.

The hangman stepped back, the body fell from view. The rope dragged taut and swayed just slightly. The voice of the priest was heard reading his prayers.

I was one of 14 newsmen-witnesses representing the public.

We were marshalled first into a long visitors' room with plastic flowers. An official warning was given: No cameras or tape recorders — 'that wouldn't be cricket'. No smoking once inside either.

Then the clock took over. At 10 minutes to eight we were led to D block. Our bodies were counted on the way, tallied at the door.

A last impression going through the door: A lot of birds singing.

Inside small fluorescent lights helped the bits of sunglow seeping through roof windows. A rope was held back up 40 ft from a green canvas-like screen. On a catwalk above, the noose lay neatly placed on a railing. Its rope ended on the thick beam above, tied around the beam in six loops.

Two minutes to eight. The prison officials' party walked on the tier catwalk above to Ryan's cell. The hangman suddenly walked quickly under the scaffold and entered behind them. A big, dark green cap — like English Soccer fans wear — pulled down low around his head. Big sun goggles over his eyes.

Forty seconds before eight. Ryan emerged. Five long paces from his cell door to the noose. Dull blue prison denims. Hands tied behind his back. A grey cloth on his head.

As the hangman fixed his rope, you could see wispy grey hair under his cap on his neck. It was a redly sunburnt neck.

Ryan, white, immobile, passive, as a wide flap from the cloth on his head was dropped over his face.

The trap door opened efficiently at eight.

[by PATRICK TENNISON
in *The Penalty Is Death*, ed. Barry Jones]

Check Your Understanding

(1) Comment on the structure of the opening sentence. Would it have been better to write, 'Ronald Ryan was put to death yesterday.'?

(2) What were Tennison's impressions as to how Ryan was trying to handle this whole procedure?

(3) What is the meaning of: (a) taut (b) marshalled (c) tier (d) immobile? Consult the back-of-the-book dictionary if you need help.

(4) What single slight change appeared to alter Ryan's composure?

(5) 'No cameras or tape recorders — "that wouldn't be cricket".' Explain the apparent irony in this statement.

(6) 'Then the clock took over.' Explain how the writing from this point onwards underscores the truth of this statement.

(7) Why was the singing of birds particularly noted by Tennison?

(8) Explain why the hangman dressed so that he could not really be seen.

(9) Which word in the final sentence appears to carry particular force? Comment on its use.

(10) Explain the difference between 'impassive' and 'passive' as they are used in this extract. Refer to the back-of-the-book dictionary if you need to.

(11) Towards the end of the description short *phrases* are used rather than complete *sentences*. Is this poor writing, because the verbs have been omitted? If not, why has the writer used this technique?

(12) How would you characterize the tone of this passage?

(13) What attitude do you feel the writer has towards this hanging? Support your answer.

(14) Evaluate the effectiveness of this passage as a description of a hanging.

(15) Has this description affected your view of capital punishment? Explain how, and outline your view.

Working with Words (11)

Senior Spelling Demons	Confusing Pairs	At Work		Increase Your Word Power
behaviour	write	playwright	engineer	undulate
necessary	rite	solicitor	geologist	extricate
guess	gate	professor	benefactor	innuendo
scarcity	gait	supervisor	philanthropist	perennial
seize	fatal	plumber	veterinarian	vestige
dissolve	fateful	musician	employee	unscathed
through	difference	chauffeur	technician	poignant
garage	deference	architect	mechanic	imbue
machinery	disinterested	pathologist	psychologist	stipulate
whether	uninterested	entrepreneur	lawyer	secluded

At Work

Line up each of the specialists in the box with the brief descriptions listed below. (Note the example.)

geologist	musician	professor	entrepreneur
playwright	plumber	psychologist	lawyer
pathologist	veterinarian	chauffeur	architect

EXAMPLE:

chauffeur   driving

(1) .... drama

(2) .... university department

(3) .... building design

(4) .... drainage

(5) .... commerce

(6) .... disease (animal)

(7) .... disease (human)

(8) .... mind

(9) .... statute

(10) .... Earth's crust

(11) .... instrument

Confusing Pairs

Match up correctly one word from each of the *Confusing Pairs* with the meaning opposite.

write/rite	ceremonial act
gate/gait	way of walking
fatal/fateful	causing death
difference/deference	respect
disinterested/uninterested	impartial

Adjectives

Write down the correct adjectives for each of the following nouns.

behaviour	....	**undulate**	....
professor	....	**difference**	....
vestige	....	**geologist**	....
pathologist	....	**philanthropist**	....
rite	....	**veterinarian**	....
supervisor	....	**psychologist**	....
musician	....	**deference**	....
technician	....		

Synonyms

Each word on the left has one word amongst those on the right that is similar in meaning. Select the word. (Note the example.)

EXAMPLE: **playwright**   novelist scribe <u>dramatist</u> character

(1) **secluded**   sombre hidden reserved rural

(2) **vestige**   allowance original garment trace

(3) **unscathed**   unhurt uncritical impractical exterior

(4) **poignant**   painful happy frenzied rushed

(5) **imbue**   alleviate maintain permeate reject

(6) **extricate**   oppose disentangle lope complicate

(7) **stipulate**   slope contain insist activate

(8) **supervisor**   bureaucrat poltroon contractor overseer

(9) **innuendo**   implement hint fragment chant

Antonyms

For each of the following sentences, provide an antonym from the lists to replace the word in heavy type.

(1) The **similarity** (................................) was striking

(2) Old Sam is a **miser** (.................................) if ever I saw one.

(3) There's an **abundance** (.................................) of wheat for export.

(4) He emerged **hurt** (.................................) from the wreckage.

(5) It is necessary to **release** (.................................) the handle when the light glows.

(6) The students turned out to be **biased** (.................................) observers.

(7) She had **sweet** (.................................) memories of the holiday.

Word Origins — 'One' words

The Greek word *monos* means 'one' or 'alone'. The following words are all derived from *monos:* **monastery, monologue, monopoly, monotone, monarch, monosyllable.** Match them up with the clues below.

(1) This person reigns alone.   mon ....

(2) Monks live here by themselves.   mon ....

(3) Exclusive control of a commodity by one person.   mon ....

(4) A word of one syllable.   mon ....

(5) A long speech by one person.   mon ....

(6) A single unchanging tone.   mon ....

Language in Action (11)

Euphemism

Euphemism is a technique in language usage which involves the use of a more pleasant word to replace a word that has unpleasant, offensive or, in some way, harsh connotations. The word derives from the Greek *eu-* ('good', 'well') and *pheme* ('speaking'). Thus, to use euphemisms is to 'speak well' of something.

The nineteenth century was an age when euphemism had its heyday — particularly in Britain. Victorian prudishness and an odd sense of refinement and delicacy made it very difficult for people openly to refer (for example) to underclothing or parts of the human body. All sorts of euphemisms were coined to enable reference to be made to these things with the necessary propriety. Chicken breast, for instance, was commonly referred to as chicken 'bosom', and the most lasting euphemism for the variety of underclothes was 'unmentionables'. 'Bulls' became 'gentlemen cows' and any girl who had a pass made at her had 'been attempted'. The motive behind most of this use of euphemism was to cloak embarrassment. Often the euphemisms were intended to be mildly humorous at the same time.

Exercise 1

Match these 19th-century euphemisms (Column 1) with their 'harsher' but unashamed synonyms (Column 2).

underlinen	legs
hose	belly
nether limbs	breasts
abdomen	underwear
posterior	buttocks
water closet	lover
chest	go to bed
a delicate state of health	stockings
retire	died
erring sister	toilet
gone to a better world	pregnancy
paramour	prostitute

Contemporary Euphemisms

Although we pride ourselves today on being 'liberated' and 'uninhibited', there are many areas in which we euphemize. This is not to be thought of as necessarily bad; the creation of euphemisms has also tended to enrich our language (because of their effect on the scope of meaning and connotation), while at times adding much humour and interest to descriptions.

Exercise 2

Match the 20th-century euphemisms in the first column with their 'harsher' counterparts in the second column.

for the fuller figure	wash
mentally handicapped	have sex indiscriminately
unemployment benefits	bombing raids
perform one's ablutions	for fat people
expectorate	garbage collector
sleep around	apartheid
an affair	dole cheque
ethnics	spit
separate development	adultery
garbologist	old-age pensioners
defensive measures	migrants
senior citizens	retarded

Dying Euphemistically

In Fritz Spiegl's *Small Book of Grave Humour,* a humorous inscription on a tombstone is cited:

> Here lies in a horizontal position the outside case of Thomas Hinde, Clock and watch maker, who departed this life wound up in hope of being taken in hand by his Maker and being thoroughly cleaned, repaired and set a-going in the world to come.

This kind of humour about death would normally seem a bit daring to us. While we smile at the pseudo-medical definition, 'Death is Nature's way of saying you have been overdoing things lately', we know that our smile is, to some extent, a cover for our fear of death. We frequently use euphemism to avoid the harsher realities of death.

For example, here is an extract from Evelyn Waugh's satirical novel, *The Loved One.*

'Can I help you in any way?'

'I came to arrange about a funeral.'

'Is it for yourself?'

'Certainly not. Do I look so moribund?'

'Pardon me?'

'Do I look as if I were about to die?'

'Why, no. Only many of our friends like to make Before Need Arrangements. Will you come this way?'

She led him through the hall into a soft passage. The *décor* here was Georgian. The 'Hindu Love-Song' came to its end and was succeeded by the voice of a nightingale. In a little chintzy parlour he and his hostess sat down to make their arrangements.

'I must first record the Essential Data.'

He told her his name and Sir Francis's.

'Now, Mr Barlow, what had you in mind? Embalmment of course, and after that incineration or not, according to taste. Our crematory is on scientific principles, the heat is so intense that all inessentials are volatilized. Some people did not like the thought that ashes of the casket and clothing were mixed with the Loved One's. Normal disposal is by inhumement, entombment, inurnment, or immurement, but many people just lately prefer insarcophagusment. That is *very* individual. The casket is placed inside a sealed sarcophagus, marble or bronze, and rests permanently above ground in a niche in the mausoleum, with or without a personal stained-glass window above. That, of course, is for those with whom price is not a primary consideration.'

Analysis

(1) Explain bluntly (non-euphemistically) the meanings of:

    (a)   Before Need Arrangements
    (b)   Essential Data
    (c)   embalmment
    (d)   inessentials
    (e)   volatilized

(2) Try to explain the differences in meaning between the euphemisms **inhumement, emtombment, inurnment, immurement** and **insarcophagusment.**

Exercise 3

Find as many euphemisms as you can for death and dying (e.g. 'to pass away', 'go to meet your Maker', etc). You could consult a Thesaurus to help you.

Euphemism and the World of Publicity

Today euphemisms are often used in advertisements to cover the poor or ordinary and to make it sound much more palatable. For example, a shabby little one-room flat with a food-stained gas-ring may be advertised as a 'bachelor apartment with cooking facilities'. The world of real-estate has its own euphemistic jargon to make everything sound desirable. Here is Jeremy Lawrence 'telling it like it is' in his book, *Unmentionables and Other Euphemisms.*

A 'hall' in the same looking-glass language is the narrow passage running between front door and kitchen; a 'garden' need not be very much more than an outsize window-box; an 'eat-in kitchen' is a convenient way of explaining that no dining-room exists; and 'well-maintained' implies that a hasty coat of paint has been slapped on the façade the day before yesterday. Seen through these rose-tinted spectacles any cramped hovel can be a 'bijou residence'. And 'Chelsea-style cottages' — or even 'Chelsea-by-the-sea style cottages' — proliferate far, far away from the precincts of the Royal Borough.

Obvious faults of construction can be glossed over — an off-hand reference to 'rain-penetration' covers the matter of a leaking roof — and unfortunate locations conjured away in some such time-honoured phrase as 'stone's throw from the sea' (cliff-top site), 'secluded' (you need an Ordnance Survey map to find it — and then re-find it the second time), and 'semi-rural with open farm-land' (adjoins sewage-farm).

This class of euphemism has behind it the motive of seeking to *persuade* people.

Exercise 4

Design your own euphemistic advertisement to describe the following piece of real-estate in a more attractive way.

'A small farm, 30 kilometres from the nearest town, accessible only by rough, narrow dirt road through steep, hilly country. Buildings include a dilapidated, small weatherboard farm-house and a tractor-shed badly in need of repairs. Price is $25 000.'

The Language of Literature (11)

THE NOT-SO-GOOD EARTH

For a while there we had 25-inch Chinese peasant families
famishing in comfort on the 25-inch screen
and even Uncle Billy whose eyesight's going fast
by hunching up real close to the convex glass
could just about make them out — the riot scene
in the capital city for example
he saw that better than anything, using the contrast knob
to bring them up dark — all those screaming faces
and bodies going under the horses' hooves — he did a terrific job
on that bit, not so successful though
on the quieter parts where they're just starving away
digging for roots in the not-so-good earth
cooking up a mess of old clay
and coming out with all those Confucian analects
to everybody's considerable satisfaction
(if I remember rightly Grandmother dies
with naturally a suspenseful break in the action
for a full symphony orchestra plug for Craven A
neat as a whistle probably damn glad
to be quit of the whole gang with their marvellous patience.)
We never did find out how it finished up . . . Dad
at this stage tripped over the main lead in the dark
hauling the whole set down smack on its inscrutable face,
wiping out in a blue flash and curlicue of smoke
600 million Chinese without a trace . . .

BRUCE DAWE

Questions — Family scenes

(1) Explain what the poet means by '25-inch Chinese peasant families'.

(2) 'Famishing' means 'being extremely hungry'. Explain what the poet means by 'famishing in comfort on the 25-inch screen'.

(3) The film was actually called *The Good Earth*. Why do you think the poet has called his poem 'The Not-So-Good Earth'?

(4) How has the poet given the impression that the suffering of the Chinese family was looked upon purely as entertainment by the family watching?

(5) What criticism of the television station is the poet making when he writes: 'Grandmother dies / with naturally a suspenseful break in the action / for a full symphony orchestra plug for Craven A . . .'?

(6) When the poet says, 'Grandmother dies / . . . probably damn glad / to be quit of the whole gang with their marvellous patience', what criticism is he making of the film and its characters?

(7) What impression is given of the Chinese when the poet writes: 'and coming out with all those Confucian analects / to everybody's considerable satisfaction'? ('Confucian analects' refers to the wise sayings of Confucius, a famous Chinese philosopher.)

(8) The poem is related in the first person by a member of the family watching the programme. What do you learn about his character and attitudes?

(9) What contrast does the poet make between the 25-inch Chinese peasant family and the family watching the programme?

(10) Did you enjoy this poem? Explain why or why not.

Writers' Workshop (1)

The aim of this 8-section strand is to assist in your development as a competent writer. The development of this particular skill must be a priority for every senior school student, since so many subject areas and life situations will require the ability to express knowledge by writing about it. Necessarily, the first few sections will treat very basic skills. However, it is essential that these be mastered if you are to become a competent writer.

Correct Sentence Structure

The sentence is the basic unit of construction in essays. The writer who is unable to express ideas in acceptable sentence-structures faces an almost impossible task in trying to write a good essay. This is an area that *must* be mastered.

The usual definition of a sentence is 'a group of words expressing a complete thought'; without becoming too technical, we can use this as a satisfactory, practical definition. On the other hand, we will want to know how the definition can be stretched at times.

The Most Frequent Errors

There are several types of incomplete sentence which cause problems for students.

TYPE A   *Incomplete sentences which start with a **connecting word** and its clause, but **omit the main clause** to which these should be connected.*

EXAMPLE: 'If only the typical business executive could slow down.'

'If only' acts as a connecting-word group whose purpose in this incomplete sentence is to join it to a main clause which will complete the thought. We find ourselves wondering, 'If only . . . , *then* what?' A completed version, for example, could be:

'If only the typical business executive could slow down, he would live longer.'

COMMON CONNECTING WORDS

although	for	when	since
though	who	not only . . . but also	even
if	whose	then	in order that
unless	whom	why	where
because	which	as	while
so that	that	before	

Note: Although 'and', 'but' and 'however' are very frequently-used connecting words, they are not included here because they may be used to start sentences which are complete — even if such usage is not always approved of.

Exercise 1

Correct the following incomplete sentences by adding a *main clause*. You may add it before or after the connecting clause.

(1) Unless people recognize the health dangers in smoking.

(2) Not only the hours of gruelling training, but also the cost to family and social life.

(3) When the world will recognize the beauty of living in the NOW.

(4) Because every nation's sense of humour has some distinctive features.

(5) Which we all know contributes to a healthy lifestyle.

(6) Although the preparation for the flight took several thousand hours.

(7) If you are especially sensitive about irritating smells.

(8) Why so many students choose courses that will never help them in later life.

(9) As the amazing Miss Piggy looked adoringly towards Kermit.

(10) Who are eager to assist you with any overseas-travel plans.

TYPE B   *Incomplete sentences which start with a **participle** and its phrase, but **omit the main clause** to which these should be joined.*

EXAMPLE: 'Running wildly across the road, ignoring the sounds of squealing tyres and tortured brakes.'

   'Running' is a present participle used to lead into a phrase, but is not linked here to any subject and main clause. We find ourselves wondering, '*Who* is running?' and 'What is there about the runner(s) that the writer wanted us to know?'. A completed version could be:

   'Running wildly across the road, ignoring the sounds of squealing tyres and tortured brakes, the dog chased its assailant.'

Exercise 2

Correct these incomplete sentences by adding a *subject* for the participle to be attached to, and a *main clause*. You may add either before or after the participial phrase.

(1) Sizing up the height of the bar, now 2.32 metres.

(2) Planning each manoeuvre with meticulous care.

(3) Buzzing with excitement at the sudden change in the game.

(4) Detested by those he had sought to serve for so many years.

(5) Burning with the desire to solve the riddle of the river's source.

(6) Watched by viewers all across the world.

(7) Taking Skippy's paw and Ron Barassi's hand.

(8) Alternately weaving to the left and to the right.

(9) Trained in the right social graces so that nothing could go wrng.

(10) Peeved at the inconsiderate behaviour of my left knee.

TYPE C *Incomplete sentences which are composed of* **extra information** *and depend for their completeness on the* **preceding sentence.**

EXAMPLE: 'The match was watched by thousands of spectators who were on holidays. As well as hundreds of others who had taken a sickie.'

Clearly, something else has been said or listed immediately before this (second) word-group. It is an addition to a main idea and needs to be joined to that main idea in the same sentence, or else reconstructed so that it can stand alone. A possible completed version could be:

'The match was watched by thousands of spectators who were on holidays, as well as by hundreds of others who had taken a sickie.'

Exercise 3

(1) Create main ideas for these incomplete sentences of the *extra information* type, and then join the two components in each case.

(a) Except for the second Friday in the month.

(b) Plus a beautiful climate and unparalleled scenery.

(c) In addition to the huge losses of troops.

(d) Including two hamburgers, a can of Coke and a meat pie.

(e) Such as books, clothing, entertainment and general living expenses.

(2) Correct each of the following incomplete sentences of the *extra information* type by joining it to its accompanying *main idea* sentence, or by reconstructing the extra-information sentence so that it makes sense on its own.

(a) The trees are beautiful native species. Mainly varieties of the eucalyptus family.

(b) *Mad* comics have published a super-special containing some really original stuff. Plus the usual assortment of articles and garbage.

(c) My mind was fuzzy and all sorts of funny things seemed to be happening to me. For example, I seemed to be floating, and I could feel a weight on my head.

(d) I remember very vividly my first attempt at skiing. Especially the hospital they took me to.

(e) The study of foreign languages seems to be on the wane in high schools. Except for a few which are moving towards the study of Asian languages.

Exercise 4

Distinguish complete from incomplete sentences in the following list. Correct all the incomplete sentences by adding main clauses, or whatever is needed. Identify the *type* of incomplete sentence in each case.

(1) Death is a subject surrounded by myths.

(2) Pounding down city streets, hot-eyed and sweaty.

(3) He was deathly pale and was bruised and bleeding on the hands. Also a cut on the side of his head.

(4) If someone laughs at you because of your clumsiness.

(5) Food becomes tasteless when you eat too many meals with a family that's quarrelling.

(6) After the guy had given me a quick tour of the insurance office.

(7) Swinging their sports-bags on the way to the stadium.

(8) Sometimes there are flashes of colour. Including all the shades and hues of the rainbow.

(9) Because of the possibility that we might all fail.

(10) A social leapfrog, hopping from person to person with small talk.

Exercise 5

Rewrite the following paragraph, correcting any incomplete sentences by joining word-groups, adding words, or altering structures as necessary.

'When the flag drops. You have 60 metres of straight to hassle for position. Jostling and colliding, trying to keep your machine on the track. You say goodbye to the only piece of straight. Except for the bit at the finish. Shifting weight to the back and bracing yourself for the crunch of landing. You roar up an inclined jump which sets you sailing free and easy. The cycle comes down spinning. While you spread your legs to maintain balance. On curves you lean dangerously. Dragging a leg in the dirt to hold your bike up. Seems insane. Other competitors crowd you.'

Language Basics (11)

Pronouns Again

Further rules to help you avoid confusion when using pronouns:

Rule 1 ● **All** is normally plural, but when 'all' means 'everything' it takes a singular verb.
      EXAMPLES: (a) All the officials <u>were</u> present.
                  (b) All <u>is</u> finished for Ronald Ryan.

Rule 2 ● For two persons or things, use **either.** For more than two, use **any one.**
EXAMPLES: (a) <u>Either</u> of the <u>two</u> journalists would make a suitable editor.
(b) <u>Any one</u> of the <u>three</u> prisoners will be chosen.
(*Note:* that 'anyone' is *one word* only when it is a synonym for 'anybody'.)

Rule 3 ● A relative pronoun should be placed as near as possible to its antecedent.
EXAMPLE: Books <u>that</u> are biased have been written about the penal system.
(*Not:* Books have been written about the penal system that are biased.)

Using the Rules

Correct the following sentences.

(1) Prisoners have been sentenced by biased juries who are really innocent.

(2) All the cells is empty.

(3) Of the three convicted women, either may be chosen for nursing duties.

(4) The prison was run inefficiently which was situated on a hill.

(5) Any one of the two prison officials may cast the deciding vote.

(6) Several warders were awarded merit badges who had been humane.

(7) Either of the three is liable for jury service.

Punctuation – Quotation marks yet again

Here are two final rules on the use of quotation marks.

1. Use quotation marks to enclose quoted statements such as proverbs, maxims, etc.
EXAMPLE: 'The punishment must fit the crime' is a saying that is often used.

2. When a number of people are speaking, enclose their actual words in quotation marks *and* begin a new line for each speaker.
EXAMPLE: 'Bring the prisoner over here,' commanded the warder.
'Yes sir,' replied the orderly smartly.

Exercise

Correct the following for quotation marks, and punctuate in any additional ways necessary.

(1) Let this be a lesson to you were the words used by the judge to finish off his sentencing remarks.

(2) What is the time asked Ryan six o'clock answered the warder.

(3) The expression crime does not pay is heard rather a lot these days.

(4) The orderly said hold out your arm but objected the prisoner I've already had an anti-tetanus injection when asked the doctor turning towards him?

(5) That wouldn't be cricket is one way of saying that you must abide by the rules

(6) The notice was 'a no smoking sign'

Unit Twelve

Comprehension (12)

Never Needle a Drug-Fiend When He's Got a Knife

A medal — or an order of a Garter or a Thistle or a Bath or whatever they give for stupendous courage in the face of unutterable menace — must be given at once to a Brisbane chemist's assistant named Carolyn Campbell.

Miss Campbell was behind the counter on Monday when the shop was stuck up by a young junkie waving a knife. He told her to hand over the contents of the drug cabinet. 'I want all the hard stuff,' he said. And: 'I haven't had a fix for two days.'

About then a customer, a paying customer, showed up; and the junkie told Miss Campbell: 'Serve him but don't do anything silly. I'll be watching you.'

Now, given that instruction by a hungering drug-fiend flashing a shiv — a combination about as stable as nitro-glycerine — anyone but a lunatic would remain not only mute but motionless, a pillar of salt. Anyone, that is, but a lunatic or a Campbell.

According to the report: 'Miss Campbell said she whispered to the customer that the shop was being robbed but he could not understand her and left with his purchase.'

I'll bet he did. At the full gallop if he had any sense. And I'm not in the least surprised to learn that he couldn't understand her. Anyone who *could* understand her would be crazy. Miss Campbell could have shouted her message into my ear and I wouldn't have heard a word.

I can imagine how that conversation went:

Customer: Er, a pack of Bandaids, please.

Carolyn (whispering): Hist! We're being robbed.

Customer: Bandaids, and a bottle of cough mixture . . .

Carolyn: Robbed, I say, robbed. Help. Call the cops.

Customer: I beg your pardon.

Carolyn: The boy up there. He's got a knife. He's a junkie. He's stealing all our drugs. Hist!

Customer: Oh, my God. Er, a Bandaid and a bottle of mix coughture and a cornplaster and, um, some of those thingummies up there, whatever they are, Eugynon, Organon, Ovulen, and a leg of lamb and four poundser steakankidney and don't forget the coffee . . .

Carolyn: Hist! Call the cops . . .

Customer: . . . and you needn't bother to wrap 'em. As a matter of fact you needn't even bother to serve 'em. I don't want 'em. I wouldn't take 'em if you gave 'em to me. Get out, leave me alone, don't touch me, hooroo . . . .

I don't suppose one should parody the poor wretch. I can't help wondering what I'd have done in the circumstances. I'll probably have nightmares about it:

Saw (entering shop): Good morning my rosy sweeting. I've just popped in to see if you can run up one of those nostrums that chemists mix for gentlemen who've had a skinful the night before and whose crapulence has . . .

Carolyn: Help. We're being robbed.

Saw: . . . reached a stage of severity so terrible as to cause serious doubts about the need to keep fighting for life and . . . EH!

Carolyn: Sssssh. Look normal. Leave the shop. Call the cops. He's got a knife.

Saw (only the whites of his eyes are showing): Knife? Eh, noh spik Angle-ish. Not onsjik Angle-ish. Not onnerstand . . .

Carolyn: Oh, please! Do stop being an ass. He's a junkie. He's got a knife. One false move and he'll slit our throats like ripe mangoes.

Junkie: Hey, what's with the whispering? I tole, you, din I? I tole you not to talk. I tole you I'd be watching.

Carolyn: Oh, be quiet, you wretched little man. And put down that knife or my friend here, who is a detective-superintendent and a commando and president of the Karate Club . . .

Saw: No I'm not! I'm an innocent bystander – or I was. Now, old pal, I'm on your side. With you all the way.

Junkie (suspiciously): She was whispering . . .

Saw: You bet she was, the sneak. She was trying to talk me into calling the cops to grab you. I refused, of course. I reckon a junkie – I beg your pardon: a connoisseur of cocaine – I reckon a connoisseur like you deserves as much respect as . . . and there's a whacking great box of gear out there and you deserve it all . . . I'll bet you you've had a hell of a life, too. Bet your old man beat you up, and your mother was . . . I mean, how could you help it? It's not fair, not fair at all.

Junkie (to Carolyn): Hurry up and get the stuff, will you?

Carolyn: I will not. I'm going straight outside to call a cop.

Saw: No you're not. Don't you! Look at that knife . . . Look, I'm a married man with kids. (His face a ghastly green, lips stretched taut, he turns to Junkie): She won't call a cop. We won't let her. I'll hold her while . . . I'll tie her up and you can rat the drug box. But don't use your knife. Please don't use your knife. You go out the back and help yourself to all those beaut drugs, old pal, old pal, and I'll just nip up the street and call you a cab. I'll even lend you the fare. I'll *give* you the fare. That's the trouble, you see. Nobody's ever given you anything. Nobody's ever been kind. That's what's made you a . . . GOOD LORD! Here are the coppers! . . . and hand over that knife you cowardly swine!

[by RON SAW
in *Forum: Contemporary Australian Essays*, edited by B. Elder]

Check Your Understanding

(1) Explain the pun in the title.

(2) In the fourth paragraph, a particular comparison is advanced within the dashes. Explain this comparison.

(3) Do you feel that the expression 'a pillar of salt' is effective? Why?

(4) The paragraph beginning, 'According to the report . . .' is a pivotal one for the story. Explain its importance.

(5) 'Anyone who *could* understand her would be crazy.' Comment on the force of *'could'* in this sentence.

(6) In the Customer/Carolyn dialogue, what use of words suggests confusion and panic?

(7) How does Saw, as the customer, attempt to use ignorance to escape the junkie's attention?

(8) What do the junkie's words in the Carolyn/Saw exchange suggest about his social and educational experiences?

(9) How does Saw undermine Carolyn's plan to deceive the junkie?

(10) What is his motive for doing so?

(11) 'I reckon a junkie – I beg your pardon: a connoisseur of cocaine . . . .' What kind of figurative device is being employed here? Why does the speaker use it?

(12) In the paragraph beginning, '*Saw:* You bet she was . . .', explain how punctuation is used to communicate hesitancy and 'second thoughts' on Saw's part.

(13) Short sentences and repetition are a feature of the last paragraph. Why?

(14) What causes the surprising change of tone in the last sentence of the passage?

(15) In what principal ways is humour created in the passage?

(16) Much of the passage is written in play form. Does this kind of presentation have any advantage over straightforward prose?

(17) Look up the following words in the back-of-the-book dictionary:
(a) unutterable (b) nostrums (c) crapulence (d) connoisseur.

Working with Words (12)

Senior Spelling Demons	Confusing Pairs	In Sickness and in Health		Increase Your Word Power
welfare	corps	diagnosis	paralysis	fortuitous
alternative	corpse	suffocation	optician	frivolous
plentiful	faint	physical	hygiene	placid
welcome	feint	surgeon	homicide	inhibit
abolition	official	physician	hysterical	assiduous
phrase	officious	medicine	pneumonia	flagrant
nephew	allusion	convalescence	penicillin	immutable
atmosphere	illusion	concussion	delirious	repudiate
system	momentary	operation	stomach	transient
despise	momentous	epidemic	infectious	discordant

Word Association

From the lists, select the words you would associate with the following.

(1) a killing ....

(2) rapid spread of disease ....

(3) to reject ....

(4) brain injury ....

(5) feverish, light-headed ....

(6) restrain or check ....

(7) due to chance ....

(8) one who sells spectacles ....

(9) highly likely to be caught (e.g. disease) ....

(10) disease of the lungs ....

(11) emotionally uncontrolled ....

(12) organ of the abdomen ....

(13) scandalous, glaringly bad ....

(14) inability to breathe ....

Confusing Pairs

Pick out two synonyms or two antonyms from each of the following.

(1) corps, wood, brigade, hull

(2) special, chronological, lasting, momentary

(3) customary, officious, political, bureaucratic

(4) illusion, reality, selection, indication

(5) allusion, prelude, epigram, hint

(6) cadaver, bush, corpse, cloister

(7) unimportant, frequent, assured, momentous

(8) limit, feint, taunt, pretence

(9) analogy, authoritative, official, increment

(10) faint, liable, strong, reconsider

Antonyms

Match up list-words on the left with antonyms on the right.

frivolous	scarce
immutable	excitable
assiduous	harmonious
abolition	serious
despise	changeable
transient	careless
plentiful	establishment
discordant	adore
placid	lasting

Changing Forms

In each of the following, change the word in heavy type into its correct form.

diagnosis procedures

medicine science

surgeon precision

convalescence home

atmosphere pressure

despise rogue

mass **hysterical**

a state of **delirious**

hygiene conditions

wild **frivolous**

a spread of **infectious**

system preparation

Miscellaneous

(1) two kinds of doctor ....

(2) a group of words lacking a finite verb ....

(3) an antibiotic ....

(4) mental and ....

(5) another possibility ....

(6) niece and ....

(7) w .... means 'well-being'

Word Origins — 'Ring-a-ring o' roses'

Ring-a-ring o' roses'
A pocket full of posies,
A-tishoo! A-tishoo!
We all fall down.

The happy children's game that we know today has a much sadder origin. It dates back to the days of the Great Plague, when a rosy rash was a symptom of the plague and posies of herbs were carried as protection. Sneezing was the last fatal symptom of the disease, and 'all fall down' was exactly what they did when they died. In the London newspaper *The Observer* on January 1949 there was a macabre parody which showed well how the original 'Ring-a-ring o' roses' might have come into being. Three and a half years after the atom bomb was dropped on Japan, someone wrote:

Ring-a-ring o' geranium,
A pocket full of uranium,
Hiro, shima,
All fall down!

Language in Action (12)

Clichés

'Another thing, Christy,' he said one night. 'You use too many clichés. Do you know what a cliché is?'

I didn't; it sounded like some kind of foreign animal or insect. But I found out that it was 'something that everybody said', a figure of speech that was in common usage, words and phrases that were used so often both in books and ordinary conversation that they had become thin and shiny, things that have been said over and over again until they become hackneyed and their original meaning lost.

When I found out this, I knew that I was frightfully guilty of this sin. Only yesterday I sat beside 'the roaring fire'; I heard 'the screeching wind'; I waited 'in an agony of suspense'; I saw she had 'lustrous eyes, full, inviting lips and a swanlike neck, and hair like floating strands of gossamer'; I 'had a lump in my throat'; and someone was 'swearing like a trooper'! I found on looking back over my manuscript that I had used so many clichés, so many times, that the number must have run into hundreds.

[from *My Left Foot* by CHRISTY BROWN]

Clichés, as we have just learnt, are hackneyed or stereotyped expressions which have lost their freshness through constant use — although when first coined they probably *were* striking and unusual. Clichés should be avoided in your own writing because they have become stale and they detract from the vitality of communication. They also tend to be associated with haste and mental laziness.

Your daily newspapers are a ready source of clichés. Here are two sentences containing clichés, taken from the sporting section of a local paper.

● The champion was *as cool as a cucumber* as he served for the match.
● *Excitement reigned supreme* in the final minutes of the game.

Matching Clichés with their Meanings

Match up the clichés in the left-hand column with their correct meanings in the right-hand column.

CLICHES	MEANINGS
To keep one's nose to the grindstone	To be in charge
To put one's foot down	To make a peace overture
To rest on one's laurels	Someone treacherous
To rule the roost	To work extremely hard
To show a clean pair of heels	To be content with past successes
To skate on thin ice	Having the same faults
A snake in the grass	To act dangerously
A storm in a teacup	To run away
Tarred with the same brush	A great fuss over nothing
To hold out an olive branch	To take a firm stand

A Crime Full of Clichés

Write down the clichés from the following dialogue between the two robbers, Jack and Bill.

Jack: I could hardly believe my eyes. I was almost at the end of my tether when I realized that we could get into the jeweller's through an air-vent. Do you want to have a finger in the pie, Bill?

Bill: Well, we can't let a chance like that slip through our fingers, can we?

Jack: You've hit the nail on the head. If we strike while the iron is hot, we can grab the chance of a lifetime.

Bill: I'll leave no stone unturned in planning a safe getaway. We'll be out of there in the twinkling of an eye.

Jack: Are you sure that you've considered all the angles?

Bill: I'll tell you man-to-man. We're both in the same boat and I'll make sure we don't get our fingers burnt this time.

Cliché Conversions

Convert all the clichés into your own words.

Old Mick: G'day, Fred. You still alive and kicking? What are you doing these days?

Old Fred: I'm at a loose end, but I suppose at eighty-two one is lucky to be able to keep the wolf from the door. I'm certainly not living in the lap of luxury.

Old Mick: Maybe I can lend a helping hand? I'm managing to keep my head above water with the occasional odd job. There are plenty around.

Old Fred: Yes, I'd like to get my teeth into some work.

Old Mick: Well, don't let the grass grow under your feet. Go and see Doctor Gordon. Her gardener has just left her high and dry.

The Language of Literature (12)

Drama — Billy Liar

Billy [*taking her in his arms*]. I love you, darling.

Barbara [*moving away*]. I love you.

Billy. Do you? Really and truly?

Barbara. Of course I do.

Billy. Are you looking forward to getting married?

Barbara *takes an orange from her handbag and peels it and eats it during the following dialogue.*

Barbara. I think about it every minute of the day.

Billy. Darling . . . [*He again attempts unsuccessfully to kiss her.*] Don't ever fall in love with anybody else.

Barbara. Let's talk about our cottage.

Billy [*simulating a dreamy voice*]. What about our cottage?

Barbara. About the garden. Tell me about the garden.

Billy. We'll have a lovely garden. We'll have roses in it and daffodils and a lovely lawn with a swing for little Billy and little Barbara to play on. And we'll have our meals down by the lily pond in summer.

Barbara. Do you think a lily pond is safe? What if the kiddies wandered too near and fell in?

Billy. We'll build a wall round it. No — no, we won't. We won't have a pond at all. We'll have an old well. And old brick well where we draw the water. We'll make it our wishing well. Do you know what I'll wish?

Barbara [*shaking her head*]. No.

Billy. Tell me what you'll wish first.

Barbara. Oh, I'll wish that we'll always be happy. And always love each other. What will you wish?

Billy. Better not tell you.

Barbara. Why not, pet?

Billy. You might be cross.

Barbara. Why would I be cross?

Billy. Oh, I don't know . . . You might think me too . . . well, forward. [*He glances at her face but can see no reaction.*] Barbara . . . ? Do you think it's wrong for people to have — you know, feelings?

Barbara. Not if they're genuinely in love with each other.

Billy. Like we are.

Barbara [*uncertainly*]. Yes.

Billy. Would you think it wrong of me to have — feelings?

Barbara [*briskly and firmly*]. I think we ought to be married first.

Billy [*placing his hand on* **Barbara's** *knee*]. Darling. . . .

Barbara. Are you feeling all right?

Billy. Of course, darling. Why?

Barbara. Look where your hand is.

Billy. Darling, don't you want me to touch you?

Barbara [*shrugging*]. It seems . . . indecent, somehow.

Billy. Are you feeling all right?

Barbara. Yes, of course.

Billy. How do you feel?

Barbara. Contented.

Billy. You don't feel . . . you know — restless?

Barbara. No.

Billy. Finish your drink.

Barbara. In a minute. [*She opens her handbag and offers it towards him.*] Have an orange.

Billy *snatching the bag from her he throws it down and oranges spill out across the floor.*

Billy. You and your bloody oranges!

Barbara [*remonstratively*]. Billy! . . . Darling!

[from *Billy Liar* by KEITH WATERHOUSE and WILLIS HALL]

Questions to Consider

(1) What is Barbara's view of love and marriage?

(2) How does Billy's attitude to love differ from Barbara's?

(3) Billy uses the word 'darling' a number of times during this short scene. Why do you think he does this?

(4) The dramatist often gives the reader of a play an insight into the characters by the use of stage directions. What does the stage direction, 'simulating a dreamy voice' show us about Billy's character?

(5) Why do you think Billy is prepared to tell Barbara the story about the garden and the lily pond?

(6) Billy uses the word 'kiddies' rather than 'children'. Can you suggest why he does so?

(7) One way we learn about a character in a play is by what he or she says. What have you learnt about the character of Billy in this short scene?

(8) Why does Billy say to Barbara, 'You don't feel . . . you know — restless?'?

(9) Why does Billy exclaim, 'You and your bloody oranges!'? Do you feel he is justified? Why?

(10) The climax in a scene or play occurs when the highest point of physical or emotional tension is reached. Where is the climax in this short scene?

(11) Have you noticed that the dialogue is made up of short, crisp sentences? Can you suggest why the dramatist has done this?

(12) How do you think an audience would react to this scene on stage? Do you think they would laugh at Billy or sympathize with him? Why?

(13) Do you think the characters of Billy and Barbara are true to life? Why or why not?

Writers' Workshop (2)

Paragraphing

If sentences are the basic building-blocks, paragraphs are the rooms of the writing 'house'. Every piece of prose writing, whether it be narrative, descriptive, persuasive or instructive, requires some structuring, some shaping. Paragraphs give writing its form — its plan.

A paragraph is usually a group of sentences, so linked because they pertain to a particular aspect of the subject being written about. These sentences show a *progression* of some sort — a development from the first to the last sentence in the paragraph. The most common progression results from expanding whatever aspect of the topic is set out in the opening sentence, through a few developmental sentences, finishing with a concluding sentence. On occasions, one sentence may stand as a pargraph on its own.

Consider the following paragraph.

> The grass is rich and matted, you cannot see the soil. It holds the rain
> and the mist, and they seep into the ground, feeding the streams in every
> kloof. It is well-tended, and not too many cattle feed upon it; not too
> many fires burn it, laying bare the soil. Stand unshod upon it, for the
> ground is holy, being even as it came from the Creator. Keep it, guard
> it, care for it, for it keeps men, guards men, cares for men. Destroy it
> and man is destroyed.
>
> [from *Cry, the Beloved Country*
> by ALAN PATON]

Notice how this, one of the opening paragraphs in *Cry, the Beloved Country,* shows a definite
progression, with each sentence building up, and developing, the description that the author
seeks to convey to us. The plan might be set out as follows:

Topic
Sentence 1   Focuses our attention on the rich grass in this part of the country.

Sentence 2   The function of the grass in retaining moisture is outlined.

Sentence 3   Careful tending of the grass is described.

Sentence 4   A request is made asking us to appreciate the holiness of the ground.

Sentence 5   This request is developed further because of the importance of the land for
the people.

Concluding   The request is succinctly and forcefully concluded with a statement of man's
Sentence 6   complete dependence upon the land.

The Topic Sentence

The sentence which lays down the topic for a paragraph is called the *topic sentence.* Normally,
of course, this is the first sentence in the paragraph, and following sentences build upon
it.

EXAMPLE: <u>We were the 'Mob' and we had everything going for us.</u> I guess every high
school has its 'in' crowd, the elite set of kids that everyone wants to belong
to. Well, in our high school — 1200 kids in all — we were it — ten guys —
the Mob. Everyone, but everyone, took notice of us.

However, it is possible for the topic sentence to be in the middle, or at the end, of its paragraph. This may be done as a variation, or sometimes to achieve a more dramatic effect.
Consider the additional impact in the following paragraph, where the topic sentence is held
over to the end and acts as a pungent conclusion.

> The men were set to work to till the soil, to build the huts, and put up
> the tents. The Reverend Richard Johnson gathered all who were willing
> under a great tree, probably on the first Sunday, to offer up thanks to
> the Lord for His great mercies. A week later he celebrated Holy Com-
> munion in an officer's tent, and another officer, Ralph Clark, whose heart
> was hot within him, asked to keep the table on which the Lord's Supper
> was first celebrated in the colony. Within a few weeks convicts had stolen
> food so shamelessly that Phillip decided to have them flogged as a warning

to both European and aborigine of his determination to defend property. When floggings failed to deter, Phillip agreed to use the last sanction of the law and launched one of the thieves into eternity. The white man had come to Australia.

> [from *A Short History of Australia*
> by MANNING CLARK]

Exercise 1

Choose four topic sentences from the following list and create another *four* sentences in each case, to expand each topic sentence into a complete paragraph.

(1) The first day confirmed my fears.

(2) I leaned forward, closing my eyes, trying to remember.

(3) Why do we need TV sets?

(4) I don't want to make a big deal out of nothing, but girls get unfairly treated at school.

(5) Exactly how do you meet a girl and get to know her?

(6) I ask myself how I became a rock musician and my mind goes back and back.

(7) Education can free people from prejudice.

(8) Death had never been so close to me before.

(9) Love can break through all barriers.

(10) I'd never actually seen a bullfight until they screened one on television.

Concluding Sentences

The final sentence in a paragraph usually rounds off the particular topic that the paragraph has been developing. In good writing, attention needs to be given to making concluding sentences thoughtful and 'strong'.

> All roads lead to Johannesburg. Through the long nights the trains pass to Johannesburg. The lights of the swaying coach fall on the cutting-sides, on the grass and stones of a country that sleeps. Happy the eyes that can close.
>
> [from *Cry, the Beloved Country*
> by ALAN PATON]

Notice the strength of the final sentence in this paragraph — the sense of completeness that it conveys.

Quite often in a piece of extended writing, the concluding sentence of a paragraph will foreshadow, or lead into, the topic sentence of the next paragraph.

> From the moment he entered it the wood seemed full of noises. There was a smell of damp leaves and moss, and everywhere the splash of water went whispering about. Just inside, the brook made a little fall into a pool and the sound, enclosed among the trees, echoed as though in a cave. Roosting birds rustled overhead; the night breeze stirred the leaves; here and there a dead twig fell. And there were more sinister, unidentified sounds, from further away; sounds of movement.

> To rabbits, everything unknown is dangerous. The first reaction is to startle, the second to bolt. Again and again they startled, until they were close to exhaustion. But what did these sounds mean and where, in this wilderness, could they bolt to?
>
> [from *Watership Down*
> by RICHARD ADAMS]

Notice that the concluding sentence of the first paragraph is strong, building an atmosphere of suspense. Notice also that it leads into the next paragraph, where the reference to 'unidentified sounds' is picked up and built upon by the new topic sentence: 'To rabbits, everything unknown is dangerous.' This is a good example of a concluding sentence leading into the new paragraph.

Exercise 2

Below are several extracts from paragraphs written by famous authors, but in each case the concluding sentence is either missing or only partly included. Try your hand at writing a strong concluding sentence of your own. Then refer to the original concluding sentences (in the upside-down box opposite) and compare them with your efforts.

(1) From *The Red Pony* by John Steinbeck.
It was a ticklish job, saddling the pony the first time. Gabilan hunched and reared and threw the saddle off before the cinch could be tightened. It had to be replaced again and again until at last the pony let it stay. And the cinching was difficult, too. [Add one sentence.]

(2) From *Lord Jim* by Joseph Conrad.
She sobbed on his shoulder. The sky over Patusan was blood-red, immense, streaming like an open vein. An enormous sun nestled crimson amongst the treetops, and the forest below . . . [Complete this sentence.]

(3) From *Hard Times* by Charles Dickens.
A year or two younger than his eminently practical friend, Mr Bounderby looked older; his seven or eight and forty might have had the seven or eight added to it again, without surprising anybody. He had not much hair. [Add one sentence.]

(4) From *The Loved One* by Evelyn Waugh.
No breath stirred the enchanted stillness of the two rooms. The leaded casements were screwed tight. The air came, like the boy's voice, from far away, sterilized and transmuted. The temperature was slightly cooler than is usual in American dwellings. The rooms seemed . . . [Complete the sentence.]

Exercise 3

Use the following topic sentences as a basis for *two paragraphs each*, in which you:

    (i) give attention to strong concluding sentences for each paragraph; and
    (ii) use the first paragraph's concluding sentence to lead into the topic for the second paragraph.

(1) The motorbike he rode had a dignified history.

(2) A town is like a wild animal.

(3) The bird looked smaller dead than it had when it was alive.

Concluding Sentences from the Originals

(1) Day by day Jody tightened the girth a little more until at last the pony didn't mind the saddle at all.

(2) ... had a black and forbidding face.

(3) One might have fancied he had talked it off; and that what was left, all standing up in disorder, was in that condition from being constantly blown about by his windy boastfulness.

(4) ... isolated and unnaturally quiet, like a railway coach that has stopped in the night far from any station.

Language Basics (12)

Adjectives and Adverbs

Remember the following rules to help you use adjectives and adverbs correctly.

Rule 1 ● Avoid double comparatives and double superlatives.
        EXAMPLES: (a) The <u>slower</u> car is despised. (*not* The more slower ...)
                   (b) The <u>fastest</u> car is prized. (*not* The most fastest ...)

Rule 2 ● Adjectives should not be confused with adverbs.
        EXAMPLES: (a) She drives <u>well</u>.
                     (*not* She drives good.)
                 (b) The police drove <u>quickly</u> to the scene of the crime.
                     (*not* The police drove quick ...)

Rule 3 ● Adverbs modify adjectives, and other adverbs.
        EXAMPLE: The owners were <u>extremely careful</u> about their cars' appearance.
                 (*not* The owners were extreme careful ...)

Rule 4 ● When you make a negative statement, do not use two negatives together.
        EXAMPLE: They did <u>not</u> tolerate <u>any</u> criticisms of their machines.
                 (*not* They did not tolerate no ...)

Rule 5 ● Use the combination 'so ... that'.
        EXAMPLE: The car is <u>so</u> common <u>that</u> every family owns one.
                 (*not* The car is that common that ...)

Rule 6 ● 'Hardly' and 'scarcely' should not be used with negatives.
        EXAMPLE: The archaeologists <u>could scarcely</u> believe what they had found.
                 (*not* The archaeologists could not scarcely ...)

Rule 7 ● 'Hardly' and 'scarcely' should be followed by 'when' or 'before' not by 'than'.
        EXAMPLE: The car had <u>hardly</u> left the garage <u>when</u> it crashed.
                 (*not* The car had hardly left the garage than ...)

Using the Rules

Correct the following sentences.

(1) Some people act very irrational when they sit behind the wheel of a car.

(2) Some cars are that powerful that they often become uncontrollable.

(3) Many cars are given the most highest degree of care and attention.

(4) Hardly had the cars raced onto the super highway than a multiple accident occurred.

(5) The scientific report did not say nothing about trains and other forms of transport.

(6) The limousine went smoother after the engine had been tuned.

(7) Each driver thought that her car was at least moderate faster than other cars on the road.

(8) The vehicle was that old that its bodywork had rusted.

(9) Unless the driver signals more clear, a collision will happen sooner or later.

(10) Scientists are usually methodical, careful sifting and assembling their findings.

Punctuation – Apostrophes

One use of the apostrophe is to indicate the omission of a letter (or letters). The shortened forms are called **contractions.**

> EXAMPLES: **wasn't** – was not
> **we've** – we have
> **you'd** – you would

Exercise A

Expand the following contractions:

it's	aren't	they'd
don't	we'll	there's

Exercise B

Form contractions from the following:

has not	they have	where is
I am	you will	she had

Unit Thirteen

Comprehension (13)

Jogging Is Fun (Or Is It?)

Running, there seems little doubt, is going to be one of the growth industries of the 1980s.

Now that's bad news, if your idea of an extremely active morning is breaking into a shuffle on your way to the letterbox for the paper.

Because if there's one thing runners, or joggers, enjoy as much as panting themselves into a state of near cardiac arrest it's telling other people about how much fun they're having.

They'll also tell you how their fitness is improved, how their chances of living longer are much better, and, if you don't walk away quickly, go into lurid details about the state of their arteries, the lack of fat on the pipes into their hearts, and the dramatic improvement in their love life.

What has to be understood about the average jogger is that he or she rapidly becomes a fanatic.

Now most fanatics can be easily recognised. They're the clean-cut young couple on your doorstep, quizzing you on your knowledge of the Bible. Or they're the people with the shaven heads and paint on their face, ringing bells and dancing in the middle of the city.

But your fanatical jogger is much more difficult to pick. Certainly a person with the build of a greyhound standing on its hind legs, and a sweatshirt with a German brandname over the heart, can be fairly easily identified as a running freak. Luckily they can be eluded with surprising ease, as most are nursing muscular injury, if not shin splints, and the normal drinking, smoking, overweight person can move around a living room or hotel bar quicker than they can.

A much trickier customer is the jogger who looks as though he's just wrapped himself around a large steak and a couple of beers.

This is the man who has got the bug very recently. The other week he almost got out for seven days in a row, and if he could get a clear run at it he'd bowl off three miles without any problems, but the trouble is that from his place no matter which way he turns it's all hills, and of course the neighbours, who probably couldn't walk around the block without lying down, are all looking with sneers on their faces, so he can't stop on those first hills, and boy, that makes it tough going once you're on the flat, so there's not much left in the old tank once a couple of miles have been covered, and he's not boring you is he, because by the look of you a few miles on the road wouldn't do you any harm, even your eyes aren't too healthy, they're sort of glazed looking.

If you're trapped with one of the fresh fanatics there's not much to be done. You could try quoting the *Playboy* story by the doctor who suggested that all that jogging will eventually jar the internal organs so much a jogger's lungs and heart might suddenly slip down towards his knees. But the jogging freak has usually got his first burst of enthusiasm from reading one of the numerous magazines that devote themselves to the pursuit of sweat, and the *Playboy* doctor ploy may only result in a burst of words about how he's just read a story suggesting the oxygen pumped through the brain while jogging could convert ordinary men into mobile geniuses.

Of course, rather in the way your children constantly suggesting you're about to die made you attempt to give up smoking, this constant barrage of pro-jogging hype may eventually persuade you to have a crack at it yourself.

Be warned! You're entering a world which will on the one hand drain your wallet, and on the other shatter your self-esteem.

There was a time when the amateur road-runner went out in old canvas tennis shoes and football shorts. To be seen in your neighbourhood now plodding along in such clothes will cause the sort of embarrassment to your children that only a father bringing a forgotten lunch into a classroom has managed to touch in the past.

You owe it to your family, your kids will tell you, to be dressed in the sort of gear the average Olympic marathon runner steps out in. The whole lot, from the ripple-soled shoes, to the silky shorts, to the hooded sweat-top, costs roughly the same as 10 days in Hawaii with continental breakfast included. Mind you, after a couple of days among the joggers you'll begin to realise how important such purchases were. As well as promoting the West German economic miracle you're also ensuring that your humiliation when a lean bronzed running machine strides past you is at least slightly cushioned by the thought that with all the stripes and flashes and trademarks on your gear the flying runner may, in his haste, have confused you with a genuine athlete.

In the early days of jogging there are some things to avoid at all costs. Try walking around the route you're planning to jog over. On the walk wear a pair of stout shoes, and carry a fair-sized stick. That way if a large German shepherd, apparently driven to a frenzy by watching re-runs of *Hogan's Heroes,* appears in a driveway you'll at least feel a little safer than you would with yards of bare flesh exposed, and only a thin layer of coloured nylon guarding you from sudden conversion to a candidate for the Vienna Boys' Choir.

Do your walking in parks and golf courses where you may only be looked on as a dirty old man who forgot his overcoat. Walking the last hundred yards to your house means you have to try to conduct a conversation with a neighbour, which can be difficult when tiny people are striking matches in both lungs and your heart is attempting to free itself from the boring restrictions imposed by your chest.

It's possible that after a while you'll actually grow to enjoy the feeling of your leg muscles suffering from the limbed equivalent of nagging toothache, that a film of sweat in your eyes will feel natural, and a burning sensation in your throat will remind you you're alive and healthy. It's at this stage you're ready for the ultimate running freak show — the marathon. The first person to run a marathon, an unfortunate Greek soldier, apparently dropped dead as soon as he reached Athens.

Most people would probably read a message in that, but the number in marathons continues to grow at such staggering rates it can only be concluded that the same self-destructive flame that burns in your teenage son when he drives your car with an arm round his girlfriend and a stolen can of your beer in the other, still flickers slightly in the heart of the aging jogger.

A favourite phrase of the great New Zealand coach Arthur Lydiard to his marathon runners was that 'the race only begins at 20 miles'. At the 20-mile mark in a marathon there are still six miles to go.

Now Mr Lydiard is, without doubt, a man who knows an awful lot about running but it would be wrong for the first-time marathon starter to place too much reliance on this particular bit of folk wisdom. The race for the novice begins at the start line, where he notices that everybody else looks half as fat and twice as fit, and the first twinges of what will develop into massive calf cramps from the halfway mark are faintly felt. The novice notices in the first few miles how tired he feels, probably the result of bloating his body in the previous couple of days with yards of spaghetti and mounds of lasagna, in keeping with the current theory that your body will need these reserves of starch along the road to the finish. The theorists also say to drink plenty of liquids right up to start time, which means that the inside of the marathon hopeful's stomach resembles a very large pot of leftover pasta, which gradually swells as the runner moves around the course.

Many other things will happen to the runner as time passes. Most of them are too painful and obscene to even mention in this magazine.

It's enough to say that if the runner does manage to finish he will not be seeking a disco that evening. More likely he will lie in a strange limbo while muscle fatigue does extraordinary things to his body.

One thought buoys him on his bed of pain. As soon as he's well enough there are all those friends out there who have never run a marathon — and now he has the chance to tell them about it ... every ... step ... of ... the ... way.

[by PHIL GIFFORD]

Check Your Understanding

(1) What does the writer mean by, 'panting themselves into a state of near cardiac arrest'?

(2) What is it that joggers seem to enjoy almost as much as running?

(3) Why are many fanatical joggers fairly easy to avoid?

(4) The writer is using a relaxed, informal, conversational style. Pick out some of the words and phrases that indicate this.

(5) What does the writer mean by the expression 'pursuit of sweat'?

(6) Explain the meaning of each of the following words in the context of this article:
(a) lurid (b) ploy (c) hype (d) novice (e) buoys.

(7) How will the jogger's children feel if he goes running in old clothes?

(8) How does the writer emphasize the runner's defencelessness when confronting a frenzied German shepherd?

(9) What metaphor is used to describe the feeling in the unaccustomed jogger's lungs following a run?

(10) Is satire, sarcasm or irony used in the paragraph beginning, 'It's possible that after a while . . . '?

(11) What were the consequences of the first marathon run, and what conclusion might most people draw from this?

(12) Why do runners often eat foods rich in carbohydrates during the last few days before a race?

(13) What does the final paragraph seem to indicate about the person who has completed a marathon?

(14) Judging from the tone of this article, how does the writer appear to feel about joggers and jogging?

(15) What is the writer's purpose in this article? How would you respond to someone who said, 'I don't find this a very adequate article on joggers and jogging'?

(16) From the evidence of the article, what type of person appears to take up jogging? Support your answer.

(17) Do you think the writer uses exaggeration? Explain your viewpoint and quote from the article.

Working with Words (13)

Senior Spelling Demons	Confusing Pairs	Actions and Reactions		Increase Your Word Power
exercise	isle	imitation	celebration	perpetually
supervise	aisle	exaggerate	penetrate	capricious
electricity	martial	occasionally	collision	elation
musician	marshal	fatigue	acquainted	terse
autograph	invaluable	recommend	accommodate	succumb
ceiling	valueless	interrupt	condemn	adamant
sovereign	affect	analysis	innovation	scepticism
champion	effect	emergency	occurrence	culminate
chaos	implicit	fortunately	benefit	ecstasy
shriek	explicit	compulsory	accomplish	emaciated

Change the Words

Change into people

(a) electricity ....

(b) supervise ....

(c) acquaint ....

(d) imitate ....

(e) benefit ....

(f) condemn ....

Change into adjectives

(a) benefit ....

(b) chaos ....

(c) musician ....

(d) scepticism ....

(e) innovation ....

(f) ecstasy ....

Change into nouns

(a) accomplish ....

(b) compulsory ....

(c) recommend ....

(d) fortunately ....

(e) culminate ....

(f) exaggerate ....

Change into verbs

(a) collision ....

(b) analysis ....

(c) imitation ....

(d) compulsory ....

(e) occurrence ....

(f) electricity ....

Change into adverbs

(a) effect ....

(b) terse ....

(c) compulsory ....

Word Power

In the *Increase Your Word Power* column, find words that have the following meanings:

(1) to reach the highest point
(2) very great joy
(3) to give way (yield)
(4) unyielding

(5) abnormally lean
(6) an attitude of doubt
(7) changeable
(8) unceasingly

Missing Words

Correctly insert the words from the box into the spaces beneath.

> emaciated   chaos   invaluable   ecstasy   fatigue   benefit   compulsory
> innovation   collision   analysis   accommodate   adamant   scepticism   exaggerate

(1) The prospector was in .... about finding the gold.

(2) The .... prisoner of war showed signs of great ....

(3) The manager displayed much .... concerning the .... suggested by his assist-ant. The manager was .... that it would fail.

(4) .... education has brought great .... to our society.

(5) Some people tend to .... their problems.

(6) The motel was unable to .... more guests.

(7) The scientist's .... of the problems provided .... answers that would assist the research programme.

(8) Considerable .... resulted from the .... of the three cars.

Finding Antonyms

Find words in the lists that are opposite in meaning to the following words. The first letters have been given to help you.

(1) harm   b...............................
(2) minimize   e...............................
(3) vitality   f...............................
(4) voluntary   c...............................
(5) plump   e...............................

(6) dejection   e...............................
(7) originality   i...............................
(8) order   c...............................
(9) resist   s...............................
(10) implicit   e...............................

Confusing Pairs

Match up correctly one of each of the pairs of confusing words with the meaning opposite.

(1)	**isle/aisle**	an island
(2)	**martial/marshal**	warlike
(3)	**invaluable/valueless**	worthless
(4)	**affect/effect**	result
(5)	**implicit/explicit**	distinctly stated

Word Origins — '-rupt' words

'Interrupt' comes from the Latin *inter* ('between') and *rumpere/ruptus* ('to break'). When we interrupt someone who is talking, we literally 'break into' that person's speech. Here are some more words derived from *rumpere* ('to break'). Match them up with their meanings.

(1)	**bankrupt**	rotten, wicked
(2)	**corrupt**	sudden
(3)	**disrupt**	unable to pay debts
(4)	**abrupt**	burst, break
(5)	**rupture**	break out
(6)	**erupt**	throw into disorder

Language in Action (13)

Propaganda

The Concise Oxford Dictionary defines propaganda as an 'Association, organized scheme, for propagation of a doctrine or practice'. Thus, propaganda is any organized scheme which deliberately promotes a one-sided view in order to gain support for a particular viewpoint, creed or belief. 'Propaganda' also denotes the *information* that is disseminated to that end — i.e. the *message* of the propagandist. During this century in particular, the word has acquired sinister overtones. It has come to be associated with such evils as deceit, treachery, manipulation — and genocide.

In our daily lives we are subjected to many 'softer' forms of propaganda. The advertisers trying to sell their products tend to use some of the techniques of the propagandists. The media are guilty of producing propaganda if they deliberately distort facts and seek to manipulate the emotions of the public.

Propaganda, of course, comes to the fore during war, when it is particularly necessary to change or channel people's attitudes. Thus the propagandist will be especially concerned to work upon the emotions of people. He will play upon their fear, their anger, their love, their hate, their hope, and their guilt.

The methods of the propagandist are simple:

- Catch the attention of the audience
- Appeal to the emotions
- Supply simple solutions
- Confine the message to a few essentials
- Use repetition and stereotyped slogans

Joseph Goebbels in action

When we think of propaganda, the names of Hitler and Goebbels readily spring to our minds. Hitler had much to say about propaganda in his book *Mein Kampf,* and put most of his ideas into practice. His approach is well summed up in the following sentences from *Mein Kampf*: 'The receptive powers of the masses are very restricted, and their understanding is feeble. On the other hand they quickly forget. Such being the case, all effective propaganda must be confined to a few bare necessities and then must be expressed in a few stereotyped formulas. . . . . Only constant repetition will finally succeed in imprinting an idea on the memory of a crowd.' Hitler blatantly acknowledged that the propagandist distorted and manipulated the truth for his own ends: 'When you lie tell big lies . . . in the big lie there is always a certain force of credibility.'

Anti-Jewish and War Propaganda

Let us look more closely at the work of the propagandist. What better manipulator of the masses can we find than the deadly Joseph Goebbels, the Nazi minister of propaganda?

> The institution of the Yellow Star, which every Jew must wear, so that he may be recognized as a Jew . . . is an extraordinarily humane regulation. . . . Jew drudges who have forgotten their duty and lost their dignity should be wearing the Yellow Star themselves. Their excuse for their shameless behaviour is always the same: 'After all, the Jews are human beings!' As if we ever denied it. So are men who steal, men who rape children, thieves and procurers. That does not make us want to walk with them down the Kurfürstendamm. . . . The flea does not become a domestic animal on the strength of living in the house. [*14 November 1941*]

Questions

(1) What is Goebbels trying to achieve with this piece of propaganda?

(2) Why does Goebbels associate the Jews with thieves and rapists?

(3) What point is Goebbels making when he argues, 'The flea does not become a domestic animal on the strength of living in the house'?

(4) What lies and distortions of truth has Goebbels put forward in this piece of propaganda?

(5) What have you learnt about the character of Goebbels himself?

Here is another piece of Goebbels propaganda, with a different theme.

> History does not give away presents. It only offers chances. Let us, therefore, go forth and fight and work until victory is ours. Do not let us ask when it will come, but let us see to it that it does come. Then one day the hour will arrive when Fate bows to us and crowns with laurels our nation and the Allies fighting with us. Then across the features of our people there will spread the bliss of the great moment for which the century is waiting. [*6 November 1941*]

Questions

(1) What do you think Goebbels was trying to achieve with this piece of propaganda?

(2) What particular words in the passage do you think would have aroused the emotions of the German people?

(3) What criticism could you make of the language used in this passage?

(4) Express in one simple sentence the propagandist's message to the German nation.

Propaganda Posters of World War I

Questions

(1) Why has the designer of the poster used a mother figure? What emotions are being aroused?

(2) Comment on the use of the word 'duty'.

(3) Would such a poster be successful today? Why?

(4) Do you think this poster is attention-getting? Why?

(5) 'Confine the message to a few essentials.' How has the writer done this?

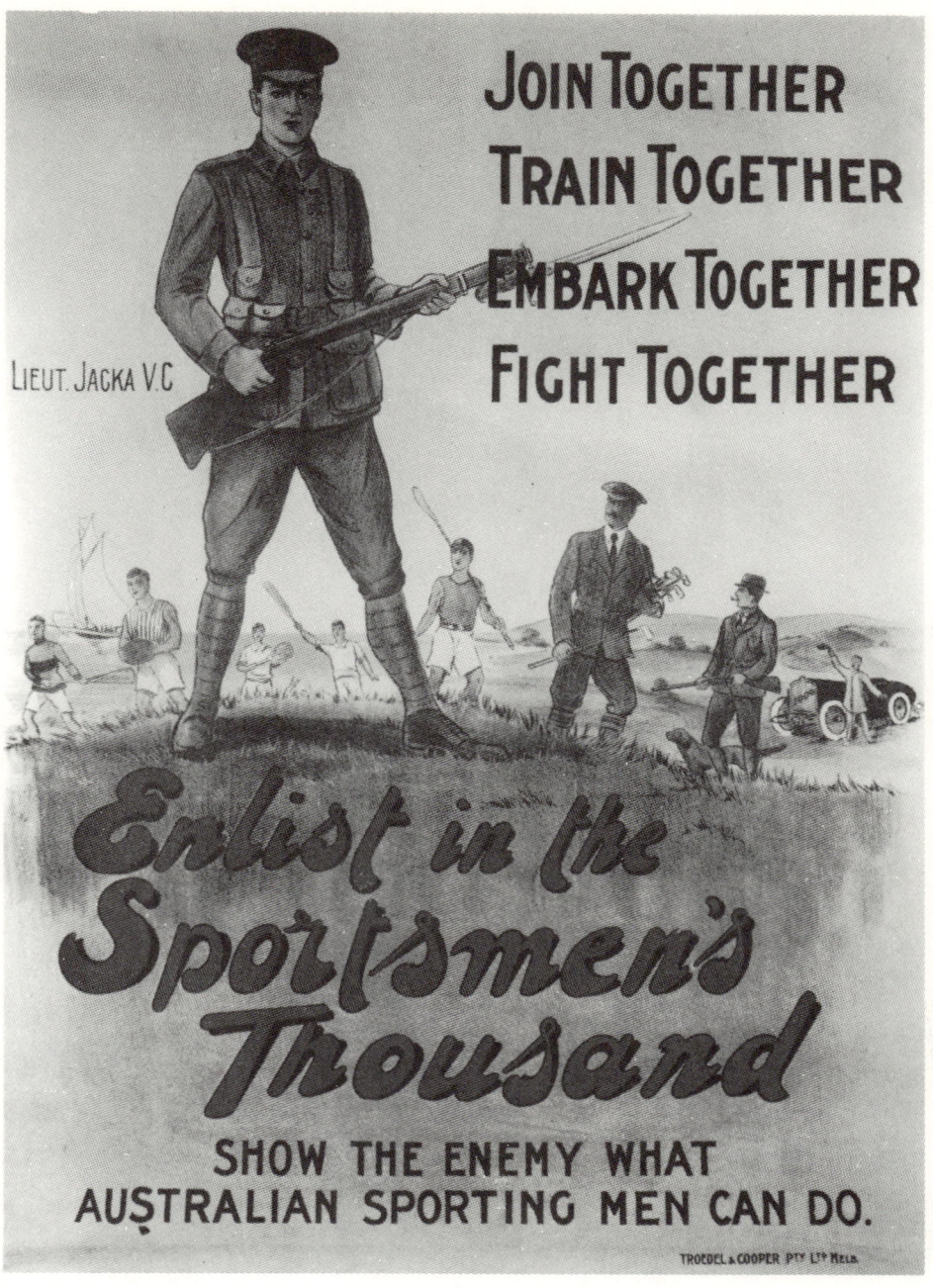

Questions

(1) Why has the poster's designer repeated 'together' so many times?

(2) With the drawings of all kinds of sportsmen, what is the artist suggesting about the war?

(3) Why do you think the artist has included a picture of 'Lieutenant Jacka VC'?

(4) How is this poster intended to manipulate its audience?

(5) Do you think the wording of the poster has been put together forcefully? Why?

A Propaganda Poster of World War II

Germany and Italy were allies in World War II. This poster, aimed at the Italian people, was designed to encourage a closer relationship between the two countries.

'GERMANY IS REALLY YOUR FRIEND'

Questions

(1) Why do you think the artist has drawn a German soldier with his gun and bayonet? Would the poster have been as effective if they had been omitted? Why?

(2) How has the artist attempted to suggest that German soldiers are friendly?

(3) Do you think this propaganda poster would have been successful? Why?

Homework.

①. Write out in paragraphs what
we did today.
               Attitude.

② Re-do last week's homework.

      FILE PAPER.

Page 18.

      Exercise A+B.

The Language of Literature (13)

THE WIDOWER IN THE COUNTRY

I'll get up soon, and leave my bed unmade.
I'll go outside and split off kindling wood
from the yellow-box log that lies beside the gate,
and the sun will be high, for I get up late now.

I'll drive my axe in the log and come back in
with my armful of wood, and pause to look across
the Christmas paddocks aching in the heat,
the windless trees, the nettles in the yard . . .
and then I'll go in, boil water and make tea.

This afternoon, I'll stand out on the hill
and watch my house away below, and how
the roof reflects the sun and makes my eyes
water and close on bright webbed visions smeared
on the dark of my thoughts to dance and fade away.
Then the sun will move on, and I will simply watch,
or work, or sleep. And evening will come on.

Coming on dark, I'll go home, light the lamp
and eat my corned-beef supper, sitting there
at the head of the table. Then I'll go to bed.
Last night I thought I dreamed — but when I woke
the screaming was only a possum ski-ing down
the iron roof on little moonlit claws.

LES A. MURRAY

For You to Consider

(1) 'I get up late now' suggests the widower didn't always arise late. Can you explain why the widower has changed his routine?

(2) Why does the poet describe the trivia of the widower's day?

(3) What picture comes to your mind when the poet writes, 'the Christmas paddocks aching in the heat'? Comment on his use of 'aching'.

(4) How does the poet suggest to the reader that time is passing?

(5) How does the expression, 'at the head of the table' emphasize the loneliness of the widower?

(6) The widower speaks of 'the dark of my thoughts'. What insight does this give you into the widower's state of mind?

(7) Do you think the poem is helped or hindered by the widower himself telling of his life? Why?

(8) What are your feelings towards the widower?

(9) What impression is given of the possum? Do you think this animal is important in the poem? Why?

(10) What do you think is the poet's intention in this poem? Has he succeeded or not? Why?

(11) Les Murray, the poet, hoped that readers would credit that he was 'out to interest and delight and challenge'. Which of these — interest, delight, or challenge — has Les Murray aroused in *you* with 'Widower in the Country'? Quote from the poem to support your answer.

Writers' Workshop (3)

Sentence Sense

When writing sentences, there are several important considerations of which you need to be aware. Your understanding of these, and the corresponding development of your skills, will add a great deal both to your appreciation of the writing of others and to the impact of your own writing.

Variety in Sentence Length

Good writing contains enough variety to maintain the reader's interest. One important aspect of this variety is *sentence length*. If sentence after sentence is of about the same length, the writing quickly becomes lifeless and boring.

Consider the use of variety in sentence length in the following extract.

> So he did it. It was difficult in the dark and once the fish made a surge that pulled him down on his face and made a cut below his eye. The blood ran down his cheek a little way. But it coagulated and dried before it reached his chin and he worked his way back to the bow and rested against the wood. He adjusted the sack and carefully worked the line so that it came across a new part of his shoulders and, holding it anchored with his shoulders, he carefully felt the pull of the fish and then felt with his hand the progress of the skiff through the water.
>
> [from *The Old Man and the Sea*
> by ERNEST HEMINGWAY]

Notice the first short sentence — just four words. The impact is strong. Our attention is focused and we want to know more. The next sentence is of medium length, giving the writer room to build his description of the action. Another carefully-controlled short sentence follows, elaborating one emotive aspect of the description — the blood running down the old man's cheek. Next, a medium-length sentence and a long sentence are added, basically describing the actions taken by the old man and, at the same time, developing something of a rhythm appropriate to the long-drawn-out struggle which has begun. This particular feature — varied sentence length — is playing an important part in the effectiveness of this paragraph, both by keeping the writing alive and by helping to create a mood.

Summary

Varying sentence length is an important skill to develop in your writing. It will add life to your writing by changing the pace, and the mood. It can enable you to achieve a dramatic effect.

But for all this, you need to avoid the sort of approach that sets out, mechanically, to alter the length of every new sentence. *Variation of sentence length should not be over-used.* Study the work of good writers to see how they use this skill, and experiment with different approaches in your own writing.

Exercise 1

Vary the sentence length in each of the following paragraphs in any way you like, so that a stronger and more interesting paragraph results.

(1) Peter Mandeling didn't actually see the incident take place on his farm. But next day when he was out repairing a gate he noticed something different. A sizeable crater had appeared just off the farm's main drive. On closer inspection Peter found that it had been caused by a falling star. He was able to dig the meteorite up and have it taken to the local university.

(2) One local store had had enough. They were tired of burglaries. They decided on a different solution. They bought a large tarantula spider. This was released in the store. A sign was put up: 'Patrolled by a Tarantula'. It seemed to work. No more burglaries occurred. No-one must have known the truth. Tarantulas are harmless to humans.

(3) A group of inmates from an Italian prison pleased their gaolers by showing a considerable interest in athletic activities, especially broad-jumping. Since the health of prisoners was of concern to their captors, they encouraged the men, even building special training broad-jump pits. Unfortunately, none of them guessed the real reason for the prisoners' sudden interest in physical activity and the hours spent developing their jumping skills. One day, confident in their new-found ability, a number of the prisoners blithely leapt 4 metres from the roof of a prison building to a roof outside the prison, and happily skipped away.

Varied Sentence Structure

The most common structure for a sentence in English is:

SUBJECT	VERB	OBJECT

EXAMPLE:

Louise	**sang**	**a song.**

By adding adjectives and adverbs we can build considerably upon this, but it will still remain the same basic structure.

EXAMPLE: **Louise,** demure yet confident, delicately **sang** a beautiful **song.**

Variation:
We can vary this basic structure by a kind of reversal procedure.

EXAMPLE: **A song** was **sung** by **Louise.**

This involves us in changes to the verb, and the addition of the preposition 'by'.

Any other variations in structure will be the result of adding different kinds of word-groups — either phrases (not containing verb-and-subject) or clauses (containing their own verb and its subject). These added word-groups allow tremendous variety because there are so many different kinds, and they can be used at different points in a sentence. Here are some examples.

(a) **Beginning the Sentence**
   ● When she had finished the speech, Louise sang a song.
   ● Slowly lifting her head, Louise sang a song.
   ● Unable to refuse, Louise sang a song.
   ● Because she felt so full of joy, Louise sang a song.
   ● Excited at the possibility before her, Louise sang a song.

(b) **In Mid-Sentence**
   ● Louise, with all eyes upon her, sang a song.
   ● Louise, looking confident and relaxed, sang a song.
   ● Louise, whose voice was known and loved by all, sang a song.
   ● Louise, while she waited for further news, sang a song.
   ● Louise, thrilled at the opportunity, sang a song.

(c) **At the End of the Sentence**
   ● Louise sang a song after the minister had finished speaking.
   ● Louise sang a song, which was well received by all.
   ● Louise sang a song in a clear, commanding voice.
   ● Louise sang a song and then sat down.
   ● Louise sang a song capturing the attention of all.

Summary

It is important that in your writing you pay some attention to varying the basic structure of sentences. Adding word-groups thoughtfully, and experimenting with different ways of starting and concluding sentences, can add considerable interest. As with variety in sentence length, however, you should avoid over-use of this skill. Too much structural variety in sentences can become distracting.

Exercise 2

Experiment with extending the structure of sentences by adding phrases or clauses to the following, in different ways.

(1) You've heard some interesting opinions today.

(2) I pushed myself into a sitting position.

(3) Your thumb-print may be the only identification needed.

(4) The worst part is the pain.

(5) He forced his eyes shut and hung on.

(6) The car was parked in the driveway.

(7) A waitress has lots of chances to learn patience.

(8) Baling hay is tough physical work.

(9) You leave a mark on other people.

(10) She was prettier than most other girls.

Exercise 3

Rewrite the following sentences, changing the way in which each sentence begins.

EXAMPLE: He saw the package and was immediately suspicious.
Suspicion filled him immediately he saw the package.

(1) I began shaking, feeling fear as the truck began to pull away.

(2) The loss of half a million of Napoleon's troops in Russia gave new confidence to the sagging hopes of other European countries.

(3) We laughed hysterically, shouting at each other and threatening to edge each other into the ditch.

(4) Jim was an incurable romantic, with an image of himself that was impossible to live up to.

(5) Terry and I huddled over the package, like two surgeons working on a live heart.

(6) The theme is expressed both in the actions and in the words of the main characters, and in the subtle use of sub-plots which throw additional light on events.

(7) His trembling hands could not hold the bowl and it fell to the ground and broke.

(8) She loved Phil and he had made such a big thing about this date because it was his birthday.

(9) People die of damage to their dignity as much as they die of medical causes.

(10) There is still considerable debate over the role played by high levels of cholesterol in the diet of the heart-attack victim.

Language Basics (13)

Comparisons

Here are some important rules that will help to make comparisons work clearly for you.

Rule 1 ● Use the **comparative** degree of the adjective or adverb to compare *two* subjects.
  EXAMPLE: Sue is the <u>better</u> jogger of the two.

Rule 2 ● Use the **superlative** degree to compare *more than two* subjects.
  EXAMPLE: In my opinion, jogging is the <u>best</u> of the non-competitive sports.

Rule 3 ● Compare subjects that are **logically linked.**
  EXAMPLE: (a) Her ripple-soled runners are as expensive as an Olympic champion.
  — *Incorrect!*

  This implies a comparison of the cost of ripple-soled runners with the cost of an Olympic champion! What is intended is a comparison of the cost of the girl's ripple-soled runners with the cost of those of an Olympic champion.

  EXAMPLES: (b) Her ripple-soled runners are as expensive as <u>those of</u> an Olympic champion.

  OR

  (c) Her ripple-soled runners are as expensive as an Olympic champion'<u>s</u>.

Rule 4 ● When a comparison is being made, use **'other'** to keep the subject distinct.
  EXAMPLE: (a) Mat sprints faster than any athlete in his club. — *Incorrect!*

  Well, as Mat himself is a club member, he would then have to be faster than himself. The use of 'other' avoids any confusion.

  EXAMPLE: (b) Mat sprints faster than any <u>other</u> athlete in his club.

Rule 5 **'Unique'** and certain other words (**'square'**, **'circular'**, **'equal'**, **'empty'** etc) defy comparison.
  EXAMPLE: Here is a <u>very unique</u> string singlet in club colours. — *Incorrect!*

  Remember, 'unique' means 'the only one of its kind'. So, 'very unique' is illogical. Be aware of other words of this type.

Using the Rules

Use the rules to correct the errors in the following sentences.

(1) When Jodie and Don jog together, Jodie is the fastest of the pair.

(2) Phil Gifford is the world's most perfect example of a backsliding jogger.

(3) The sweatshirt with the German brandname over the heart indicates more clearly than any shirt that a running freak is upon you.

(4) Muscular injuries caused by jogging on hard surfaces can be as painful as a skier.

(5) There are ten of you on the run — may the better jogger win!

(6) What we have to do is find the most circular track to time ourselves over the kilo-metre.

(7) Let's hold a contest to decide the best of the two runners. The judges will run a final heat.

(8) These days any jogger's headband, silky shorts and hooded sweat-top may be comparable in quality with an Olympic champion.

Punctuation — More apostrophes

Another use of the apostrophe is to indicate possession. Here are some rules to follow.

1. To indicate possession in the singular form of a noun, add **'s** to the noun.
    EXAMPLE: The jogger's gear. [*One jogger owns the gear.*]

2. To indicate possession in the plural form of a noun ending in 's', add only **'**.
    EXAMPLE: The joggers' club. [*A lot of joggers have the club.*]

3. To indicate possession in the plural form of a noun not ending in 's', add **'s**.
    EXAMPLE: The children's race. [*Children have the race.*]

4. To indicate possession in the singular form of a noun that already ends in 's' add **'** OR **'s**, whichever style you prefer. (But be consistent.)
    EXAMPLES: (a) Mr Jones' shirt.
                     (b) Mr Jones's shirt.   [*Mr Jones owns the shirt.*]

Exercise

Correct the following sentences by applying the rules above.

(1) The societys emblem was stitched on Les shirt.

(2) The district boys school has put jogging on its timetable.

(3) Womens sizes are displayed in many of our stores windows.

(4) The jogging club has a childrens section.

(5) Employees canteens have notice-boards for joggers.

(6) The girl stitched badges to her jeans pockets.

Unit Fourteen

Comprehension (14)

The Ghost Train

In this extract from *The Ghost Train*, Lawrence Durrell gives a dramatic account of the ride experienced by a group of visiting dignitaries on a Yugoslav train specially built to extol the triumph of Yugoslav heavy industry.

'We entered and found our reserved carriages which seemed normal enough. The band played. We accepted a wreath or two. Then we set off in the darkness to the braying of donkeys and cocks and the rasping of trombones. We were off across the rolling Serbian plains.

'Two things were immediately obvious. All this elaborate woodwork squeaked and groaned calamitously, earsplittingly. How were we to get any sleep? But more serious still was the angle of inclination of the second coach with the Heads of Mission in it. It was about thirty degrees out of centre and was only, it seemed, held upright by the one immediately before and behind it. It was clear that the Yugoslav heavy industry had mislaid its spirit-level while it was under construction. People who looked out of the windows on one side had the illusion that the ground was coming up to hit them. I paid Polk-Mowbray* a visit to see if he was all right and found him looking rather pale, and drawn up on the higher elevation of the coach like someone on a sinking ship. The noise was so great that we couldn't speak — we had to shout: "My God," I heard him cry out, "what is to become of us all?" It was a little difficult to say. We were now gathering speed. The engine was a very old one. It had been abandoned before the war by an American film company and the Yugoslavs had tied it together with wire. Its gaping furnace, which was white hot, was being passionately fed by some very hairy men in cloth caps who looked like

_____
*the head of the British diplomatic mission.

Dostoevsky's publishers. It seemed to me that the situation had never looked graver. Despite its age, however, it had managed to whip up a good forty-five. And every five hundred yards it would groan and void a bucketful of white clinker into the night which set fire to the grass on either side of the track. From far off we must have looked like an approaching forest fire.

'Another feature of the "Liberation-Celebration Machine" was an ingenious form of central heating which could not be turned off, and as none of the windows opened, the temperature inside the coaches rapidly mounted into the hundreds. People were fanning themselves with their tall hats. Old man, never have I seen the Corps subjected to such a strain. Sleep was impossible. The lights would not turn off. The wash basins appeared to empty into each other. And all the time we had the ghastly thought of all the Heads of Mission in the Hanging Coach, drinking brandy and gibbering with fright as we sped onwards through the night.

'The chance of some frightful accident taking place was far from remote and consequently nobody was able to relax. We did not even dare to get into pyjamas but sat about in that infernal racket staring desperately at one another and starting at every regurgitation of the engine, every shiver and squeak of the coaches. The American Ambassador was so overcome that he spent the night singing "Nearer My God to Thee". Some said that he had had the forethought to take a case of rye into his compartment with him. Madame Fawzia, the Egyptian Ambassadress, spent the night on the floor of her compartment deep in prayer. I simply did not dare to think of Polk-Mowbray. From time to time when the wind changed the whole train was enveloped in a cloud of rich dense smoke containing fragments of half-digested coal the size of hailstones. But still the ghoulish crew in the engine-cab plied their grisly shovels and on we sped with mournful shrieks and belches.

'At two in the morning there was a ghastly rending noise as we entered the station of Slopsy Blob, named after the famous Independence fighter. The Hanging Coach somehow got itself engaged with the tin dado which ran along the roof of the station and ripped it off as clean as a whistle, by the same token almost decapitating one of the drivers. The noise was appalling and the whole Corps let out a unified shriek of terror. I have never heard diplomats scream like that before or since — and I never want to. A lot of cherubs and floral devices were ripped off the Hanging Coach in the encounter and the people in the rear coaches found themselves assailed by a hail of coloured fragments of wood which made them shriek the louder. It was all over in a moment.

'Then we were out in the night once more racing across the dark plain, the brothers Karamazov still plying the engine with might and main. . . . '

[from *The Ghost Train* by LAWRENCE DURRELL]

Check Your Understanding

(1) What evidence can you find to indicate that a special occasion is being described?

(2) What seemed to prevent the main carriage from tipping over?

(3) What is suggested by the words 'had mislaid its spirit-level'?

(4) Express in your own words what you understand by: 'Its gaping furnace . . . was being passionately fed by some very hairy men in cloth caps who looked like Dostoevsky's publishers.'

(5) What might the reference to the men looking 'like Dostoevsky's publishers' indicate about the speaker?

(6) What is 'clinker'?

(7) The name 'Liberation-Celebration Machine' is an example of: (a) metaphor (b) colloquial speech (c) euphemism (d) slang?

(8) Is the author a senior diplomat or does he hold some other post? Explain your deduction.

(9) Find a phrase that indicates that this is a spoken account.

(10) What emotions do the diplomats experience as they travel in the 'Liberation-Celebration Machine'? Identify two fairly extreme individual reactions to this experience.

(11) Express in more forceful language: 'The chance of some frightful accident taking place was far from remote'.

(12) What are the meanings of the following words as they are used in the passage: (a) calamitously (b) inclination (c) void (d) gibbering (e) regurgitation (f) infernal?

(13) Did you find Durrell's story humorous? Why?

(14) What picture do these words call to your mind: 'the ghoulish crew in the engine-cab plied their grisly shovels'?

(15) Explain the meaning of: (a) 'the people in the rear coaches found themselves assailed by a hail of coloured fragments of wood' (b) 'with might and main'.

(16) What do you think was Lawrence Durrell's purpose in writing the story?

Working with Words (14)

Senior Spelling Demons	Confusing Pairs	Food and Drink		Increase Your Word Power
auxiliary	current	nutritious	luscious	cadaverous
execute	currant	sustenance	edible	complacent
parallel	sensitive	delicious	gourmet	conservative
scissors	sensible	consumption	delicacy	elite
artificial	imaginary	palatable	exquisite	didactic
application	imaginative	etiquette	alcohol	extrovert
faithfully	astronomy	restaurant	beverage	facet
surrender	astrology	sumptuous	chocolate	gesticulate
irrelevant	confident	connoisseur	tomato	immortalize
corridor	confidant	exorbitant	spaghetti	impede

Changing Forms

Change the words in heavy type into their correct forms in the context.

(1) Some religions stress the idea of **immortalize.**

(2) The speech **impede** was curable.

(3) His **complacent** in the face of all that criticism was astounding.

(4) It is necessary to **conservative** our wildlife for future generations.

(5) The fly has a **multi-facet** eye.

(6) It was an **exquisite** beautiful piece of jade.

(7) Her **gesticulate** was meant to convey disgust.

(8) Vitamins are necessary to **sustenance** life.

(9) This wine has a distinctive and delicate appeal to the **palatable.**

(10) I'm afraid the cost is going to be **astronomy.**

Plurals

Change the following words into their plural forms.

> tomato, auxiliary, army, story, scarf, bus, radius, photo, hero, lady, tooth, bureau, lens, ceremony, crisis, thief, loaf, roof, piano, woman, half, child, mouse, knife, dinghy

Confusing Pairs

Supply the correct word-endings for the following.

(1) **curr**..........   flow of water or electricity

(2) **curr**..........   small dried fruit

(3) **curr**..........   happening at the present time

(4) **sens**..........   responsive to slight changes

(5) **sens**..........   possessing common sense

(6) **imagin**..........   possessing ideas

(7) **imagin**..........   not real, not in fact there

(8) **astr**..........   the foretelling of events by the stars

(9) **astr**..........   the study of heavenly bodies

(10) **confid**..........   full of assurance

(11) **confid**..........   someone entrusted with secrets

People

Form people from the following words. (Note the example.)

EXAMPLE: **astronomy**   astronomer

consumption	....	**alcohol**	....
execute (2 possible)	....	**application**	....
	....	**restaurant**	....

Find the Word

Fill in the spaces with list-words.

(1) give up   ....

(2) like a dead person   ....

(3) able to be eaten   ....

(4) the accepted code of good manners ....

(5) having a lesson to impart   ....

(6) an expert in matters of taste   ....

(7) excessive, especially in cost   ....

(8) anything that assists or helps   ....

(9) not on the topic   ....

(10) one whose personality is outgoing   ....

(11) a special, privileged group   ....

(12) hot chocolate as a drink   ....

TOME, TOME ON THE RANGE..

Word Origins — 'Sandwich'

John Montagu, fourth Earl of Sandwich (1718–92), was a compulsive gambler whose political life was almost as corrupt as his private one was scandalous. He often refused to leave the card table for a meal during a game and instead ordered his servant to bring him a slice of meat between two pieces of bread — the first sandwich.

Language in Action (14)

Advertising Techniques

All advertisers are trying to 'sell' something — a product, an idea, a service, an attractive image. The final success will be: did the advertisement produce the desired response in people?

Persuasive Language

The words in advertisements usually do more than merely provide information: the intention of the message is to convey feelings, arouse emotions or associate ideas and needs with the product. Brand names are often carefully chosen in the hope that customers will identify with an image, and the accompanying slogan is intended to be striking. Esso could have said 'puts power in your car' but preferred 'put a tiger in your tank', Nescafé said '43 beans in every cup' rather than 'richer flavour', and Colgate chose 'the ring of confidence' rather than 'makes your teeth whiter'. Where there are many brands not very different from each other, the jargon becomes more sophisticated. In the soap-powder and detergents market, we have 'whiter than white', whatever that means; 'cleans in depth'; 'lemon charged'; or alleged links with scientific knowledge — 'scientifically formulated to give washable woollens the special care they need', and those 'germ-killing enzymes'.

The language of commercials must be consistent with the mood. Qantas has used the romanticism of a smooth aircraft take-off backed by the slow line 'something in the way we move'.

Television commercials employ sight and sound — the camera never lies when showing that super-efficient clothes brush, close-shave razor, delicious whipped cream in a second! In the American Tupperware commercials the mood and message were created without words — products were shown in close-up with fingers pressed against the top of the storage container. Viewers saw the way it closed, heard the snap as it shut, then heard the vacuum of air released when opened.

Appeal to a Way of Life

Some commercials suggest that most people, or the 'best people', use a product and are better off for doing so, or can't do without it. This may take the form of 'keeping up with the Joneses' in the need for colour television, or feature a celebrity who praises the product — Rolf Harris trusts British Paints while John Meillon keeps on keeping on for Berger Paints. Ockers in beer commercials suit the relaxed, outgoing, working-class image which the advertiser wants to associate with the product. In the highly competitive cigarette market, images of lifestyle are associated with particular brands. The Australian Council on Smoking and Health profiled the smokers:

The Marlboro man — masculine, rugged and independent. A man with a horse, all the freedom in the world, to be what he wants, to do what he wants. An image every urbanized, frustrated man carries within him.

The Winfield man — a rebel at heart, the down-to-earth dinkum Aussie. Mr Average who made it, proving every man is as good as the next one, but proving every man can make it.

The Peter Stuyvesant person — for the person who has never been overseas, but is envious of friends who have. It is a prop, a statement, and admittance to the international set.

The Dunhill woman — she cultivates quietly refined status symbols, in the classic and conservative style, from tailored, pure-fibre clothes to tailored cars: if not a Rolls, then BMW. She is a dominant woman and men, at least in the ads, play a secondary role.

The Benson & Hedges woman — if not the golden touch, she likes the gilt. The showy clothes from *avant-garde* boutiques, flashy cars, a Mercedes sports, and her fantasy life revolves not around her husband, but the playboy image of the commercial.

Repetition

Once an image or style is decided upon for an advertisement, the same formula is repeated for as long as the advertising budget permits. The maxim 'if you keep talking about something for long enough eventually people pay attention' is widely accepted in advertising. This is sometimes referred to as the 'drip-drip effect' of the media: just as moving water gradually sculptures into a different shape the stone over which it passes, advertisements may eventually 'do something' to their audiences. The repetition of the same commercial within the same programme, or a sustained advertising campaign over a week, or the same advertisement placed on several consecutive pages in a newspaper — these are tactics designed at least to ensure that the brand name will be recalled. It is considered inadvisable to vary the form of presentation — the same layout, typeface and copy are used over and over again.

Honesty in Advertising

Phillip Adams, an authority on advertising, maintains that it is possible for advertisers to create honest and positive advertisements:

I believe that there is a place for honest, straightforward, simple, intelligent advertising. A very big place. A growing place. Furthermore, I believe that sort of advertising can sell. It can not only move goods, it can almost move mountains. Whenever I think of this area I think of the Volkswagen story in America. There, automotive advertising was always characterized by the wildest fantasies. Motorcars were treated as if they were objects of religious veneration; photographed in strange surreal surroundings; adorned and accessorized by beautiful women. The cars themselves were designed to be fantasies with tail-fins and monstrous grilles and voluptuous upholstery.

Then along came the VW. Ugly, small, practical. If the American car was a dream, surely this was a nightmare. But VW were lucky to appoint a very brilliant advertising agency in Doyle Dane Bernbach and rather than use trick photography and stage settings to make it appear glamorous, that agency dramatized the truth. They showed the car in stark simplicity and they called it a bug. The advertisements they did were shocking, but those advertisements made a virtue out of truth. Here at last the American people were offered a car that didn't tell them lies; a car without a single frill or flourish or concession to fantasy. And backed with intelligent advertising, they took that car to their hearts. Imagine what would have happened to Volkswagen sale figures in America if they'd ... advertised in any other way.

[from *Adams with Added Enzymes* by PHILLIP ADAMS]

Two Examples

Study the advertisements that appear on pp. 210–213, and then consider the questions posed in connection with each.

Analysing the Advertisement (Triumph TR7)

(1) Does the advertiser work on any need or desire the consumer might have? What need(s) or desire(s)?

(2) What attention-getting features has the writer used in this advertisement?

(3) What is the tone of this advertisement?

(4) Why do you think the advertiser has left out the verbs in the sentences, 'Same spoked alloy wheels. Same sports steering wheel. Same arresting stripes.'?

(5) How does the advertiser give the impression that he is talking personally with the reader?

(6) Why do you think the use of repetition is important in advertising? What examples of repetition can you find in this advertisement?

(7) '. . . you may think we're trying to pull a fast one on the constabulary.' Explain the writer's pun on the words, 'trying to pull a fast one'.

(8) What is the advertising writer suggesting when he says that 'there may not be enough to go around'?

(9) Why do you think the advertiser has used the word 'nab' rather than 'get' or 'obtain'?

(10) Do you think this is a successful advertisement? Why?

THE LIMITED EDITION TR-7 AS THE LAW SEES IT.

One look at the limited edition TR-7 and you may think we're trying to pull a fast one on the constabulary.

The limited edition TR-7 looks exactly like the racing edition TR-7, currently being raced by the likes of Bond and Morris.

Same spoked alloy wheels. Same sports steering wheel. Same arresting stripes.

And undercover, the same race and rally proven motor.

Inside, the limited edition TR-7 is dressed for racy action of a different kind.

With a powerful, all-enveloping radio/cassette sound system, reclining seats and sneaky touch control interior lights.

The crowning glory is the price.

You certainly won't have to rob a bank to buy one which, by the way, is precisely why you'll have to be quick to nab one.

The limited edition TR-7 is strictly limited in number.

While there may not be enough to go around, there'll be enough to keep the law on their toes.

Analysing the Advertisement (BHP)

(1) What attention-getting devices does this advertiser use?

(2) Why does the advertiser ask the question, 'Steel is restricting?'?

(3) What kind of person could be interested in this advertisement?

(4) Can you suggest why the advertiser has enclosed businessmen rather than people from other walks of life in the McShane portable sheepyard?

(5) Is this advertisement making an emotional appeal to the reader, or is it appealing to the logic of the reader? Explain your viewpoint.

(6) What does the advertiser mean by, 'Pick our brains on steel'?

(7) Why do you think the advertiser has focused the advertisement on Peter McShane's invention?

(8) The advertiser gives detailed information about the fence and its assembly. Can you suggest why?

(9) What is the advertiser's purpose in this advertisement?

(10) Do you think it is a successful advertisement? Why?

Steel is restricting?

Never. Steel is a material with which you can create innovative and exciting designs. Like the automatic portable sheepyard shown here.

One driver can re-load the basic yard in just four minutes.

It is the brainchild of a Tasmanian grazier, Peter McShane. Peter realized that time and effort were being wasted moving the sheep to and from the sheepyards; so he designed a sheepyard he could take to the sheep.

It is constructed from fifty-eight gates made of steel tubing with 'weld mesh' inlay. They are carried upright on a specially constructed trailer hinged together in such a way that when laid from the moving trailer, they become a self-supporting fence.

One man with a vehicle can unload and form a basic yard in just two minutes. Reloading can take four minutes.

BHP are proud to be involved with Peter McShane's automatic portable sheepyards. Early sales results from A.R.C. Engineering* indicate that it will achieve all the success it deserves.

<u>Pick our brains on steel.</u>

Naturally, BHP want to encourage innovative use and design of steel. Please feel free to talk to us on creative and technical issues. Make our resources work for you, and hear of the latest developments in steel. You may be surprised.

Sydney 239 0333, Melbourne 60 0701, Adelaide 212 6700, Brisbane 31 1041, Perth 325 9633, Hobart 23 2986.
*Sole Distributors.

BHP
Surprising Steel

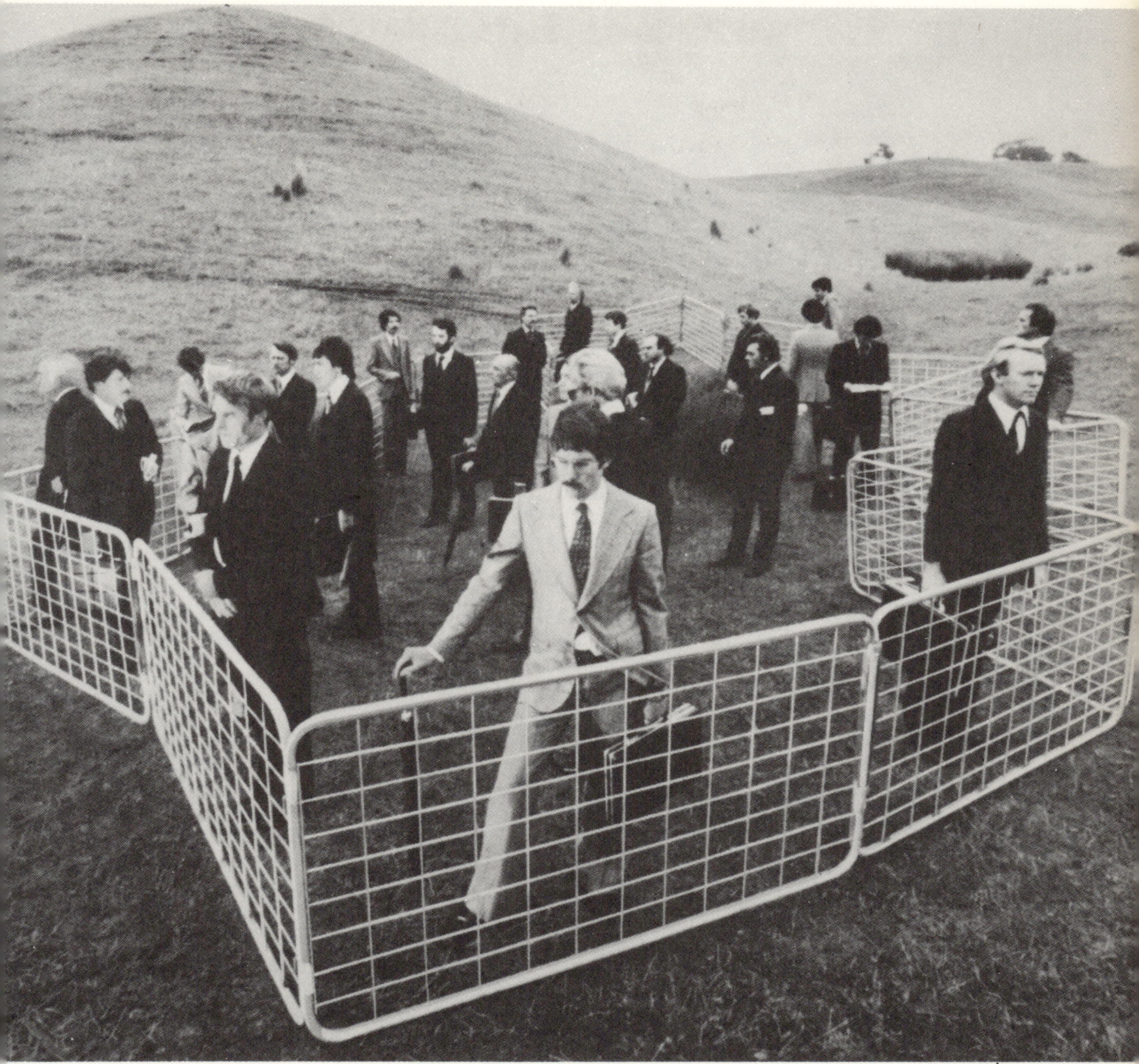

The McShane Weldmesh Portable Sheepyards - to restrict the sheep, not the innovator.

The Language of Literature (14)

Characters in Fiction — Uriah Heep

Memorable characters throng the pages of Charles Dickens's novels. Here are three descriptions of the odious Uriah Heep from *David Copperfield*. Read them, and answer the questions alongside each.

David Copperfield's first impression of Uriah Heep

When the pony-chaise stopped at the door, and my eyes were intent upon the house, I saw a cadaverous face appear at a small window on the ground floor (in a little round tower that formed one side of the house), and quickly disappear. The low arched door then opened, and the face came out. It was quite as cadaverous as it had looked in the window, though in the grain of it there was that tinge of red which is sometimes to be observed in the skins of red-haired people. It belonged to a red-haired person — a youth of fifteen, as I take it now, but looking much older — whose hair was cropped as close as the closest stubble; who had hardly any eyebrows, and no eyelashes, and eyes of a red-brown, so unsheltered and unshaded, that I remember wondering how he went to sleep. He was high-shouldered and bony; dressed in decent black, with a white wisp of a neckcloth; buttoned up to the throat; and had a long, lank, skeleton hand, which particularly attracted my attention, as he stood at the pony's head, rubbing his chin with it, and looking up at us in the chaise.

Questions

(1) The first sentence gives an unfavourable impression of Uriah Heep — the word 'cadaverous' is responsible for this. What idea of physical appearance does the word call up in the reader's imagination?

(2) How is our unfavourable impression reinforced in the sentence beginning, 'It was quite . . . '?

(3) ' . . . in the grain of it there was that tinge of red . . . ' The word 'grain' is not normally associated with human skin. Can you suggest why Dickens might have chosen it?

(4) What peculiarities linked with Uriah's eyes does David notice? What do they cause him to wonder about?

(5) In the last sentence, what words catch up and carry on the cadaverous image of Uriah Heep?

(6) In this passage one character is seen through the eyes of another character. The description focuses on physical features. Which three of the following words would you select to describe David's reaction to Uriah: repugnance, tolerance, sympathy, repulsion, superciliousness, respect, aversion?

The 'humbleness' of Heep

But, seeing a light in the little round office, and immediately feeling myself attracted towards Uriah Heep, who had a sort of fascination for me, I went in there instead. I found Uriah reading a great fat book, with such demonstrative attention, that his lank forefinger followed up every line as he read, and made clammy tracks along the page (or so I fully believed) like a snail.

'You are working late to-night, Uriah,' says I.

'Yes, Master Copperfield,' says Uriah. . . .

'I suppose you are quite a great lawyer?' I said, after looking at him for some time.

'Me, Master Copperfield?' said Uriah. 'Oh, no! I'm a very umble person.'

It was no fancy of mine about his hands, I observed; for he frequently ground the palms against each other as if to squeeze them dry and warm, besides often wiping them, in a stealthy way, on his pocket-handkerchief.

'I am well aware that I am the umblest person going,' said Uriah Heep, modestly; 'let the other be where he may. My mother is likewise a very umble person. We live in a numble abode, Master Copperfield, but have much to be thankful for. My father's former calling was umble. He was a sexton.'

'What is he now?' I asked.

'He is a partaker of glory at present, Master Copperfield,' said Uriah Heep. 'But we have much to be thankful for.'

Uriah Heep as David's guest

I led him up the dark stairs, to prevent his knocking his head against anything, and really his damp cold hand felt so like a frog in mine, that I was tempted to drop it and run away. . . .

As he sat on my sofa, with his long knees drawn up under his coffee-cup, his hat and gloves upon the ground close to him, his spoon going softly round and round, his shadowless red eyes, which looked as if they had scorched their lashes off, turned towards me without looking at me, the disagreeable dints I have formerly described in his nostrils coming and going with his breath, and a snaky undulation pervading his frame from his chin to his boots, I decided in my own mind that I disliked him intensely. It made me very uncomfortable to have him for a guest, for I was young then, and unused to disguise what I so strongly felt.

Questions

(1) 'Uriah Heep, who had a sort of fascination for me . . .' In view of what has already been given on Uriah, what do you think is the nature of the fascination David feels?

(2) What does the adjective 'lank' suggest about Uriah's forefinger?

(3) How is a simile used to give a vivid image of the way Uriah Heep is reading?

(4) Uriah Heep's favourite word is 'umble'. What effect (intended by Dickens) does its constant repetition have on the reader?

(5) Comment on Dickens's use of verbs to present a powerful picture of Heep in the paragraph beginning, 'It was no fancy . . .'.

(6) What use does Uriah make of euphemism towards the ends of this extract?

Questions

(1) Comment on the aptness of the comparison made in the first sentence.

(2) Details of Uriah's appearance and behaviour follow each other in quick succession in the second paragraph. What impact does this accumulation of detail have?

(3) Comment on the positioning of the topic sentence in the second paragraph.

(4) There is a hypnotic quality present in this description of Uriah Heep. What use of words and phrases achieves this? (Mention alliteration in your answer.)

(5) To what creature is Uriah Heep implicitly linked in the second paragraph?

(6) What view of life is inherent in the last sentence?

Maria

From *For Whom the Bell Tolls,* a novel by Ernest Hemingway about a guerilla band planning and executing the destruction of a bridge during the Spanish Civil War, comes the girl partisan, Maria.

In this passage Robert Jordan, an American volunteer who has joined the guerillas, meets Maria for the first time.

The girl stooped as she came out of the cave mouth carrying the big iron cooking platter and Robert Jordan saw her face turned at an angle and at the same time saw the strange thing about her. She smiled and said, '*Hola,* Comrade,' and Robert Jordan said, '*Salud,*' and was careful not to stare and not to look away. She set down the flat iron platter in front of him and he noticed her handsome brown hands. Now she looked him full in the face and smiled. Her teeth were white in her brown face and her skin and her eyes were the same golden tawny brown. She had high cheekbones, merry eyes, and a straight mouth with full lips. Her hair was the golden brown of a grain field that has been burned dark in the sun, but it was cut short all over her head so that it was but little longer than the fur on a beaver pelt. She smiled in Robert Jordan's face and put her brown hand up and ran it over her head, flattening the hair which rose again as her hand passed. She has a beautiful face, Robert Jordan thought. She'd be beautiful if they hadn't cropped her hair.

'That is the way I comb it,' she said to Robert Jordan and laughed. 'Go ahead and eat. Don't stare at me. They gave me this haircut in Valladolid. It's almost grown out now.'

She sat down opposite him and looked at him. He looked back at her and she smiled and folded her hands together over her knees. Her legs slanted long and clean from the open cuffs of the trousers as she sat with her hands across her knees and he could see the shape of her small, up-tilted breasts under the grey shirt. Every time Robert Jordan looked at her he could feel a thickness in his throat.

[from *For Whom the Bell Tolls* by ERNEST HEMINGWAY]

Questions

(1) Even the first sentence arouses our immediate interest in the girl's appearance. How?

(2) What is curious about the girl's appearance?

(3) Jordan is 'careful not to stare and not to look away'. What would have been the effect of either action?

(4) Why is the description of the girl's hands unusual?

(5) The girl emanates a feeling of life and vitality. What choice of words and phrases contributes to this effect?

(6) How is figurative language used to present us with a striking image of one aspect of the girl's appearance?

(7) How does Maria show that she is fully aware of Robert Jordan's appraisal of her cropped hair?

(8) The second description of the girl ('Her legs . . . grey shirt.') is far more detached and objective than the first. Comment on the way the author has achieved detachment and objectivity. Mention, in particular, verbs and adjectives.

(9) 'Every time Robert Jordan looked at her he could feel a thickness in his throat.' Why is Robert Jordan reacting in this manner?

(10) What method of character revelation is used, almost exclusively, in relation to Maria?

Captain Queeg

The Caine Mutiny by Herman Wouk introduces us to Captain Queeg, USN, a giant of a character — in notoriety — in recent American fiction. His bizarre and inconsistent behaviour, and final failure as Captain of the *Caine*, lead to morally questionable mutiny on the high seas by his officers.

In this passage, the officers meet their new captain for the first time.

'I'm simply observing,' said Keefer, 'that our new captain has a sense of drama. I thoroughly approve.'

'Knock it off,' whispered Maryk, as the knob of the captain's door turned. Gorton came out and looked around the table. 'All present, Captain,' he called through the open door. Queeg entered the wardroom. With a scrape of chair legs the officers stood. The *Caine* officers had not performed this courtesy in a year; several of them had never done it; but they all rose instinctively.

'Sit down, sit down, gentlemen,' said Queeg in a light, joking tone. He sat in his chair, laid a fresh pack of cigarettes and a packet of matches in front of him, and looked around with a smile as his officers took their seats. He tore open the pack deliberately, lit a cigarette and took the two steel balls out of his pocket. Rubbing them softly back and forth in his fingers, he began to speak. Occasionally he glanced up at their faces; other-wise he kept his eyes on the cigarette or the steel balls.

'Well, gentlemen, I just thought we ought to get acquainted. We're going to be shipmates for a long time. You're probably wondering about me, and I confess I'm a little curious about you, though I've formed some pretty good first impressions. I think we're going to have a good cruise, and I hope, as Captain de Vriess put it, some good hunting. I intend to give you every co-operation, and I expect the same in return. There is such a thing as loyalty upward, and such a thing as loyalty downward. I desire and expect to get absolute loyalty upward. If I do, you'll get loyalty downward. If I don't — well, I'll find out why, and I'll see to it that I do.' He laughed, indicating that this was a joke, and the officers nearest him smiled.

[from *The Caine Mutiny*
by HERMAN WOUK]

Questions

(1) What overall effect is Wouk aiming at by giving an item-by-item description of Queeg's acts, beginning, 'He sat in his chair . . . '?

(2) At what point does Queeg's behaviour depart somewhat from what would normally be expected?

(3) What change in Queeg's tone occurs as he puts forward his philosophy of command?

(4) Exactly how does the author use language to inject more than a suggestion of incoherence into Queeg's exhortation to loyalty?

(5) A character is revealed in three main ways:
    (a)   by direct description of appearance, thoughts and actions;
    (b)   through the eyes of another character;
    (c)   by self-revelation — through the character's own thoughts, words and actions.
To what extent is Queeg, as a character, revealed by each of these three methods in the passage quoted?

Writers' Workshop (4)

Rhythmic Balance in Sentences

One of the fairly intangible, yet important, aspects of good writing is rhythmic balance in sentences. One sentence may flow smoothly and appear to be 'just right'; another may appear jerky and disjointed. Almost certainly the difference lies in the balance of the sentence. The balance of a sentence derives from the way the words and word-groups are placed in relation to each other to give a satisfying rhythmic effect.

> Go placidly amid the noise and haste, and remember what peace there may be in silence. As far as possible without surrender be on good terms with all persons. Speak your truth quietly and clearly; and listen to others, even the dull and ignorant; they too have their story. Enjoy your achievements as well as your plans. Keep interested in your own career, however humble; it is a real possession in the changing fortunes of time. Be yourself.
>
> [from *Desiderata*]

Note the use of balance in this extract. Here are some observable features.

(i) **Conjunctions** such as 'and' and 'as well as' act to balance one word against another or one word-group against another. Notice 'amid the noise *and* haste'. Notice also the 'and' which balances the first clause ('Go placidly . . . ') with the second clause ('remember . . . ').

(ii) **Groups of three** — either single words or word-groups — often act to give a sense of completeness and aptness in sentences. Note the three clauses balanced against each other: 'Speak your truth . . . '; 'and listen to others . . . '; 'they too have their story'. Here, semicolons are used to separate the three. Often, commas are used for the same purpose.

Summary

The most common technique used to achieve a sense of aptness in the rhythm of a sentence is to balance one word against another, or one word-group against another. Either a conjunction or some punctuation mark such as a comma is used to separate, and yet link, the two. *Avoid* balancing a single word against a group of words, as this tends to create a disjointed feel to the sentence.

Another common technique used in sentence balance is to list things in groups of three. This is most commonly done by separating the first two in the list with a comma, and the second and third with 'and'.

EXAMPLE: He wore a dirty sombrero, a faded shirt and incredibly patched trousers.

Sometimes, commas or semicolons may be used between each of the three, though this is less common.

EXAMPLE: I came, I saw, I conquered.

Note: Awareness of sentence balance and skill in writing balanced sentences are valuable assets for your writing, but do not *over-use* the specific techniques listed here. They need to be blended thoughtfully with other techniques and features, such as variety of sentence length, in order to produce the desired effect.

Exercise 1

Rewrite the following sentences to achieve a more satisfying rhythmic balance. Sometimes you will need to add or remove a word or two, or change a structure.

(1) The trap moved, gaped a little and at last I saw it come widely open.

(2) He paused, embarrassed by the large eyes and the way his companion's face looked so thin and weary.

(3) With all its sham and drudgery and broken dreams, it is still a beautiful world.

(4) All around the house you could hear feet running, doors opening and you could also hear a loud voice shouting.

(5) He saw the old man, bemused with age, liquor, sorrow, go shambling across the snow, and with his whimpering dog at his heels.

(6) He stood irresolute, as well as wondering what to do next.

(7) He spoke very well about decency and how important having a companion is to animals.

(8) I have neither come to wrangle nor am I going to seek reconciliation.

(9) Santiago will be remembered as a man who faced life with courage, endurance and without losing hope.

(10) The mood of the passage is pleasant, while the tone is in some parts melancholy, some parts joyful and still in others it was depressing.

Choosing the 'Right' Word

The choice of an incorrect or 'not-quite-right' word can have a jarring, distracting effect in written work. Often this problem shows itself in essays or creative-writing pieces in which a student is trying to use impressive words without being completely sure of their meaning. Sometimes the result may be complete misuse of a word, a *malapropism:* 'He strongly resembled [instead of 'resented'] the insulting remark.' Sometimes it may be the use of a word that just doesn't quite fit into the sentence in which it is employed. It may occasionally be a made-up word, even an incorrect spelling of an otherwise correct word. The 'right' word, on the other hand, will convey the precise meaning desired, and will be appropriate to the whole mood and tone of the passage.

Exercise 2

Alter any of the words you consider inaccurately or inappropriately used in the following statements. In each case make sure that the word you use is 'correct' or more appropriate.

(1) The poem builds upon the subject of a young person who lives life carefreely and carelessly.

(2) I have sited evidence which should establish the guilt of this person.

(3) The hero portraits himself as loyal and humble but the image that he transfers to the reader is quite different.

(4) The small VW sympathized with the character of its owners, being both economical and brightly coloured.

(5) They stopped before a home which was the epitome of the residence of a working-class Australian family.

(6) The young boy's face, ludicrous and sad, painfully sought to ascertain his situation.

(7) Her most apparent quality, however, would appear to be her unyielding, unquenching spirit.

(8) With insightful perspicacity Nurse Susan Edgely chose the decision to administrate the drug to the young child before her.

(9) Slowly an awareness of unmeasurable ambition within him began to intrude its way into his thoughts.

(10) Only too well did he understand the importance of being adapt with the sails.

Exercise 3

In each of the following sentences, several possible words are offered. Choose the one you consider to be most appropriate and be prepared to justify your choice. Often you will be required to make fairly subtle judgements.

(1) As Robin attempted to right the yawing craft, he found he had to [**spend/expend/deplete/disperse**] every ounce of strength.

(2) Reading the map accurately required [**intense/minute/diligent**] concentration.

(3) The main character is [**portrayed/depicted/described**] as a villain of the most evil kind.

(4) The judge was affronted by the prisoner's air of [**audacity/arrogance/impudence**] as he listened to the charges being read.

(5) The task of the referee is to judge with no [**partiality/predilection/predisposition**] the extent to which the play of both teams conforms to the rules.

(6) The present [**opulence/richness/affluence**] of Western society is unlikely to be maintained as raw materials become used up.

(7) When the complete explanation was heard it was apparent that the actions were fully [**exonerated/vindicated/justified**].

(8) Overcome with [**desperation/despondency/pessimism**], the elderly couple chose to end their lives.

(9) The selection of the 20-year-old centre from the ACT to [**substitute for/supersede/supplant**] the injured player proved a masterly stroke.

(10) Roles in the drama were [**disposed/assigned/distributed**] according to how well the participants had handled the play-reading.

Summary

In seeking to be an effective writer, use words that you are sure of. By all means work at extending your vocabulary, but do not experiment with words when writing something that will be judged. Develop a feel for the 'right' word, always matching its meaning with your purpose and with the situation you are writing about.

Language Basics (14)

The Conjunction

Here are some rules to guide you in the correct use of conjunctions.

Rule 1 ● Maintain the following pairs in your sentences:

> both ... and
> whether ... or
> either ... or
> neither ... nor
> so ... that
> no sooner ... than

> EXAMPLE: <u>Both</u> the Ghost Train <u>and</u> its driver were exceptional.

Rule 2 ● **'Like'** should not be used as a conjunction. Instead, use **'as'**.
> EXAMPLE: Do it <u>as</u> I do it.

Using the Rules

Correct the following sentences.

(1) Fix it like the plumber fixes it.

(2) The drivers did not know whether to stoke the boilers and put on the brakes.

(3) The diplomats were that afraid that they were unable to sleep.

(4) You'd better keep it going like the mechanics instructed.

(5) No sooner had the train stopped when the ambassador stumbled out.

(6) The driver was neither drunk or mad.

Punctuation – The dash

1. A dash is used to indicate a break or an abrupt change of thought in a sentence.
   EXAMPLE: 'That is why I – oh, it doesn't matter,' she said tiredly.

2. Dashes are used to insert secondary matter into a sentence, in effect interrupting the sentence temporarily.
   EXAMPLE: One of the boys – he was as swift as a rabbit – raced up the track.
   [Parentheses could be used here instead, but would not carry the same 'immediacy' in this context.]

3. A dash is used to gather together a number of items.
   EXAMPLE: Diplomats, politicians, officials and assistants – all were present.

4. A dash is used within a sentence to introduce a phrase, clause or sub-sentence that acts as a significant 'afterthought'.

EXAMPLES: (a) He knew the arrival-time — after all, he was the stationmaster!
(b) The train had not arrived — not yet.

Exercise

Correctly insert dashes into the following sentences.

(1) The 'Liberation-Celebration Machine' it had to be seen to be believed made the diplomats suffer great anxiety.

(2) 'Because he no, you wouldn't understand', she sighed dejectedly.

(3) Buildings, signals, rails, fences all raced past the windows.

(4) One of the diplomats he was certainly afraid of dying spent the night singing, 'Nearer My God to Thee'.

(5) Her next statement it was not what we anticipated showed how prepared she was.

(6) The 'Liberation-Celebration Machine' was an I'd better not say what!

(7) He was middle-aged not old and not young.

Unit Fifteen

Comprehension (15)

Race Memories

As a child of fourteen, I remember how my guts twisted with bitterness as I dug the skeletons of black women and children out of the sands of the Murrumbidgee and examined the squashed and bullet-riddled skulls. Many black families have some story, some horror story of racial massacre in their district. It is not that long ago that the last 'shoot-ups' occurred in blacks' camps — the local whites having themselves some fun. It's not that long ago that Aborigines were roped off in picture houses from the rest of the audience, that they couldn't get service in cafes etc. In some areas it still goes on. In more recent times, the figures on the number of black babies dying in the outback were ignored while this country gave generous millions to nations like Pakistan. Blacks know this. They know how little time has elapsed since they were not counted in the census. They lived through the shame of being 'second class' people in a country that denied them the right to social services, the right to walk into the country's lowest institutions, the pubs. Very few blacks have any land security as yet. Police victimization and disadvantages before the law are attested to by the enormous disproportion of blacks in jail.

White man, you may well speak to the Aborigine of your 'democracy' and 'justice' and 'Christianity'. But your reality is a little at variance with your theory. The Aborigine snarls his disbelief of your words as he slinks away unmanned. Often he holds silence, for such is the beggarly state that society and circumstance have reduced him to — and this includes the 'respectable' blacks who have been singled out for white favour — that he will fawn obsequiously at your lies and half-truths. Once his fathers were men. Now he hopes, by fawning, to remain reasonably agreeable in your sight so that he may beg from you, borrow, or if he is one of the favoured ones, be given a more lucrative sinecure tomorrow. Underneath it all there is frustration, obsequious resentment, divided loyalties, uncertain values. There is no real belonging, no real identification except to the memory of misery. It is true that the modern Aborigine is sick, very sick. But let no white person use this as an excuse to denigrate him even further. You cannot look down on black people while you understand the historical reasons that have reduced them to what they are — the reasons of which I have here sketched only a tiny, general, impressionistic fraction. Remember that the Aborigine's sickness has been forced upon him. Yours you not only tolerate, but structured into the very fibres of your society.

[from *Because a White Man'll Never Do It*
by KEVIN GILBERT]

Check Your Understanding

(1) Account for the emotional reaction of the author to the incident that occurred when he was fourteen.

(2) What was a 'shoot-up'?

(3) To whom is this extract addressed?

(4) Explain the purpose of the writer in this extract.

(5) Identify three examples of fairly recent discrimination against Aborigines.

(6) What fact is used to support the claim that there exists police victimization of Aborigines?

(7) What is the meaning of, 'your reality is a little at variance with your theory'?

(8) What is the meaning of 'fawn obsequiously'?

(9) Why does the writer particularly identify as worthy of comment the tendency of white people to talk about 'democracy', 'justice' and 'Christianity'?

(10) 'There is no real belonging, no real identification except to the memory of misery.' Explain what is meant.

(11) What overall 'sickness' does the writer see in Aborigines? What 'sickness' does he identify in whites?

(12) Which 'sickness' does the writer feel deserves the harsher judgement? Explain his reasons.

(13) What is the meaning of the following as they occur in the passage: (a) variance (b) unmanned (c) lucrative sinecure (d) denigrate (e) impressionistic fraction? Consult the back-of-the-book dictionary where necessary.

(14) What emotions on the part of the writer are conveyed by the tone of this passage? Why does he feel these emotions?

(15) What impact does this extract have upon you? Is it at all likely to change your attitudes towards Aborigines?

Working with Words (15)

Senior Spelling Demons	Confusing Pairs	Buying and Selling		Increase Your Word Power
superstition	construct	depreciate	guarantee	impunity
society	construe	accumulate	counterfeit	impasse
obstacle	verbal	prestigious	monopoly	irascible
mystery	verbose	integrity	magnate	lethargy
military	mantle	currency	mortgage	loquacious
explorer	mantel	commodity	revenue	insignia
reputation	superfluous	impecunious	recession	malinger
manufacture	superficial	exorbitant	scrupulous	moribund
surpass	luxurious	subsidy	courteous	introvert
catalogue	luxuriant	supersede	association	insinuate

Change the Words

Change into nouns

(a) depreciate ....

(b) prestigious ....

(c) courteous ....

(d) exorbitant ....

(e) scrupulous ....

(f) superficial ....

Change into verbs

(a) subsidy ....

(b) insinuation ....

(c) explorer ....

(d) association ....

(e) recession ....

(f) monopoly ....

Change into adjectives

(a) lethargy ....

(b) mystery ....

(c) construct ....

(d) superstition ....

(e) recession ....

Change into adverbs

(a) courteous ....

(b) verbal ....

(c) superficial ....

Write the plurals of

(a) society ....

(b) revenue ....

(c) cargo ....

(d) monopoly ....

(e) brother-in-law ....

(f) man-eater ....

Find the Word

Replace the words in heavy type with list-words.

(1) The old man was **without any money.**

(2) The price was **far too high.**

(3) The car had begun to **go down in value.**

(4) The bookseller was **very talkative.**

(5) He was able to rob cars with **no punishment resulting.**

(6) The real-estate agent had a **distinguished** colonial home for sale.

(7) A politician should always retain his **uprightness.**

(8) The businessman had begun to **pile up** a fortune.

(9) The dairy industry received a **grant of money** from the government.

(10) The government had the **sole right** of the importation of Arabian oil.

(11) The criminal had a bundle of **forged** ten-dollar notes.

(12) There has been a **temporary decline** in the building industry.

(13) The secretary was **conscientiously correct** in her management of the company's finances.

(14) The colonel wore his **emblems of rank** on his new uniform.

(15) His **lack of energy** prevented him from working.

(16) The union discussions with the prime minister reached an unfortunate **deadlock.**

(17) He tried to **imply** that we had not been working.

(18) Difficulties made him **hot-tempered.**

(19) He was always **polite and gracious** to others.

(20) Her home was **rich and exquisite.**

Confusing Pairs

Write down the following sentences, inserting into the blank spaces the correct words from the brackets.

(1) The engineer had been employed to .... the bridge. [**construe/construct**]

(2) The politician's speech was monotonous and .... [**verbose/verbal**]

(3) There was a .... of snow on the ground. [**mantle/mantel**]

(4) The boy's understanding of the problem was .... [**superfluous/superficial**]

(5) There was a .... growth of grass on the tennis courts. [**luxuriant/luxurious**]

Missing Words

Correctly insert words from the box into the spaces in the sentences that follow.

currency	magnate	integrity	monopoly	scrupulous	impecunious
exorbitant	prestigious	supersede	counterfeit	mortgage	

(1) The shipping .... had a .... of the world's largest oil-tankers.

(2) A person of .... does not produce .... money.

(3) Taking out a .... on one's home can be helpful if one is ....

(4) The cost of petrol is becoming ....

(5) The new *de luxe* model, which will .... your model, is a .... motorcar.

(6) The new cashier was .... in his handling of the foreign ....

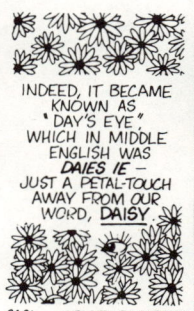

Word Origins — Some handy words

Manus is the Latin word for 'hand'. Many years ago when something was 'manufactured' it was made by hand. Strangely enough, the word 'manure' is related to *manus*, because fertilizer used to be mixed by hand. Now match up the following *manus* ('hand') words with their correct meanings.

WORDS	MEANINGS
manicure	handwritten book or document
manual	a handcuff
manipulate	grooming of the hands and nails
manacle	done by hand
manuscript	to handle with skill

Language in Action (15)

Satire

Satire is speech or writing which sets out to hold up human foolishness and weakness to ridicule. Satire seeks to expose aspects of human behaviour such as hypocrisy, folly, and

If it wasn't for Winsom, I wouldn't smoke.

I also wouldn't cough. And my breath wouldn't smell. And my fingers wouldn't be stained yellow. And my hair and my clothes wouldn't stink from stale smoke. And my taste buds wouldn't be deadened. And my nose wouldn't run and my eyes wouldn't tear and—

The Surgeon General Is Amazed That Cancer, Emphysema, High Blood Pressure and Heart Disease Weren't Even Mentioned In This Ad

PHOTOGRAPHY BY IRVING SCHILD

expedience. By adopting an attitude of scornful amusement towards the quality or person under examination, and by the use of such tools as irony, sarcasm, innuendo, lampooning and scorn, it seeks to induce readers or hearers to reconsider and (ideally) alter their behaviour in regard to the particular characteristic being satirized.

Sent Up in Smoke?

(1) What particular aspect of human behaviour is being satirized in this 'advertisement'? What company is also the target of the satire?

(2) What similarities are there between this ad and a normal cigarette advertisement? Explain why they are important in this piece of satire.

(3) Summarize the techniques being used by the satirist.

(4) What effect is this satirical advertisement intended to have on the reader? Explain why you feel it is effective or not.

Satire Old and New

The following extracts illustrate the style of two great British satirists — Jonathan Swift and George Orwell.

Swift (1667–1745), writing in the early eighteenth century, is acknowledged to be, in many respects, the 'father' of Western satire. Using ridicule, irony, sarcasm, invective, scorn, caricature and a variety of such techniques, he satirized the people and events of his time. It is an irony he probably wouldn't have enjoyed that his greatest satire, *Gulliver's Travels*, is nowadays all-too-often treated as just a children's story. When writing it, Swift intended the book to reflect upon the nature of man, in particular exposing the folly of his snobbishness. In the extract that follows, Gulliver is in Lilliput, the land of tiny people. He is privileged to witness one of the kingdom's great diversions, Rope Dancing....

This Diversion is only practised by those Persons, who are Candidates for great Employments, and high Favour, at Court. They are trained in this Art from their Youth, and are not always of noble Birth, or liberal Education. When a great Office is vacant, either by Death or Disgrace, (which often happens) five or six of those Candidates petition the Emperor to entertain his Majesty and the Court with a Dance on the Rope; and whoever jumps the highest without falling, succeeds in the Office. Very often the chief Ministers themselves are commanded to shew their Skill, and to convince the Emperor that they have not lost their Faculty. *Flimnap*, the Treasurer, is allowed to cut a Caper on the strait Rope, at least an Inch higher than any other Lord in the whole Empire. I have seen him do the Summerset several times together, upon a Trencher fixed on the Rope, which is no thicker than a common Packthread in *England*. My Friend *Reldresal*, principal Secretary for private Affairs, is, in my Opinion, if I am not partial, the second after the Treasurer; the rest of the great Officers are much upon a Par.

These Diversions are often attended with fatal Accidents, whereof great Numbers are on Record. I my self have seen two or three Candidates break a Limb. But the Danger is much greater, when the Ministers themselves are commanded to shew their Dexterity: For, by contending to excel themselves and their Fellows, they strain so far, that there is hardly one of them who hath not received a Fall; and some of them two or three. I was assured, that a Year or two before my Arrival, *Flimnap* would have infallibly broke his Neck, if one of the *King's Cushions*, that accidentally lay on the Ground, had not weakened the Force of his Fall.

[from *Gulliver's Travels* by JONATHAN SWIFT]

George Orwell (1903–1950) is acknowledged as one of the greatest satirists of the twentieth century. His *Nineteen Eighty-Four* and *Animal Farm* are two of the world's widest-selling political satires. *Animal Farm,* from which the next extract is taken, was written in 1945, and uses a fable involving animals to satirize the emptiness of man's hopes for Utopia via the proletarian revolution and Communism. Lofty ideals are lost in power struggles, corruption, and lies.

Several nights a week, after Mr Jones was asleep, they held secret meetings in the barn and expounded the principles of Animalism to the others. At the beginning they met with such stupidity and apathy. Some of the animals talked of the duty of loyalty to Mr Jones, whom they referred to as 'Master', or made elementary remarks such as 'Mr Jones feeds us. If he were gone, we should starve to death.' Others asked such questions as 'Why should we care what happens after we are dead?' or 'If this rebellion is to happen anyway, what difference does it make whether we work for it or not?', and the pigs had great difficulty in making them see that this was contrary to the spirit of Animalism. The stupidest questions of all were asked by Mollie, the white mare. The very first question she asked Snowball was: 'Will there still be sugar after the Rebellion?'

'No,' said Snowball firmly. 'We have no means of making sugar on this farm. Besides, you do not need sugar. You will have all the oats and hay you want.'

'And shall I still be allowed to wear ribbons in my mane?' asked Mollie.

'Comrade,' said Snowball, 'those ribbons that you are so devoted to are the badge of slavery. Can you not understand that liberty is worth more than ribbons?'

Mollie agreed, but she did not sound very convinced.

The pigs had an even harder struggle to counteract the lies put about by Moses, the tame raven. Moses, who was Mr Jones's especial pet, was a spy and a tale-bearer, but he was also a clever talker. He claimed to know of the existence of a mysterious country called Sugarcandy Mountain, to which all animals went when they died. It was situated somewhere up in the sky, a little distance beyond the clouds, Moses said. In Sugarcandy Mountain it was Sunday seven days a week, clover was in season all the year round, and lump sugar and linseed cake grew on the hedges. The animals hated Moses because he told tales and did not work, but some of them believed in Sugarcandy Mountain, and the pigs had to argue very hard to persuade them that there was no such place.

Their most faithful disciples were the two cart-horses, Boxer and Clover. These two had great difficulty in thinking anything out for themselves, but having once accepted the pigs as their teachers, they absorbed everything that they were told, and passed it on to the other animals by simple arguments. They were unfailing in their attendance at the secret meetings in the barn, and led the singing of 'Beasts of England', with which the meetings always ended.

[from *Animal Farm*
by GEORGE ORWELL]

Analysis

(1) In each extract, identify the particular group of people and the particular aspect of human behaviour being satirized.

(2) Identify the purpose of the author in each piece of satire.

(3) Evaluate the satirical effectiveness, for you, of each extract.

(4) What similarities and differences can you see in these two examples of satire?

Discuss

'The best satire is relevant to every generation.' Do these extracts still have relevance for us? As a class, discuss the statement and try to reach some sort of conclusion.

Assignments

(1) Choose some aspect of human folly, hypocrisy or weakness which is current and write a brief satire upon it. In each case make sure you have a clear purpose — a particular reader-response that you want to create. Aim at achieving this effect with your satire.

(2) Collect cartoons that satirize current political or social activity and, in a class session, discuss the techniques being used and the effectiveness of the cartoons.

(3) Design your own satirical cartoon relating to a current political or social event. Compare your results with those of others and comment on them in a class session, evaluating each cartoon in terms of its purpose and impact.

The Language of Literature (15)

GRANDPARENTS

They're altogether otherworldly now,
those adults champing for their ritual Friday spin
to pharmacist and five-and-ten in Brockton.
Back in my throw-away and shaggy span
of adolescence, Grandpa still waves his stick
like a policeman;
Grandmother, like a Mohammedan, still wears her thick
lavender mourning and touring veil,
the Pierce Arrow clears its throat in a horse-stall.
Then the dry road dust rises to whiten
the fatigued elm leaves—
the nineteenth century, tired of children, is gone.
They're all gone into a world of light; the farm's my own.

The farm's my own!
Back there alone,
I keep indoors, and spoil another season.
I hear the rattly little country gramophone
racking its five foot horn:
'O Summer Time!'
Even at noon here the formidable
Ancien Régime still keeps nature at a distance. Five
green shaded light bulbs spider the billiards-table,
no field is greener than its cloth,
where Grandpa, dipping sugar for us both,
once spilled his demitasse.
His favourite ball, the number three,
still hides the coffee stain.

Never again
to walk there, chalk our cues,
insist on shooting for us both.
Grandpa! Have me, hold me, cherish me!
Tears smut my fingers. There
half my life-lease later,
I hold an *Illustrated London News*,
disloyal still,
I doodle handlebar
mustaches on the last Russian Czar.

ROBERT LOWELL

Questions

(1) 'They're altogether otherwordly now' suggests complete and final separation. Yet, how true is this for the poet?

(2) Two very clear memories of the habits of the poet's Grandpa and Grandmother are presented towards the middle of the poem. What is the first memory?

(3) Grandpa and Grandmother are remembeed in living, vivid detail. What are some of the words and phrases that illustrate this?

(4) 'Grandpa still waves . . .' and 'Grandmother . . . still wears . . . ' What is the significance of 'still' in these lines?

(5) How is the car given the attributes of a living creature in the first stanza?

(6) The use of punctuation in a poem is often significant. The dash towards the end of the first stanza marks a great change in the poet's thoughts and mood. Explain the change in mood that takes place.

(7) Repetition of a word or phrase is usually significant in a poem. What is the significance of the repetition of 'the farm's my own'?

(8) Explain how the words, 'the farm's my own' link the first and second stanzas of the poem.

(9) The term *'Ancien Régime'* usually refers to the old order of pre-revolutionary France. Can you see any connection between this meaning and the one in the poem?

(10) The poet talks about the world of his grandparents keeping 'nature at a distance'. However, the poet does describe an indoor scene which suggests that his grandparents have made their own kind of nature. What words and phrases depict this?

(11) What humorous and endearing traits and habits of the poet's grandfather are described in the second and third stanzas?

(12) What feelings does the poet express at the beginning of the third stanza?

(13) Why does the poem end with a seemingly insignificant, childish action?

(14) What is the poet's intention in this poem? To what extent has he succeeded?

Writers' Workshop (5)

Style

A writer's style is made up of all the aspects of writing we have looked at, and yet it is more than the sum of these technical aspects. Choice of words, rhythm in sentences, variety in sentence structure and length, the way sentences are woven into paragraphs, figures of speech – all of these play a part in determining style. But beyond them, style is the unique and personal blending that develops out of the many features of writing, and unfolds as the writer becomes increasingly skilled and aware of the impact of his work.

Ideally, style in writing is matched to
- the situation
- the purpose of writing
- the people involved in the situation

Here are two passages on sharks. Note the contrasting styles.

PASSAGE 1

He was a very big Mako shark built to swim as fast as the fastest fish in the sea and everything about him was beautiful except his jaws. His back was as blue as a swordfish's and his belly was silver and his hide was smooth and handsome. He was built as a swordfish except for his huge jaws which were tight shut now as he swam fast, just under the surface with his high dorsal fin knifing through the water without wavering. Inside the closed double lip of his jaws all of his eight rows of teeth were slanted inwards. They were not the ordinary pyramid-shaped teeth of most sharks. They were shaped like a man's fingers when they are crisped like claws. They were nearly as long as the fingers of the old man and they had razor-sharp cutting edges on both sides. This was a fish built to feed on all the fishes in the sea that were so fast and strong and well armed that they had no other enemy. Now he speeded up as he smelled the fresher scent and his blue dorsal fin cut the water.

[from *The Old Man and the Sea*
by ERNEST HEMINGWAY]

PASSAGE 2

The typical shark is a long-bodied fish with a flattened head that slopes to the pointed snout. Its mouth lies on the under-side of the head and the powerful jaws are armed with strong, sharp teeth. The shark has well-developed shoulder and hip, or pelvic, paired fins, and it has one or two fins on its back. There is a small fin, called the anal fin, on the under-side near the anal opening. The tail is usually two-lobed; the upper lobe is larger than the lower one. On each side of the shark's body, back of the head, lie openings that lead to the inside of its mouth. These are called gill openings, or gill clefts. When the shark 'breathes in', water is taken in at the mouth. When it 'exhales', water is forced out of the gill clefts; as the water passes out it bathes the gills, which extract the oxygen held in it.

[from *The Book of Popular Science*]

Exercise 1

(1) What is the purpose of each passage? How has this affected the style of the writing?

(2) Comment on the effectiveness of the particular style used by each writer, in terms of their purpose.

(3) What obvious differences between the two passages are there in the words used?

(4) What overriding image of the Mako does Hemingway's choice of words create?

(5) What is the overall image of the shark conveyed by the second passage?

(6) Comment on sentence length in the Hemingway passage.

(7) Comment on any distinctive features you see in the second extract.

(8) Does the Hemingway extract fit in with the style said to be characteristic of Hemingway — short sentences and simple words?

Matching Purpose and Style

Writing may serve numerous purposes. Furthermore, one piece of writing may, at times, have more than one objective. Some fields of writing may come under more than one 'heading'. Here are some suggested categories.

1. WRITING WHICH IS INTENDED TO PERSUADE
   e.g. essays, letters (to newspapers)

2. WRITING WHICH IS INTENDED TO INFORM
   e.g. reports, descriptions, letters, reviews

3. WRITING WHICH IS INTENDED TO CREATE OR RE-CREATE
   e.g. creative writing (short stories, novels, poems, plays), biography, narrative, descriptions

4. WRITING WHICH IS INTENDED TO INSTRUCT
   e.g. textbooks, specialized books on arts and crafts (cookery, stamp-collecting, music)

Note that the style used in good writing will suit not only the particular person, but also the readers for whom the writing is intended. The difficulty of words and the complexity of thoughts will be considered in the light of the intended audience.

The Varieties of Style

Any look at the writers who have achieved fame over the centuries, whatever their country of origin, will show that a tremendous variety of styles of writing exists. Many attempts to draw up categories of the varieties of style have been made, yet the lists are always inadequate. This is because the style of a writer is to some extent a unique entity. However, when we try to describe the style of a piece of writing, we *will* find ourselves using words such as:

> forceful, graceful, delicate, intense, realistic, impressionistic, simple, unadorned, dignified, terse, grandiose, abstract, concrete, lively, animated, wordy, verbose, flowery, humorous, satirical, surrealistic

Exercise 2

Read each of the three extracts that follow and carry out these analytical tasks for each.

(1) How, in broad terms, would you describe the style of this piece of writing?

(2) In what way do words and their particular usage contribute to the style?

(3) Comment on the length of sentences, balance of sentences, and variety of sentences, wherever this seems important.

(4) Comment on any relevant features of paragraphing that you may note.

(5) Point out any particular devices, such as figures of speech, that you notice the writer using.

(6) What is the overall rhythm of the extract? If you have not done so already, explain how it is achieved.

(7) Make a summary statement about the effectiveness of the piece of writing. For example, how appropriate is the style to the situation?

Extract 1

Lovingly and meticulously he assembled the rifle — breech and barrel, upper and lower component of the stock, shoulder-guard, silencer and trigger. Lastly he slid on the telescopic sight and clipped it fast.

Sitting on a chair behind the table, leaning slightly forward with the gun barrel resting on top of the upper cushion, he squinted through the telescope. The sunlit square beyond the windows and fifty feet down leapt into focus. The head of one of the men still marking out the standing positions for the forthcoming ceremony passed across the line of sight. He tracked the target with the gun. The head appeared large and clear, as large as a melon had looked in the forest glade in the Ardennes.

[from *The Day of the Jackal* by FREDERICK FORSYTH]

Extract 2

I am told that punctual persons are a terrible nuisance to their friends. Quite! But an honest man is a terrible nuisance to a thief. I am told also that punctual persons are the slaves of time. Not so. It is the unpunctual who are the slaves of time, which constantly rushes them to and fro with whips and scourges. Further, unpunctual persons are unmannerly. To be late is to be selfish and silly, because the late person wastes other people's time for his own inconvenience.

[from 'Hustle' in *The Savour of Life* by ARNOLD BENNETT]

Extract 3

I raised my eyes when he spoke, and I saw him as though I had never seen him before. I saw his chin sunk on his breast, the clumsy folds of his coat, his clasped hands, his motionless pose, so curiously suggestive of his having been simply left there. Time had passed indeed: it had overtaken him and gone ahead. It had left him hopelessly behind with a few poor gifts: the iron-grey hair, the heavy fatigue of the tanned face, two scars, a pair of tarnished shoulder-straps; one of those steady, reliable men who are the raw material of great reputations, one of those uncounted lives that are buried without drums and trumpets under the foundations of monumental successes.

[from *Lord Jim* by JOSEPH CONRAD]

Exercise 3

In the box below are the essential facts of an incident which you are asked to describe more fully, using a variety of styles. Try to vary your style to suit the demands, in turn, of each of these:

(a) A description of the event as given in a politician's speech.

(b) A description of the event written as a formal report.

(c) A description given by a wordy gentleman to a friend.

(d) A description given by a poorly educated farmer.

INCIDENT

It is late afternoon. A strange light appears over a country town. It is blue-green. It seems to stand still for a few minutes, then suddenly move at great speed across the sky. It changes direction several times, before disappearing from view. It is seen by a number of people. No-one is able to explain the phenomenon.

Language Basics (15)

Verbs

Keep the following rules in mind for correct verb usage.

Rule 1 ● **Transitive verbs** (those having a direct object) govern nouns and pronouns in the objective case.
EXAMPLE: The doctor gave Mary and <u>me</u> an injection. [*not* 'Mary and I']

Rule 2 ● **'Teach'** and **'learn'** should not be confused.
EXAMPLES: (a) The Deputy <u>teaches</u> our class. [*not* 'learns']
(b) The whole class <u>learns</u> to swim.

Rule 3 ● **'Can'** and **'may'** should not be confused. 'Can' relates to ability, 'may' to permission.
EXAMPLES: (a) <u>Can</u> I operate this kind of stove?
(b) <u>May</u> I offer you a seat?

Using the Rules

Correct the following sentences.

(1) 'I have matches. Can I light the campfire, please?'

(2) She learnt the children the way to track in the bush.

(3) Tony followed you and I into the bush.

(4) He learned us the way to fish.

(5) 'Can I ask a question,' said the student taking out his notebook.

(6) They noticed Mark and he running towards the river.

(7) All the teenagers were learnt to survive in the bush.

Punctuation — Brackets

Brackets are used to enclose a word, phrase or clause *within* a sentence with which it may have some thought-connection, but of which it is grammatically independent. If the words within the brackets were left out, the basic structure and meaning of the sentence would not be changed. (Of course, a complete sentence can also be put in brackets.)

EXAMPLE: She completed her novel in 1980 (but only after three unsuccessful attempts) and had it published in 1984.

Note: Strictly speaking, the correct name for brackets is **parentheses.**
True brackets look like this: [ ]

Exercise

Correctly insert brackets in each of the following sentences.

(1) Kevin Gilbert not to be confused with Sir Arthur Gilbert, who is also an author wrote *Because a White Man'll Never Do It.*

(2) The author made a statement quoted on page ten condemning the atrocities of the white man.

(3) There will come a time and we hope it will be soon when the Aborigines have the same rights as white people.

(4) The tribal people carrying woomeras throwing-sticks walked in from the desert.

(5) We went on to the next big town Cowra by train.

(6) When you encounter prejudice I doubt whether you will in this city try to overcome it.

Unit Sixteen

Comprehension (16)

Young Donald

As one expects from a child, my love for my parents was ideal. The three of us seemed undivided, except when my father beat me, or when he lost his temper with my mother ... My earliest memories of my parents — pre-Muswellbrook memories — are solely of my father. I can remember how, as a very young child, I sat on the bed and leant forward to touch his cheek and his black hair, and to look at his brown eyes: he then sang a song for me. I adored talking to him, or listening, watching his tobacco smoke spiral and turn blue in a shaft of sunlight, or pottering around with him in the garden, probably getting in his way. I loved his carnations so loyally that I beat up my cousin for pulling a bloom off one of them. As I got older, it was still holding with him what seemed to me to be serious conversations that I enjoyed most. I also greatly admired him in company when he made people laugh or sang a song, although there were other times — when people were talking about their motor-cars or their businesses — when he seemed inadequate: but when talk switched to the Great War, which it often did, he more than stood his ground. I respected his importance at the Muswellbrook school, where he was second in charge, and when he blew his whistle in the playground we would all stand still; and as a sportsman, although this was more remote and sometimes dull. He called me 'Donald'. My mother called me 'Don'. Although there was sometimes a certain sudden reserve in my father's manner, a thud of silence as if he were suddenly contemplating something within himself, my mother's personality invariably flowed out into her surroundings. I have not one early memory of her, but as a growing schoolboy I admired and associated myself with her huge appetite for hospitality and her incessant desire to do some-

thing. When my mother talked we would all shout inconsequentially, hopping from one subject to the next as if we were playing hunt-the-slipper in a game in which we were never to find the slipper. However, it was not all that often that the three of us were able to enjoy our own company together. Some of my most contented times were at the evening meal when the three of us would sit in the kitchen with no one else there, the tennis party behind us, the bridge party still to come.

[from *The Education of Young Donald* by DONALD HORNE]

Check Your Understanding

(1) What does the writer mean by, 'my love for my parents was ideal'?

(2) What evidence can you find in the passage to suggest that Donald Horne deeply loved his father?

(3) What faults does he find with his father?

(4) What was the occupation of Donald's father?

(5) 'He called me "Donald". My mother called me "Don".' Can you explain this difference in the way the parents addressed their son?

(6) What does the writer mean by 'a thud of silence'? What is the effect of his use of the word 'thud'?

(7) What aspects of his mother's personality did Donald particularly like?

(8) What does the writer mean by, 'hopping from one subject to the next as if we were playing hunt-the-slipper in a game in which we were never to find the slipper'?

(9) How does the writer give the impression that life was very busy for Donald and his family?

(10) What contrast is there between the personalities of Donald's mother and father?

(11) What do you think was the writer's purpose in this passage?

(12) Explain the meanings of the following: (a) 'my mother's personality invariably flowed out into her surroundings' (b) 'we would all shout inconsequentially'.

Working with Words (16)

Senior Spelling Demons	Confusing Pairs	Actions and Reactions		Increase Your Word Power
skilful	adversary	disdain	abolish	altruist
successful	adversity	allege	technique	analogy
discuss	compliment	beseech	persevere	adroitly
accidentally	complement	surpass	repeat	agnostic
committee	heredity	participate	achieve	chronological
immediately	hereditary	diligent	exasperate	recuperate
usually	dissent	exuberant	disintegrate	truculent
definite	descent	notoriety	anticipate	animosity
thoroughly	precede	obsession	maintain	anomaly
endeavour	proceed	relegate	recognition	versatile

Suffixes

Add the suffix **-ion, -ance, -ence**, or **-ment**, to make nouns of the list-words that follow.

(Note: in some cases you will need to change the form of the word before adding the suffix.)

> definite, allege, maintain, truculent, repeat, abolish, discuss, achieve, proceed, diligent, persevere, exasperate, exuberant, anticipate, disintegrate

Confusing Pairs

Put in the correct word to complete each of the following sentences.

(1) In .... she showed she had a strong will to survive. [**adversary/adversity**]

(2) I want to .... you on your success. [**compliment/complement**]

(3) .... will determine whether the kitten will have green or blue eyes. [**heredity/hereditary**]

(4) The Parliamentarian rose and strode from one side of the House to the other, thus showing his .... in regard to the Bill under consideration. [**dissent/descent**]

(5) The school captain will .... to harangue the assembly. [**precede/proceed**]

Synonyms

Each list-word in the left-hand column has a synonym in the right-hand column. Match them up.

exuberant	industrious
animosity	expect
recuperate	completely
abolish	infuriate
beseech	exceed
diligent	entreat
technique	enmity
thoroughly	effusive
exasperate	recover
participate	method
surpass	end
anticipate	partake

'NOW A QUESTION ON DRIVEL . . . . .'

Word Quiz

Give a list-word in answer to each of the following.

(1) A synonym for skilfully is ....

(2) An antonym for deliberately is ....

(3) Arranged in time-sequence, or ....

(4) Fame in a bad sense is ....

(5) One who believes that we cannot know about the existence of God is an ....

(6) A habitually unselfish person is an ....

(7) If you have an .... you have an abnormally persistent urge or idea.

(8) To .... is to transfer something or someone to an inferior grade or position.

(9) Another word for 'irregularity' is ....

(10) If you have many different skills you're ....

Changing Forms

Supply the form of the list-word asked for in the brackets.

(1) **achieve** [*noun*] ....

(2) **usually** [*adjective*] ....

(3) **repeat** [*noun*] ....

(4) **disdain** [*adjective*] ....

(5) **recognition** [*verb*] ....

(6) **maintain** [*noun*] ....

(7) **notoriety** [*adjective*] ....

(8) **versatile** [*noun*] ....

(9) **definite** [*adverb*] ....

(10) **immediately** [*noun*] ....

(11) **obsession** [*adjective*] ....

(12) **anomaly** [*adjective*] ....

Word Origins — 'Safety Razor'

American travelling salesman King Camp Gillette spent much of his early life thinking about the man who had invented the disposable bottle-cap and who had said: 'The thing to do is to invent something which people have to have but which they can use, throw away, and then buy another.' Gillette was forty when he came up with his idea for a product which fitted exactly into this category — a cheap, disposable razor-blade.

Said Gillette: 'I rushed out and bought some pieces of brass, some steel ribbon used for clock springs, a small hand vise and some files.' That was in 1895, and the Gillette Safety Razor Company began business in 1901 above a fish shop in Boston, Massachusetts. The design and technical problems posed by Gillette's idea were overcome by an ingenious engineer who had invented the pushbutton lift, William Nickerson.

Gillette was not the first man to invent a safety razor. In 1762 Frenchman Jean-Jacques Perret had put a guard along one side of a cut-throat razor-blade to stop it slipping into the skin. And it was an Englishman, William Henson, who invented the modern form of safety razor by setting the blade at right-angles to the handle. The first electric razor was patented in 1923 by Colonel Jacob Schick.

Although men have been shaving their faces for thousands of years, soldiers were for a long time discouraged from growing beards because it gave the enemy too good a handhold in battle. The navy is the only one of the three services which has always allowed its men to sport a beard, reasoning that nobody should be compelled to shave in a ship lurching through a heavy sea.

Language in Action (16)

Irony

Irony is a particular use of language in which the words employed by a speaker or writer convey an opposite or different meaning. It often involves the use of language which has an 'inner' (secret) meaning as well as the 'outer' (face-value) meaning, of which only some among those listening — or reading — are aware.

Exercise 1

(1) Explain the irony in this cartoon.

(2) How is this irony conveyed to us?

(3) Does Thor appear to see any irony in his own words?

The Dramatic Impact of Irony

The use of irony is frequently a tool for achieving considerable dramatic impact in literature. Perhaps nowhere is this better illustrated than in Mark Antony's speech after the death of Caesar in Shakespeare's *Julius Caesar*. Caesar has been murdered by a group of Roman Senators who considered him too ambitious. Among the murderers was Brutus, a Roman whose integrity everyone trusted.

FRIENDS, ROMANS, COUNTRYMEN

Antony:
Friends, Romans, countrymen, lend me your ears;
I come to bury Caesar, not to praise him.
The evil that men do lives after them;
The good is oft interred with their bones;
So let it be with Caesar. The noble Brutus
Hath told you Caesar was ambitious:
If it were so, it was a grievous fault;
And grievously hath Caesar answer'd it.
Here, under leave of Brutus and the rest,—
For Brutus is an honourable man;
So are they all, all honourable men,—
Come I to speak in Caesar's funeral.
He was my friend, faithful and just to me:
But Brutus says he was ambitious;
And Brutus is an honourable man.
He hath brought many captives home to Rome,
Whose ransoms did the general coffers fill:
Did this in Caesar seem ambitious?
When that the poor have cried, Caesar hath wept:
Ambition should be made of sterner stuff;
Yet Brutus says he was ambitious;
And Brutus is an honourable man.
You all did see that on the Lupercal
I thrice presented him a kingly crown,
Which he did thrice refuse: was this ambition?
Yet Brutus says he was ambitious;
And, sure, he is an honourable man.
I speak not to disprove what Brutus spoke,
But here I am to speak what I do know.
You all did love him once, — not without cause:
What cause withholds you, then, to mourn for him?
O judgment, thou art fled to brutish beasts,
And men have lost their reason! — Bear with me;
My heart is in the coffin there with Caesar,
And I must pause till it come back to me.

[from *Julius Caesar*, Act III Scene ii]

Exercise 2 — Analysis

(1) Which particular line is the focus of Mark Antony's use of irony?

(2) How does Antony build the dramatic impact of this use of irony?

(3) What did Antony want his listeners really to conclude from his ironic monologue?

Discussion

(1) Is tone of voice important in effective spoken irony? How would Antony have spoken these words?

(2) Rewrite the lines that are ironic, so that they become straightforward statements of what Antony really believes and wants others to believe. Have someone read this 'unmasked' version of the speech. As a class, discuss the difference in impact between the ironic and non-ironic versions.

How to Bring Up Your Child

At different times, writers have made effective use of irony in drawing up 'Ten Commandments' on such issues as 'How to Bring Up Your Child'. One list, attributed to the Police Department in Houston, Texas, includes such rules as:

- Quarrel frequently in front of him — he then won't be shocked when the home breaks up.
- Be careful that the cutlery and crockery are sterilized, but let his mind feast on garbage.
- When he gets into trouble apologize for yourself by saying 'I never could do anything with him'.

The use of irony enables us to see that, really, these 'commandments' are advocating the opposite approach, by showing us what will happen if we follow these 'rules'. The gentle humour in such use of irony is almost certainly a more vivid and powerful way of pointing people in the right direction — and much more thought-provoking — than a straight, 'non-ironic' list of direct guidelines.

Exercise 3

Make up your own list of 'Ten Commandments', using irony, for one of the following. An example is provided in each case; use it as the 'First Commandment'.

SITUATION 1 — **'How to Get the Most out of Camp'**
   1. Never get out of bed when they call you in the morning. A man once died getting out of bed early.

SITUATION 2 — **'How to Be a Good Driver'**
   1. Always honk and shake your fist at any driver who does something wrong. Fools who can't control their driving shouldn't be on the roads.

SITUATION 3 — **'How to Pass Exams Well'**
   1. Don't follow a programme of study. Good textbooks can wear out if they are opened too much.

Sarcasm

Sarcasm is an extreme use of irony in which the speaker or writer intends to be deliberately hurtful or spiteful. The aim of sarcasm is to belittle whoever (or whatever) is the target of the sarcasm.

Exercise 4

(1) Whom does the speaker in the last frame of this cartoon-strip intend to belittle?

(2) Explain his use of sarcasm.

Exercise 5

The insults that follow depend upon the use of sarcasm to achieve a humorous (?) belittling of the person being spoken about. Combine the START OF INSULT in each case with the appropriate SARCASTIC FINISH from the jumbled list alongside. The first one has been done for you as an example.

START OF INSULT   SARCASTIC FINISH

START OF INSULT	SARCASTIC FINISH
E.g. She's so dumb that every time she gets into a taxi	the driver keeps the 'Vacant' sign up.
(1) They have their home in a nice location:	she comes back with a sunburnt tongue.
(2) He cultivates his friendships like a garden —	that's the only kind that would take him.
(3) She said she felt like a young colt,	it would only be a minor operation.
(4) I'd engage in a battle of wits with you,	but she looked more like an old forty-five.
(5) Every time she goes to the beach	they rushed her to a maternity hospital.
(6) She's so thin that when she recently swallowed an olive	to pieces.
(7) He says he'd only marry a girl who can take a joke —	on the outskirts of their income.
(8) He's so narrow-minded	that gives failure a bad name.
(9) They pick their friends —	when a butterfly kicked him in the head.
(10) He gives the kind of performance	with continuous little digs.
(11) If he had his conscience taken out	that he won't even listen to both sides of an LP.
(12) He's so dumb that he lost his mind	but you're only half-prepared.

The Language of Literature (16)

THE SURFER

He thrust his joy against the weight of the sea,
climbed through, slid under those long banks of foam—
(hawthorn hedges in spring, thorns in the face stinging).
How his brown strength drove through the hollow and coil
of green-through weirs of water!
Muscle of arm thrust down long muscle of water.
And swimming so, went out of sight
where mortal, masterful, frail, the gulls went wheeling
in air, as he in water, with delight.

Turn home, the sun goes down; swimmer, turn home.
Last leaf of gold vanishes from the sea-curve.
Take the big roller's shoulder, speed and swerve.
Come to the long beach home like a gull diving.

For on the sand the grey-wolf sea lies snarling;
cold twilight wind splits the waves' hair and shows
the bones they worry in their wolf-teeth. O, wind blows,
and sea crouches on sand, fawning and mouthing;
drops there and snatches again, drops and again snatches
its broken toys, its whitened pebbles and shells.

JUDITH WRIGHT

Analysing the Poem

(1) What are the surfer's feeling in the first stanza?

(2) What do you understand by, 'hawthorn hedges in spring, thorns in the face stinging'?

(3) Why does the poet refer to the seagulls as both 'mortal' and 'masterful'?

(4) What similarities can you find between the surfer and the seagulls?

(5) Explain how the mood of the poem abruptly changes at the beginning of the second stanza.

(6) Explain what Judith Wright means by, 'Last leaf of gold vanishes from the sea-curve'.

(7) How does she show that the sea is dangerous and unfriendly to the swimmer?

(8) In what ways is the sea similar to a wolf?

(9) Do you think the poem is meant to be no more than a description of the surfer? Explain your viewpoint.

(10) Explain what the poet means by 'shows the bones'?

(11) What was your reaction to this poem?

Writers' Workshop (6)

The Importance of Planning

Much of the writing required of you as a senior student is essay-writing. Your normal task in an essay is to assemble the knowledge you have about a subject, shape it into a planned form of some kind, and present it as convincingly as you can. The importance of spending some time working out a plan for your essay cannot be overstressed. An essay written to a plan is going somewhere; an essay written 'off the top of your head' runs the danger of rambling and losing its impact.

The Task

There is a considerable difference between an essay set as homework by a teacher, and an essay you have to write under exam conditions. But both of them require planning. For the homework essay, you have the opportunity to use textbooks and collect material before planning. In an exam you have to assemble as much information *as you can remember*, and fit it in with a plan.

(a) ASSEMBLY OF INFORMATION
After receiving the essay topic and considering exactly what it requires of you, write brief notes on the information you have. This will become clearer with an example, so here is an essay topic.

> **Topic:** *'From a consideration of two of his poems that you have studied, outline the distinctive characteristics of the poetry of Gerard Manley Hopkins.'*

In response to this topic a student jotted down the following notes, taking two or three minutes to do so.

- Sprung rhythm — the rhythm of natural speech (?)
- Tendency to omit words — compresses language — vitality.
- Sometimes makes up words — compound words — 'dapple-dawn-drawn falcon'.
- A poetry of 'sound' — use of alliteration, etc.
- Emphasis on religion and nature.
- Complexity — vitality.
- 'Inscape' (?)

(b) SHAPING THE ESSAY
Having jotted down the rough ideas, the next task is to structure them into a plan which will allow you to write a purposeful, tight essay, *answering the question*. This step should take three or four minutes in an exam.
Here is how the student shaped the information in point-form (above) into an essay plan.

Characteristics of Hopkins's Poetry

<u>Introduction</u> — a difficult poet — uses words as artist uses colours.

1. <u>Use of language</u>
   Overall Purpose — desire to capture essence of what he describes — 'inscape'.
   (i) Omission of words — urgency (e.g. 'There lives the dearest freshness deep down things').
   (ii) Creation of new words, compound words (examples).
   (iii) Concentration on 'sound' of words — hence alliteration, etc (examples).

2. <u>Themes</u>
   (i) Nature
   (ii) Religion } (examples)

3. <u>Rhythm</u> — sprung rhythm — explain — effect.

4. <u>Conclusion</u> — on the topic!

(c) WRITING THE ESSAY

Notice that the plan offers a structure which the student was then able to follow in answering the question. Other students will have followed a different plan, perhaps highlighting different aspects of Hopkins's poetry that they saw as distinctive. The important thing here is that the two or three minutes spent planning the essay provided a *form* that gave the final product a sense of progress and purpose.

These three steps, then — **assembling, shaping, writing** — make up the essential on which successful essay-writing is built.

Planning a Creative Essay

Since essay-planning is a skill that needs practice, choose three easy topics from the broad lists that follow and write down a plan for each. Incorporate several points, and list sub-points where necessary. Pick topics you are interested in, or have some knowledge of, as this will make the task easier. An example of a plan for the first topic is worked out for you.

Topics

(1) 'A Frustrating Experience'
   EXAMPLE: *1.* <u>The situation</u> — looking forward to visit friend in hospital.
   2. <u>The problem</u> — caught at railway crossing — train coming.
   3. <u>Increasing frustration</u> — shunting back and forth — 4 times.
   4. <u>What I did</u> — ate peppermints; composed letter to local paper; fumed; looked for way out, but none.
   5. <u>Further frustration</u> — gates opened, but give way to all cars on right!
   6. <u>Conclusion</u> — what I did — you guessed it — nothing!

(2) 'Someone I'll Always Remember'

(3) 'Talk About an Incredible Coincidence!'

(4) 'A Job I Enjoyed'

(5) 'The Holiday That Went Wrong'

(6) 'Recollections of Childhood'

(7) 'TV's Most Super-Boring Programme'

(8) 'The Car — Servant turned Tyrant'

(9) 'Hate Makes the World Go Round'

(10) 'Steps to Overcome Worry'

(11) 'The Sport I Love'

(12) 'Making Use of Leisure Time'

(13) 'My Dabblings in Horticulture'

(14) 'Advice for Novice Daters'

(15) 'The Right to Strike in Australia'

(16) 'The Day I Made a Fool of Myself'

(17) 'Divorce — an Evil Necessity?'

(18) 'Woman v. Man'

(19) 'Informative v. Persuasive Ads'

Essays on Set Works

To further practise the planning of essays, choose three of the following topics and set yourself the task of working out plans for them. In each case:
  (i) Begin by assembling information. Jot down your rough ideas, in any order, as they come to you.
 (ii) Shape the essay. Look over your rough notes and work out possible plans that you could follow for the essay. Write them down.
(iii) Choose one of the essay plans and proceed to write the essay, allowing yourself a time-limit of around thirty minutes.

Topics

(1) Choose a short crucial extract from a play that you have studied this year and explain how it contributes to the theme of the play.

(2) Use evidence from a play that you have studied this year to outline the important features of the playwright's style.

(3) 'The essence of drama is conflict, but in many important dramas this conflict is within characters, not between them.' Discuss the accuracy of this statement in relation to one play you have studied this year.

(4) 'Good plays are built on good stories.' Using a play you have studied this year as a guide, evaluate the truth of this statement.

(5) Outline the qualities that are portrayed in *two* leading characters from a play you have studied this year. How real are these characters, and how successfully has the playwright brought them to life?

(6) Choose a novel you have studied this year and explain its main theme. How does the writer bring this theme out in the novel?

(7) 'Believable characters, a good story and something important to say; these are the features of a successful novel.' Evaluate the success of one novel you have studied, in the light of these three criteria.

(8) From one of your novels, select the incident that you feel is most crucial to the development of the novel's theme. Explain the importance of the incident.

(9) 'In life, people change; in a good novel, the same thing should happen.' Outline the important changes that take place in one character from a novel you have studied this year.

(10) Refer to features of a novel you have studied this year in summarizing the main elements of the author's style.

Language Basics (16)

More on Verbs

Rule ● You should be careful not to use a past participle instead of the past-tense form of the verb, or the past-tense form instead of a past participle.

   EXAMPLES: (a) Young Donald <u>ate</u> breakfast. [*not* Young Donald eaten . . .]
   (b) Young Donald had <u>eaten</u> breakfast. [*not* Young Donald had ate . . .]

Exercise

Given one of the three, PRESENT TENSE, PAST TENSE or PAST PARTICIPLE, fill in the other two blank spaces for each of the verbs. Note the example using 'swim'.

PRESENT TENSE	PAST TENSE	PAST PARTICIPLE
swim	swam	swum
am		
	arose	
		begun
	bit	
blow		
break		
		chosen
		done
	drew	
drink		
	drove	
	fell	
fly		
forbid		
	forgave	
	froze	
		given
	grew	
hide		
know		
		lain

PRESENT TENSE	PAST TENSE	PAST PARTICIPLE
ride		
	rang	
	rose	
		shaken
	showed	
shrink		
	sang	
		slain
smite		
sow		
	sprang	
		stolen
	strove	
swear		
		taken
tear		
	threw	
	trod	
		woken
wear		
	wove	
write		

Punctuation – The colon

Three important uses of the colon are:

1. To introduce a **list.**
   EXAMPLE: The school ordered the following: 20 cartons of chalk, 40 exercise books, 3 tape recorders.

2. To introduce a **series of ideas.**
   EXAMPLE: The school assembly was told of many problems: the difficulties of going co-ed, the need for a new uniform, the prevalence of truancy, and so on.

3. To introduce a **quotation or statement.**
   EXAMPLE: The principal opened the speech night with the words: 'Your school will look after you and expects you to look after your school.'

Exercise

Insert colons into the following sentences, where they are needed, and add any other necessary punctuation.

(1) We recommend that each student bring a toothbrush a towel and comb and a camera.

(2) I shall always remember the headmaster's three fateful words that changed my whole life Consider yourself expelled!

(3) The lecturer covered the following topics the school in the community ways of teaching reading the teacher and his class.

(4) Burns wrote this famous line 'O, my Luve's like a red, red rose

(5) Get me these students Bill Drake Jill Noosa Ralph Booth.

(6) Remember turn off the electricity lock the doors shut the gate.

Unit Seventeen

Comprehension (17)

Pitying Animals

If one listens to the remarks of the visitors in any of the larger zoos one will frequently find that people are in the habit of wasting sentimental pity on animals that are absolutely contented with their lot, while the genuine suffering, which is to be found in every zoological gardens, may pass unnoticed. People are specially apt to pity those animals which, owing to their particular emotional associations, play a prominent role in literature, like the nightingale, the lion or the eagle. . . .

The lion is [an] animal very often misrepresented in literature, both as to habitat and to character. The English call him King of the Jungle — thus relegating him to much too wet a locality, while the Germans, with customary thoroughness, go to the other climatic extreme and deposit him in the desert, calling him *'Wüstenkönig'* (Desert King). In reality, he prefers the happy medium and lives in steppes or savannahs. His majesty of bearing, to which he owes the first part of his title, is due to the simple fact that, being a hunter of large animals of the open plains, he habitually surveys the far distance and disregards everything moving in the foreground.

The lion suffers less under close confinement than most other carnivores of equal mental development, for the simple reason that he has a lesser urge for movement. To put it crudely, the lion is about the laziest of the predatory beasts: he is indeed quite enviably indolent. Under natural conditions he covers enormous distances, but obviously only under pressure of hunger and not from any inward drive. Therefore, it is seldom that a lion in captivity is seen pacing restlessly to and fro in his cage as wolves and foxes will do for hours at a stretch. If the pent-up drive for locomotion urges him, for once, to walk up and down the length of his cage, his movements bear the character of a leisurely after-

dinner stroll and have nothing of the frantic haste with which captive canine carnivores discharge their frustrated urge to cover large distances. In the Berlin Zoo, a huge paddock with desert sand and yellow rocky crags was made for the lions, but this expensive construction proved very nearly useless; a gigantic model with stuffed beasts might have served the same purpose, so lazily did the lions lie about in their romantic surroundings.

And now for the eagle! I hate to shatter the fabulous illusions about this glorious bird, but I must adhere to the truth: all true birds of prey are, compared with passerines or parrots, extremely stupid creatures. This applies particularly to the golden eagle, 'the eagle' of our mountains and our poets, which is one of the most stupid among them, much more so indeed than any barnyard fowl. This, of course, does not preclude this proud bird from being beautiful and impressive and embodying the very essence of wild life; but here we have to deal with the mental qualities of the creature, its supposed love of freedom and its imaginary suffering in captivity.

I still remember what disappointment was caused me by my first and only eagle, an imperial eagle which I bought, out of pity, from a wandering menagerie. She was a beautiful female bird, nearly matured in colour, a sign that she boasted several years. She was completely tame and greeted her keeper, and later myself, with a curious gesture of affection in which she turned her head upside down, so that the fearful curve of her beak pointed perpendicularly upwards. At the same time, the creature spoke in tones so quiet and docile as to be worthy of a turtle dove; moreover, compared with the latter, she was a veritable lamb . . . . I originally bought her because I intended to train her for hawking, as many Asiatic peoples are known to do with eagles. I did not flatter myself that I should acquire any particular success in this noble sport, but I hoped, if only by using a domestic rabbit as bait, to make observations on the hunting behaviour of one of these large birds of prey. This plan failed because my eagle, even when she was hungry, refused to harm a hair of the rabbit's body.

[from *King Solomon's Ring* by KONRAD Z. LORENZ]

Check Your Understanding

(1) What mistake do some people visiting zoos make about animals such as the lion and the eagle?

(2) Explain what is meant by 'animals which . . . play a prominent role in literature'?

(3) Why is it erroneous to refer to the lion as 'King of the Jungle' and 'Desert King'?

(4) What is the meaning of: (a) habitat (b) relegating (c) predatory? (Consult the back-of-the-book dictionary if you need help.)

(5) What does the author mean by 'His majesty of bearing'?

(6) What does 'indolent' mean? Why does the writer refer to the lion as 'enviably indolent'?

(7) Under natural conditions, what causes the lion to cver enormous distances?

(8) What does the writer mean by 'pent-up drive for locomotion'?

(9) What contrast is there between a lion in captivity and other captive carnivores?

(10) What is said by the writer concerning the physical appearance of the eagle and its mental ability?

(11) What does Lorenz mean by 'fabulous illusions'?

(12) Why does the writer refer to the imperial eagle's gesture of affection as 'curious'?

(13) Write down two phrases that suggest that this imperial eagle was very tame.

(14) Why did the writer wish to train the imperial eagle for hunting?

(15) What did you learn about the writer himself from this extract?

(16) What do you think was Lorenz's purpose in writing the book from which the extract is taken?

Working with Words (17)

Senior Spelling Demons	Confusing Pairs	The Law		Increase Your Word Power
appropriate	difficulty	delinquent	judgement	survillance
suicide	dilemma	judicial	witness	retrograde
severely	censor	prosecution	acquittal	formidable
occasional	censure	condemn	defiance	exquisite
anniversary	wave	innocent	homicide	discernible
unfortunately	waive	persevere	investigation	fidelity
interesting	referee	allegation	evidence	squalor
nuisance	reverie	apprehend	dishonesty	dissension
decision	deficient	comprehend	adjourn	writhe
accustomed	defective	testify	authority	astute

Change the Words

Change into people

(a)   prosecution   ....

(b)   investigate   ....

(c)   dissension   ....

Change into nouns

(a)   comprehend   ....

(b)   severely   ....

(c)   appropriate   ....

(d)   testify   ....

(e)   persevere   ....

(f)   condemn   ....

Change into verbs

(a)   prosecution   ....

(b)   allegation   ....

(c)   judicial   ....

(d)   acquittal   ....

(e)   discernible   ....

(f)   decision   ....

Change into adjectives

(a)   decision   ....

(b)   squalor   ....

(c)   apprehend   ....

(d)   authority   ....

(e)   homicide   ....

(f)   condemn   ....

Change into adverbs

(a)   occasional   ....

(b)   astute   ....

(c)   homicide   ....

Form the plurals of

(a)   witness   ....

(b)   difficulty   ....

(c)   valley   ....

(d)   mosquito   ....

(e)   echo   ....

(f)   ratio   ....

Find the Word

Replace the words or phrases in heavy type with words from the lists.

(1) The prisoner had been placed under **a close watch.**

(2) **Faithfulness** is especially important in marriage.

(3) The reasons for the building's collapse were not **able to be seen.**

(4) The **filth and wretchedness** of the surroundings astounded the reporter.

(5) The publisher of the James Bond books must have been very **shrewd and sharp.**

(6) There was no **disagreement** amongst the social workers about the evils of the excessive consumption of alcohol.

(7) The police made an **assertion without proof** that the demonstrator had broken the law.

(8) It was considered a **backward** plan to lower the school leaving age.

(9) The accident victim had begun to **twist violently** in agony.

(10) It is difficult to **understand** why some motorists don't wear safety belts.

(11) The police tried to **catch** the robber.

(12) He seemed to be walking in a kind of **dream.**

Missing Words

Correctly insert the words from the box into the spaces below.

surveillance	censor	delinquent	investigation	formidable
deficient	witness	homicide	exquisite	acquittal

(1) The film .... decided to cut a scene from the film.

(2) The police .... showed that the manager was guilty of ....

(3) To the weaker batsmen, the fast bowler appeared ....

(4) The actress received an .... necklace.

(5) The diet of the refugees was .... in most vitamins.

(6) On the evidence of the ...., the defendant received an ....

(7) The juvenile .... had been placed under police ....

Confusing Pairs

Correctly match up one word from each of the confusing pairs with its meaning opposite.

difficulty/dilemma   a choice between two unpleasant alternatives
censor/censure   blame, criticize
wave/waive   not insist upon, forgo
referee/reverie   an umpire
deficient/defective   faulty

Word Origins — Permutations

Per is the Latin word meaning 'through'. Match up the following *per* words with their correct meanings.

PER WORDS	MEANINGS
perforate	to puzzle
perturb	to continue steadfastly
permit	to sweat (breathe through the skin)
permanent	to spread through
perspire	to make holes through
pervade	to throw into confusion
persevere	to let or allow
perplex	lasting indefinitely

Language in Action (17)

The Pun

> Two young men established a beef-cattle station and called it 'Focal Point'. When asked by their father why they had given it such a name, they explained: 'Focal point — why, that's where the sun's rays meet.' [*sons raise meat*]

This example illustrates what a pun is. It is a *play on words* in which words having the same sound — but different meanings — are used. The reader, or listener, is able to perceive both meanings and thus appreciate the wit involved. In the passage above we have an example of a triple pun — three words being used, each with an appropriate double-meaning. Puns are examples of quick wit (some would say, of a distorted sense of humour!) and are usually 'clever' rather than side-splittingly funny.

Questions

(1) Which is the pun-word in this strip?

(2) What are the two meanings of the word?

Bending Words to Make a Pun

Often, in order to make the pun, a word may have to be slightly distorted or altered. If this is excessive the pun will be laboured and will lose its sense of spontaneity and 'cleverness'. However, if the distortion is within acceptable limits, the distorted pun may be seen as even more humorous than a straight pun.

An example would be the response of the grain farmer who was asked by the Grain Board if he would be able to increase his production quota. 'Just sago and I'll rice to the occasion!' he replied. (I imagine he could barley wheat to do so! But that *would* be a case of pushing things a bit too far. . . .)

Questions

(1) Which word forms the pun in this strip?

(2) What is the other word the pun reminds us of?

(3) Why is it an appropriate pun?

Make-A-Pun

In the exercise below you are given two WORDS alike in sound, but different in meaning, to be used as the basis for a pun. Then, a SITUATION and an INITIAL COMMENT are provided and you are required to write a REPLY which turns the first comment into a pun. Try your hand at creating your own puns!

Pun-Word	Situation	Initial Comment	Pun Reply
EXAMPLE: **where's/wears**	Two sailors scrubbing the deck	*Sailor 1:* 'Where's the soap?'	*Sailor 2:* 'Yes, doesn't it!'
1. **hi/high**	Two tourists at top of Empire State Building	*Tourist 1:* 'Hi!'	*Tourist 2:* ....
2. **conviction** = belief **conviction** = proven charge	Two people discussing someone else	*Person 1:* 'He's a man of convictions?'	*Person 2:* ....
3. **prays/ preys**	Two acquaintances discussing a third	*Person 1:* 'He prays on his knees every Sunday.'	*Person 2:* ....
4. **rear** = to bring up **rear** = the back section	Two men discussing a woman	*Person 1:* 'She's pretty well reared.'	*Person 2:* ....
5. **moving** = emotional **moving** = getting up and going	Two playgoers discussing an actor	*Person 1:* 'I found his performance moving.'	*Person 2:* ....

More Punishment

Identify the two words upon which the pun in each of the following lines depends, and explain their separate meanings.

(1) Her waistline is definitely of her own chewsing.

(2) He sticks with his friends until debt do them part.

(3) One of these days he'll get caught in his own mouthtrap.

(4) You could describe nuclear fallout by calling it fission chips.

(5) 'Do you smoke while studying?'
    'I don't know, I've never looked.'

The Language of Literature (17)

'Sons and Lovers'

This novel is based on Lawrence's own adolescence. Walter, Gertrude and Paul Morel, and Clara and the other characters, work out the novel's twin themes: the effect of the prolonged love of a mother on a son's emotional development, and the unbridgeable differences between physical and spiritual love. The passage below focuses on conflict between husband and wife. Walter Morel comes home late and drunk. He enters a household in which the baby is unwell, and Gertrude (his wife) is unable to endure his presence.

She sighed, hearing him coming, as if it were something she could not bear. He, taking his revenge, was nearly drunk. She kept her head bent over the child as he entered, not wishing to see him. But it went through her like a flash of hot fire when, in passing, he lurched against the dresser, setting the tins rattling, and clutched at the white pot knobs for support. He hung up his hat and coat, then returned, stood glowering from a distance at her, as she sat bowed over the child.

'Is there nothing to eat in the house?' he asked, insolently, as if to a servant. In certain stages of his intoxication he affected the clipped, mincing speech of the towns. Mrs Morel hated him most in this condition.

'You know what there is in the house,' she said, so coldly it sounded impersonal.

He stood and glared at her without moving a muscle.

'I asked a civil question, and I expect a civil answer,' he said affectedly.

'And you got it,' she said, still ignoring him.

He glowered again. Then he came unsteadily forward. He leaned on the table with one hand, and with the other jerked at the table drawer to get a knife to cut bread. The drawer stuck because he pulled sideways. In a temper he dragged it, so that it flew out bodily, and spoons, forks, knives, a hundred metallic things, splashed with a clatter and a clang upon the brick floor. The baby gave a little convulsed start.

'What are you doing, clumsy, drunken fool?' the mother cried.

'Then tha should get the flamin' thing thysen. Tha should get up, like other women have to, an' wait on a man.'

'Wait on you — wait on you?' she cried. 'Yes, I see myself.'

'Yis, an' I'll learn thee tha's got to. Wait on *me,* yes, tha sh'lt wait on me—'

'Never, milord. I'd wait on a dog at the door first.'

'What — what?'

He was trying to fit in the drawer. At her last speech he turned round. His face was crimson, he eyes bloodshot. He stared at her one silent second in threat.

'P-h!' she went quickly, in contempt.

He jerked at the drawer in his excitement. It fell, cut sharply on his shin, and on the reflex he flung it at her.

One of the corners caught her brow as the shallow drawer crashed into the fireplace. She swayed, almost fell stunned from her chair. To her very soul she was sick; she clasped the child tightly to her bosom. A few moments elapsed; then, with an effort, she brought herself to. The baby was crying plaintively. Her left brow was bleeding rather profusely. As she glanced down at the child, her brain reeling, some drops of blood soaked into its white shawl; but the baby was at least not hurt. She balanced her head to keep equilibrium, so that the blood ran into her eye.

Walter Morel remained as he had stood, leaning on the table with one hand, looking blank. When he was sufficiently sure of his balance, he went across to her, swayed, caught hold of the back of her rocking-chair, almost tipping her out; then, leaning forward over her, and swaying as he spoke, he said, in a tone of wondering concern:

'Did it catch thee?'

He swayed again, as if he would pitch on to the child. With the catastrophe he had lost all balance.

'Go away,' she said, struggling to keep her presence of mind.

He hiccoughed. 'Let's — let's look at it,' he said, hiccoughing again.

'Go away!' she cried.

'Lemme — lemme look at it, lass.'

She smelled him of drink, felt the unequal pull of his swaying grasp on the back of her rocking-chair.

'Go away,' she said, and weakly she pushed him off.

He stood, uncertain in balance, gazing upon her. Summoning all her strength she rose, the baby on one arm. By a cruel effort of will, moving as if in sleep, she went across to the scullery, where she bathed her eye for a minute in cold water; but she was too dizzy. Afraid lest she should swoon, she returned to her rocking-chair, trembling in every fibre. By instinct, she kept the baby clasped.

Morel, bothered, had succeeded in pushing the drawer back into its cavity, and was on his knees, groping, with numb paws, for the scattered spoons.

Her brow was still bleeding. Presently Morel got up and came craning his neck towards her.

'What has it done to thee, lass?' he asked, in a very wretched, humble tone.

'You can see what it's done,' she answered.

He stood, bending forward, supported on his hands, which grasped his legs just above the knee. He peered to look at the wound. She drew away from the thrust of his face with its great moustache, averting her own face as much as possible. As he looked at her, who was cold and impassive as stone, with mouth shut tight, he sickened with feebleness and hopelessness of spirit. He was turning drearily away, when he saw a drop of blood fall from the averted wound into the baby's fragile, glistening hair. Fascinated he watched the heavy dark drop hang in the glistening cloud, and pull down the gossamer. Another drop fell. It would soak through to the baby's scalp. He watched, fascinated, feeling it soak in; then, finally, his manhood broke.

'What of this child?' was all his wife said to him. But her low, intense tones brought his head lower. She softened: 'Get me some wadding out of the middle drawer,' she said.

[from *Sons and Lovers*
by D. H. LAWRENCE]

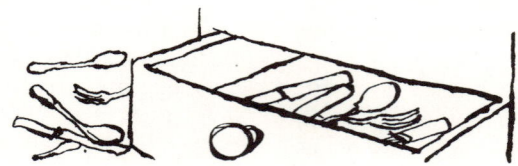

Thinking about Language

(1) Though she does not wish to see her husband, Mrs Morel is intensely aware of his drunken presence. How do we know this?

(2) What tone in Walter Morel's language causes his wife to react impersonally?

(3) Can you suggest why Morel should affect 'the clipped, mincing speech of the towns' when he is drunk?

(4) Words such as 'clang' and 'clatter' occur in the paragraph describing the spilling of the drawer. What effect is achieved by the use of such words?

(5) What emotion parallels Walter Morel's switch from the 'clipped, mincing speech of the towns' to broad Midlands dialect?

(6) When Gertrude addresses her husband as 'milord', is she really showing respect towards him or is it something else?

(7) 'I'd wait on a dog at the door first.' How does Morel react to this reply?

(8) 'To her very soul she was sick . . . .' What advantage or force is gained by using this construction rather than the more usual, 'She was sick to her very soul'?

(9) What tone does Morel use in speaking to his wife after she has been injured?

(10) In the sentence beginning, 'As he looked at her . . . .', how is figurative language used to convey an image to us?

(11) What causes Morel's 'feebleness and hopelessness of spirit'?

(12) 'Get me some wadding out of the middle drawer' is both an unemotional and a normal piece of communication. What has apparently resolved their conflict?

(13) What is the final effect on Morel of watching the blood soak in?

(14) 'Tha should get up, like other women have to, an' wait on a man.' Comment on the kind of society that could produce such an attitude. Was there, or is there, any justification for such an attitude?

(15) After reading this passage, what comments would you be prepared to make about the character of (a) Walter Morel, and (b) Gertrude Morel?

Writers' Workshop (7)

Supporting Assertions with Evidence

One of the most damaging omissions in any essay occurs when the writer makes assertions without providing supporting evidence. It is *absolutely vital* that you understand the importance of this in examination essays — and in all essays which require you to argue a case, or take a particular stance. In such writing you are aiming to convince the reader of the correctness of what you are saying. The only way to do this is to offer specific evidence to support every assertion, every point, that you make!

The Importance of Specific Evidence

By providing specific evidence from the play, novel, poem, experience or situation in question, three things are accomplished:
  (i) Your depth of understanding is demonstrated.
 (ii) Your assertions are supported and thus have greater force.
(iii) Reader interest is more easily maintained. (Nothing becomes more quickly boring than a succession of general statements with no concrete specific material in support!)

Consider the paragraph that follows.

> The poetry of Gerard Manley Hopkins is strikingly original. He has written many beautiful and powerful poems which, though difficult to understand at first, will richly repay the serious student. He is at pains to try to express the essence of the subject he writes about and this usually accounts for his originality. He tends to make up words at times, whenever he finds that normal language cannot express all that he wants to express.

Comments

The student who has written this paragraph obviously has some knowledge of the poetry of Hopkins, but *nowhere* does she offer any *specific evidence* to support the assertions she makes. In fact, the paragraph consists of one claim after another about Hopkins's poetry, none of which is backed up with evidence. When the task is to *convince* the reader of the *'rightness'* of what is being said, supporting evidence must be given. An essay written like this cannot possibly achieve a high mark.

Now look at the following.

> The first point I would like to make about the distinctive characteristics of Hopkins's poetry is about his remarkably fresh, vital use of language. In 'Spring' there is life and urgency in lines such as
>
> > ...and thrush
> > Through the echoing timber does so rinse and wring
> > The ear, it strikes like lightnings to hear him sing;
>
> In 'Pied Beauty' he piles descriptive word upon descriptive word:
>
> > All things counter, original, spare, strange;
>
> and
>
> > ...swift, slow; sweet, sour; adazzle, dim;
> > He fathers-forth whose beauty is past change:
> > > Praise him.
>
> By creating his own compound word 'fathers-forth', meaning 'creates or brings to life', Hopkins develops the reader's sense of freshness and vitality in the poem's language. The 'Praise him', which closes the poem, carries this same mark of forceful vitality.

Comments

This paragraph has its faults, among them a fairly weak introductory statement, but at least support is offered for the points being made. The student has concentrated on making *one* point, and has tried to find specific evidence to back it up. The concluding sentence does tend to move the argument along a little further and, while the observation could have begun a new paragraph, it does suggest that the student may be making more than one point. On balance, the student is headed towards a reasonable mark — if he continues to provide support for his assertions.

How Do You Support a Point with Evidence?

In an essay based on a text or a poem, there are *two* kinds of specific evidence which can be introduced to support a general assertion. You may:

(i) *quote a line or two from the text or poem*
The important points here are that the quotation must be **accurate** (including spelling and any internal punctuation!) and that it must be **relevant.** No purpose at all is served by introducing a quotation which is unrelated to the point being made!

(ii) *refer to a specific incident or a significant point-of-development in the text or poem*
For example, in a novel you may refer to an incident in the story which illustrates a point you have just made. Again, this supporting evidence must be *relevant.*

The most obvious way to support claims with specific evidence is to make each new assertion the topic sentence of a new paragraph. The developing sentences of each paragraph then take up the presentation of the supporting evidence. This approach will provide you with a safe and structured method of backing up your argument.

Exercise 1

Use each of the following general assertions as the topic sentence of a paragraph. Develop your paragraph by building subsequent sentences upon specific evidence which you offer in support of the general point.

(1) There's nothing worse than being unemployed.

(2) The world would be considerably poorer without rainbows and sunsets.

(3) We certainly pay a high cost for our use of motorcars these days.

(4) A girl with a good sense of humour has a lot going for her.

(5) The kind of food we consume is more important than most of us would admit.

(6) Owning a horse is great, but you need plenty of leisure time.

(7) Deafness would be even harder to bear than blindness.

(8) Not many Australians really appreciate snow.

(9) You can learn a lot by watching children play.

(10) Bushwalking has a lot to offer anyone who takes it up.

Exercise 2

Using a text or texts (novel, poetry, drama, short stories, essays) that you have studied this year, write a paragraph for each of the following.

(1) Make a general assertion about the kind of person the hero/heroine is, and then support the point with quotations or by referring to incidents in the action.

(2) Make a general assertion about the author's theme and support your point with specific evidence.

(3) Make a general assertion about the use of language, and support it with specific evidence.

Language Basics (17)

Prepositions

● Some prepositions go with verbs and other parts of speech to form idiomatic expressions.

EXAMPLES: (a) Many people believe <u>in</u> pitying animals <u>in</u> captivity.

(b) Some scientists have been searching <u>for</u> evidence <u>of</u> the eagle's mental capacity.

Exercise

Supply the prepositions that are commonly used and accepted to complete the following sentences.

(1) I am obliged .... make mention .... several animal fallacies.

(2) It is hardly possible to accede .... his request for a full scientific enquiry .... the habits .... the lion.

(3) The world has bestowed great but undeserved distinction .... the king of the beasts.

(4) Some zoologists are unfitted temperamentally .... be animal behaviourists.

(5) Other scientists are deserving .... praise for their patience and dedication.

(6) We must become reconciled .... the fact that some of our animal heroes are fakes.

(7) Associated .... further research is further insight .... the habits .... the king of birds.

(8) A professor .... zoology is surely qualified .... give an answer!

(9) Some pronouncements on animals are devoid .... sense.

(10) We must insist .... flawless evidence.

(11) Ignorance is fraught .... peril.

(12) We must refrain .... any impetuous moves with large carnivores.

(13) Zookeepers are indebted .... the great zoologists .... a substantial amount .... information.

(14) Eagles are capable .... sudden and brilliant power-dives.

(15) Prior .... the report, there were thought to be hundreds .... lions in the park.

(16) In fable, lions are superior .... other large carnivores.

(17) Russian zoologists have agreed .... their American counterparts.

(18) Great numbers had been reported .... Park Rangers.

(19) The theory must comply .... the facts as they stand.

(20) As a result .... recent discoveries, we may soon be able to communicate .... some animals.

Punctuation — More on the colon

Two more rules for the use of the colon are:

1. A colon is used **between two clauses** when the second resolves ('explains') the first.
   EXAMPLE: We now understand why some animals hunt at night: there is far less competition around.

2. A colon is used **between the title and subtitle** of a book.

    EXAMPLE: *The Way We Were: A Social Comment* is a most interesting book.

Exercise

Put colons into the following sentences where needed.

(1) One more thought on the subject a bird in the hand is worth two in the bush.

(2) *Remembering The Story of My Childhood*

(3) His explanation was simple he had left the key inside the house.

(4) *Trees A Lifelong Study,* by Edgar Maple and Floyd Oakpine.

(5) There was a reason for the lecturer's pause she drank a glass of water for the sake of her throat.

Unit Eighteen

Comprehension (18)

Adland — the Magic Mountain

Advertising is to business what the toilet is to the home — a handy facility in times of need. It affords quick access and, usually, quite satisfying results. Sometimes even a sense of achievement. It also comes in a range of shapes, sizes, colours, sounds, costs, to cater for most tastes. It flushes the economy and helps to maintain a healthy tone.

Unhappily, advertising has tended to be regarded by many as a dodge of the devil, spawning false lusts, pandering to unworthy passions. This phenomenon has been accentuated in the last quarter of a century — coincidental with the introduction of television. Aversion is particularly acute among those who suffer from the pains of other people's acquisitive urges. It manifests itself mostly in predictable protest that has, at its core, a deep-seated conviction that other people (it is always 'they') have no adequate protective mechanisms in their make-up to resist the lure of advertised temptations.

That there are baits and traps is readily conceded. That most people have their own resources to deal with the situation is also asserted.

Guilt-transference, nonetheless, abounds and it is sometimes terrible to behold. Avenging angels, unfortunately, often display a selective incapacity to isolate wrongdoers. The innocent — represented by the main body of advertising — are herded in with the guilty. Still, the tests of survival demand such trials and it is probably part of the Plan of the Great Account Executive in the Sky to make one of us all before the final reckoning.

Meantime, during periods of non-need, screening filters are normally at work. If yours are a bit faulty and you have this awful feeling, all the time, that advertising is sapping your will to resist, it is perfectly legitimate to kick in the set, cancel your newspaper subscription. If that doesn't work, get a second opinion. You may be suffering from the advertising ague. It is not really serious and can easily be remedied by sitting in a dark corner for half an hour each day and saying to yourself, over and over, 'No! No! No!'

[from *Soft Soap, Hard Sell* by R. R. WALKER]

Check Your Understanding

(1) Comment on the appropriateness or inappropriateness of the opening comparison.

(2) What is the effect sought by the writer by the use of this comparison?

(3) What particular event appears to be linked to the emergence of unfavourable connotations in regard to advertising?

(4) Find two phrases that suggest that many critics of advertising are narrow, moralistic people.

(5) Would the writer feel that the demand by some critics that advertising should be banned (in order to protect consumers) is a legitimate one?

(6) 'Avenging angels, unfortunately, often display a selective incapacity to isolate wrong-doers.' Explain this in your own words.

(7) ' . . . to make one of us all . . . . ' Explain what is indicated by 'one'.

(8) What options are offered for the person who feels that advertising is sapping his/her will?

(9) Explain the purpose behind the action of sitting in a corner saying 'No!' over and over.

(10) What is implied by the parenthetical statement 'it is always "they" '?

(11) Explain the meaning of the following words as used in the passage (consulting the dictionary at the back of the book if necessary): (a) spawning (b) pandering (c) accentuated (d) ague.

(12) Explain the difference between 'conceded' and 'asserted' as used in this passage.

(13) What attitude towards advertising is expressed by the writer of this passage? Support your answer.

(14) What strengths and weaknesses can you see in this piece of writing?

(15) Comment on the style of the writer as displayed in this extract.

Working with Words (18)

Senior Spelling Demons	Confusing Pairs	Conflict		Increase Your Word Power
miniature	stationary	annoyance	discipline	benign
precision	stationery	boundary	opponent	hypocrisy
concise	emigration	controversy	challenge	conceivable
intimidate	immigration	rebellious	disastrous	repugnant
illuminate	creditable	warfare	treachery	calamitous
intervene	credible	torture	retaliate	tangible
possession	collision	equipment	casualty	insatiable
dominant	collusion	ammunition	deterrent	indiscriminate
adolescent	veracious	cemetery	massacre	derogatory
academic	voracious	quarrel	aggression	spontaneous

Confusing Pairs

Use words from the *Confusing Pairs* column to complete the following.

(1) A newsagent often sells ...., while a stalled car is ....

(2) Leaving a country in order to settle overseas is called ...., whereas entering a country to settle there is called ....

(3) If something can be believed, it is .... On the other hand, an action that brings honour or trust can be called ....

(4) .... is secret cooperation for some unsavoury purpose, while .... is violent impact.

(5) The shark is sometimes called ...., while to be truthful is to be ....

Prefixes
Form the opposites of the following list-words by using the prefixes **in-, im-, dis-, un-**.

> possession, conceivable, academic, creditable,
> precision, credible, discipline, tangible

Antonyms
Find list-words that are antonyms for: (a) **planned** (b) **malignant** (c) **ally** (d) **peace** (e) **darken.**

Synonyms
Find list-words that are synonyms for: (a) **argue** (b) **dispute** (c) **tiny** (d) **succinct** (e) **controlling.**

Change the Words

Change into people

(a)	possession	....
(b)	rebellious	....
(c)	hypocrisy	....
(d)	emigration	....
(e)	discipline	....
(f)	aggression	....

Form nouns from

(a)	spontaneous	....
(b)	veracious	....
(c)	calamitous	....
(d)	retaliate	....
(e)	dominant	....
(f)	adolescent	....
(g)	disastrous	....
(h)	intervene	....

Form verbs from

(a)	opponent	....
(b)	dominant	....
(c)	collision	....
(d)	possession	....

Form adjectives from

(a)	retaliate	....
(b)	quarrel	....
(c)	precision	....
(d)	controversy	....
(e)	aggression	....
(f)	treachery	....

Meanings

Select, from the brackets accompanying each sentence, the word or phrase nearest in meaning to the heavy-type word in that sentence.

(1) There is **tangible** evidence for the existence of the Tasmanian wolf.
[*retrenched, tactful, real, tentative*]

(2) The teacher made a **derogatory** comment about my son.
[*conventional, furtive, frivolous, injurious*]

(3) The nuclear arsenal of each nation can be called a **deterrent.**
[*positive measure, preventative, effective, elaborate hoax*]

(4) After a time, living the frugal existence of a student became **repugnant** to him.
[*offensive, uplifting, spurious, lax*]

(5) The emu and the ostrich are both noted for their **insatiable** appetite.
[*flagrantly curious, resourceful, impossibly greedy, resolute*]

(6) In the **conceivable** future there will be Earth colonies on other worlds.
[*ridiculous, looming, preventable, thinkable*]

(7) If you hit him he's obviously going to **retaliate.**
[*simulate, strike back, prevaricate, opt out*]

(8) **Hypocrisy** is liable to creep in when doctors begin to think more of their fees than of their patients.
[*pretence of virtue, lack of skill, impossible conditions, unrelieved tension*]

Word Origins — 'Soccer'

The idea of two teams pushing a ball backwards and forwards to each other began in ancient Egypt as a fertility rite. The Roman army of Julius Caesar introduced it to Britain, where the savages took to it quickly; and today's Association Football, or soccer, is the direct descendant of Roman football and the forerunner of all the other football codes. The word 'soccer' came from an abbreviation of Association, which students called 'Assoc'.

The first extensive description of English football dates back to 1175 in London. Rules in those days were considerably more lax than today, and games frequently ended in wild brawls with broken limbs and even the occasional death. The number of players could exceed 500 and a game could last all day.

The birth of modern soccer took place in London in October 1863 when the Football Association was formed, and in the following few years the rules as we know them were largely adopted.

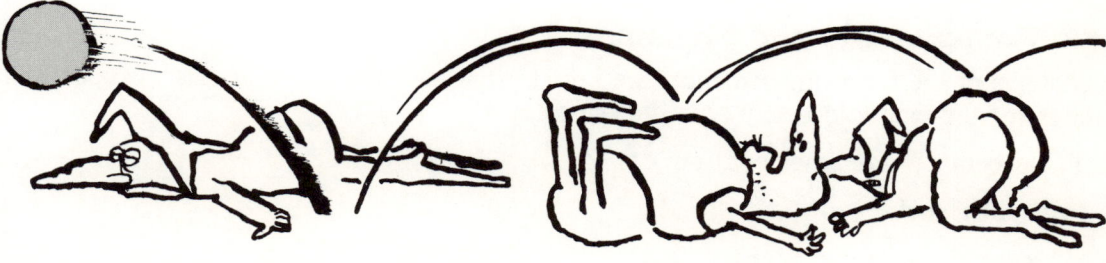

Language in Action (18)

Context

Verbal Context

One of the best ways of working out the meaning of a word is to see it used in a sentence. This is known as its verbal context. Thus the meaning of 'aroma' becomes much clearer when we read, 'The delicious aroma of the hot scones filled her nostrils'.

Physical Context

If we are swimming at the beach and someone on the shore yells out, 'Shark!' our emotional response is genuinely one of fear as we look around for the ominous fin. However, when we are on the tennis court and our partner yells out, 'Shark!' we know we are being reproached for playing a ball meant for her.

Social Context

The social context of a word relates to the way it is used by various groups in the community. Some social groups consider 'dough' to be money, some refer to a 'pad' as a house, others look upon 'a nut' as a stupid person, and still others view a girl as 'a bird'.

The Psychological Context

The psychological context of words has already been discussed in another section of the book. Our comments here will be brief. A person's past experiences have an important role in assigning a personal context (or 'connotation') to the meaning of words. Someone who has had enjoyable experiences at the beach will give the word 'sea' a meaning different from that of a country person who has never seen and fears the sea.

THE WIZARD OF ID   By Parker and Hart

Vague Contexts, Blurred Meanings

The contexts of the following sentences are not clearly defined. Suggest at least two possible meanings for the words in heavy type in each case.

(1) You'd better put another **coat** on.

(2) **Pull your socks up!**

(3) He gave his girlfriend **a ring.**

(4) We've been told to go to another **court.**

(5) What a nice **bird!**

(6) **Keep your shirt on.**

(7) The scientist was most concerned about the problem of his **culture.**

(8) That's **funny!**

(9) She's **skating on thin ice.**

(10) **Fire!**

(11) He's **stuck his neck out.**

(12) She's **got green fingers.**

Context and Meaning

By examining the context, explain the variation in meaning of the word 'dog' in the following sentences.

(1) The dog barked loudly.

(2) The old man was leading a dog's life.

(3) 'You've done for me! you dog. I'm beat! one hit before I go.'

(4) Since his wife left him, Joe has gone to the dogs.

(5) In the football competition I always barrack for the underdog.

(6) While there's peace and quiet in the office, it's best to let sleeping dogs lie.

By examining the context, explain the variation in meaning of the word 'light' in the following sentences.

(1) Turn the light on.

(2) The parcel was light.

(3) We need to shed more light on our financial problems.

(4) The girl was light-hearted while she was dancing at the party.

(5) We'll have some light refreshments.

The Language of Literature (18)

A Poet's Anxieties

The poet is sitting on the beach observing her children surfing. She is also reading a newspaper.

CHILDREN

Long-summer scorched, my surfing children
Catch random waves or thump in dumpers,
Whirling, gasping, tossed, disjointed.
I, watching, fear they may be broken—
That all those foaming limbs will never
Reassemble whole, together.

All under such a peaceful sky.

All under such another sky

The pictures show some village children
Caught at random, tossed, exploded,
Torn, disjointed, like sticks broken,
Whose jagged scorching limbs will never
Reassemble whole, together.

NANCY KEESING

Reacting to the Poem

(1) In your own words describe what is happening in the first half of the poem.

(2) What does 'long-summer scorched' tell you about the poet's children?

(3) What do you understand by 'foaming limbs'?

(4) What does the sound of the words 'thump in dumpers' suggest about the children in the waves?

(5) Why is the poet afraid for her children?

(6) How does the poet prepare the reader for a change of scene?

(7) What evidence can you find in the second part of the poem to suggest that there is a war in progress?

(8) Explain the difference between 'catch random waves' and 'caught at random'.

(9) Why are the village children '. . . disjointed, like sticks broken'?

(10) What do you think was the poet's purpose in writing 'Children'?

(11) How successful did you find the poem?

Writers' Workshop (8)

Writing an Essay as a Home Assignment

Before considering the features of the homework essay, it is important to remind ourselves that the fundamentals are the same for both homework essays and examination essays. Material should be generated, a plan should be roughed out, assertions should be supported with specific evidence, and so on.

Yet there are some obvious differences between having to write an essay in an exam and as a home assignment. The home assignment does not have to be completed in around 35 minutes, reference books can be consulted; more time can be put into planning and writing. Clearly, because of these differences, a higher standard is usually expected for the home-assignment essay. Let us suppose, in the following outline, that the set essay involves a literary text.

1. Assembling Material

Having made sure that you understand the question set, your first task is to draw together the relevant ideas that you will weave into the essay. This means involving yourself in
  (i) looking over relevant parts of the text;
 (ii) consulting critics who have written relevant material;
(iii) looking back over any relevant class notes or study guides;
 (iv) in the light of all this, bringing to bear on the question your own considered reflections.

As relevant points or ideas are noticed, jot them down. At the same time jot down any evidence that you are aware of in support of each point. If you can't think of the evidence at this stage, note 'Needs evidence!' alongside the particular point. If, after later reflection, you are unable to find evidence to support a point, it is important to ask whether or not the point is correct. A valid point should have evidence to support it!

2. Planning and Organization

The relevant material you now have must be shaped so that it purposefully sets forth an answer to the question asked.

Look back over your notes and begin to organize them. You may choose to organize your points:
  (i) **in order of importance** (from the most important to the least important, or vice versa); or
 (ii) **in order of occurrence** (i.e. following the order in which they emerge in the novel, play, poem, etc).

Make sure that *sub-points* are organized under their relevant *major point*, and not tacked on as an unrelated observation later in the essay. Careful thought at this organizational stage should remove that danger.

3. Writing a Draft and Rewriting

For the home assignment, it is particularly important to write a rough-draft copy of the essay. This should follow the essay plan, but should tend to be written fairly quickly, without becoming bogged down on specific issues or slavishly worrying about technicalities.

The draft copy serves a very important function in crystallizing and clarifying your thoughts for the finished essay. It is comparable in its role to an architect's rough sketch of a building. Suddenly, your thinking is stimulated. Now, with a rough copy in front of you, you can see changes that *must* be made; you can see what the 'finished building' needs to be like! Before the rough sketch was provided, ideas may have been hard to come by; now they flow.

The importance of a draft cannot be overstated. It sometimes happens that the final essay is quite different from the draft in structure, simply because the draft itself has generated a better plan, a different method of organization, another approach.

The draft copy is a workman's document. If its structure is not going to be altered too much in the finished essay, then it should be worked over — improving expression, restructuring sentences, adding evidence, correcting spelling and punctuation. From this corrected draft, the final essay is written.

Although this process is time-consuming, it is imperative if you are to produce your best in a homework essay. You just cannot produce your very best in a once-off piece of writing. You must begin to develop the habit of refining and reworking your effort until it has become a polished product.

Assignment

Have your teacher set an essay topic for you and follow through the three stages outlined in this approach. Include your plan and draft copy as part of the product you hand in for assessment. Discuss as a class any areas of difficulty you experience and work out ways of overcoming them.

Language Basics (18)

Mixed Metaphors

- Figurative language often enlivens communication. However, when metaphors are mixed and images are distorted the clarity of communication suffers. Here is an example of mixed metaphors:

  An avalanche of commercials in the programme nearly drowned the viewers.

  Notice that an *avalanche* image is mixed with a *drowning* image. The sentence can be improved by modifying either metaphor so that it matches the other.

  An avalanche of commercials in the programme nearly buried the viewers.

- Sometimes, however, clear meaning can only be achieved by omitting one or more of the metaphors. Thus,

  We can see the light at the end of the tunnel with regard to the spiralling costs of colour TV sets.

  becomes much clearer and neater as:

  We can foresee an end to the spiralling costs of colour TV sets.

Exercise

Rewrite the following sentences so that images are undistorted.

(1) You can't expect to burn the candle at both ends and still avoid upsetting the apple cart.

(2) Red tape in the industry is excessive and cannot be expected to bite the dust for quite a few years yet.

(3) Our aim is to give our young people's minds a chance to rub shoulders with older, wiser heads.

(4) Those who poke their noses into other people's business are likely to have their fingers burnt.

(5) He has a chip on his shoulder that could flare up at any moment.

(6) Since all of us are in the same boat, we had better start coming to heel.

Punctuation — The semicolon

Here are some rules for the correct use of the semicolon.

1. A semicolon should be used to separate statements so closely linked that a comma would be too weak and a full stop would be too strong.
    EXAMPLE: TV is fascinating; radio is interesting; films are educational; and life is too short to take it all in.

2. Use the semicolon between pairs of main clauses not connected by a coordinating conjunction such as 'but' or 'and'.
    EXAMPLE: You can buy it; I can't afford it.

3. Where two main clauses are joined by a coordinating conjunction, a semicolon may be used if the clauses are long.
    EXAMPLE: Presently, from away off in the forest a mellow bugle-note came floating; then all of a sudden a multitude of dogs burst out of that forest.

4. A statement introduced by words such as 'however', 'then', 'therefore', 'so', 'nevertheless', 'consequently', 'otherwise' can usually be separated from a preceding statement by a semicolon.
    EXAMPLE: There is a government ban on violence in TV programmes; however, it is not enforced.

Exercise

Insert semicolons where needed in the following sentences.

(1) The manager is out the secretary is in.

(2) I like TV, I need it but I do not trust it.

(3) TV stars are in demand consequently, they command high salaries.

(4) You may believe her I will not.

(5) Radio talkback shows are popular nevertheless, they are frequently mindless.

Dictionary

The following abbreviations for parts of speech are used throughout this dictionary:

adj adjective	*adv* adverb	*n* noun	*n pl* noun plural
pp past participle	*pr p* present participle	*v* verb	

abstain *v* refrain, keep away [*from*]

abundance *n* great quantity, plenty

accentuated *pp* emphasized, made prominent

acquiesce *v* agree, accept [*in*]

adamant *adj* unyielding

adept *adj* (or *n*) proficient, expert, skilled

admonition *n* reproof, warning

adroitly *adv* dexterously, skilfully

adversary *n* opponent, enemy

aggressive *adj* inclined to attack, forceful

agnostic *n* (or *adj*) one who believes that the existence of anything (e.g. God) beyond material phenomena cannot be known

ague *n* acute fever

altruist *n* one who places regard for others above selfish concerns

amiable *adj* friendly, likeable, good-natured

analogy *n* similarity, description of one thing by reference to another

animosity *n* enmity, hostility

anomaly *n* irregularity

appeasement *n* pacification by making concessions

ardent *adj* fervent, zealous

articulate *adj* (or *v*) clear and coherent in expression

artifice *n* clever trick or device

aspire *v* desire earnestly, seek to reach [*to*]

assail *v* attack

assiduous *adj* diligent, persistent

assimilation *n* absorption (into a system), incorporation

astute *adj* keen-minded, sagacious, shrewd

avert *v* turn away; ward off

barbarous *adj* uncivilized, coarse; cruel

belligerent *adj* (or *n*) waging war; hostile

benign *adj* gentle, kindly

bigot *n* one who holds blindly and intolerantly to a belief or opinion

boycott *v* (or *n*) refuse any dealings with, in order to punish or coerce

brusquely *adv* bluntly, offhandedly, roughly

cadaverous *adj* corpse-like

cajole *v* coax or persuade by flattery or deceit

calamitous *adj* disastrous

capricious *adj* inconstant, guided by whim

chagrin *n* (or *v*) keen disappointment, mortification

chant *v* (or *n*) sing, intone

chronological *adj* arranged in order of time

coherent *adj* consistent, clear, not rambling

coincidence *n* notable concurrence of apparently unconnected events

complacent *adj* self-satisfied

conceivable *adj* thinkable

connoisseur *n* discriminating person (in art, food, etc)

conservative *adj* (or *n*) inclined to preserve or maintain what is established; cautious

contemptuous *adj* scornful, showing contempt

contrite *adj* penitent, broken in spirit by sense of sin

cranium *n* skull

crapulence *n* gross intemperance, over-indulgence; its ill after-effects

culminate *v* reach highest point, climax [*in*]

culpable *adj* blameworthy

culprit *n* offender

cult *n* system of belief or worship, often with devotion to significant person or thing

curfew *n* time after which people are not allowed on the streets

deity *n* a god; divine status

delude *v* deceive, mislead

deluge *n* flood; downpour

demeanour *n* bearing, outward conduct

demoralized *pp* with morale or resolution undermined

denigrate *v* defame, blacken

derisive *adj* expressing mockery or ridicule

derogatory *adj* tending to discredit, disparage

diligent *adj* industrious, assiduous, hard-working

diminutive *adj* very small

dirigible *n* airship

discernible *adj* able to be perceived or distinguished

discerning *adj* having keen discriminating insight

discordant *adj* harsh, dissonant; in disagreement or strife

dissension *n* disagreement in opinion, discord

dissuade *v* advise or persuade against [*from*]

diversion *n* detour, deviation; feint, distraction; amusement, pastime

divulge *v* reveal

docile *adj* manageable, submissive

dogmatic *adj* asserting arrogantly or authoritatively with scant regard for proof

dominant *adj* strongest, prevailing

ecstasy *n* rapture, great joy

elation *n* high spirits, joy

élite *n* select group

eloquent *adj* fluent and forcible in expression

emaciated *pp* (or *adj*) wasted, lean

epithet *n* adjective or descriptive term expressing a characteristic quality of a person or thing

escapade *n* reckless or wild adventure

euphemism *n* mild or vague term used in place of accurate but distasteful one

exasperate *v* irritate strongly

exigency *n* urgent need

exonerate *v* free from blame

exquisite *adj* of great excellence or beauty; intense

extricate *v* disentangle, free, release [*from*]

extrovert *n* outgoing person

facet *n* one side or aspect; one segment of a compound eye; one surface of a gem

fastidious *adj* very fussy, hard to please

fatality *n* a death by accident, in war, etc.

fervour *n* zeal, passion, intense feeling

fidelity *n* faithfulness

flagrant *adj* scandalous, glaring, shamefully obvious

flared *pp* blazed up; burst into sudden anger

formidable *adj* hard to overcome; giving cause for dread

fortuitous *adj* happening by lucky accident or chance

frivolous *adj* silly, not serious

gesticulate *v* make lively gestures, wave hands about

graphic *adj* expressed by visual symbols; vividly descriptive

gratitude *n* gratefulness

gullible *adj* naive, believing too readily

habitat *n* natural home or conditions of plant or animal

hypocrisy *n* pretence of virtue, two-facedness, insincerity

imbue *v* impregnate, inspire, saturate [*with*]

immobile *adj* unmoving, not mobile, fixed

immortalize *v* endow with eternal life or fame

immutable *adj* unchangeable

impasse *n* blind alley, situation with no outlet

impassive *adj* not expressing any emotion

impede *v* hinder, retard

impervious *adj* not permitting passage or penetration [*to*]

implore *v* plead, beg

impressionistic *adj* giving general tone — impression — without elaborate detail

impunity *n* exemption from punishment

inane *adj* empty, silly

inanimate *adj* not having life

inception *n* beginning

inclement *adj* severe, merciless; cold or stormy

incongruous *adj* out of place

indefatigable *adj* tireless

indict *v* charge with a crime [for]

indifference *n* lack of concern, absence of interest

indignity *n* unworthy treatment, insult, affront

indiscriminate *adj* making no distinctions, random

indulgent *adj* yielding (to wishes), compliant, tolerant

infamous *adj* of ill fame, shameful, notorious

inflexible *adj* unbending

inhibit *v* restrain, hinder (e.g. through sense of the forbidden)

initiate *v* (or *n*) set going; admit (with special rites or forms) to membership

innuendo *n* indirect (unfavourable) hint, insinuation

insatiable *adj* unsatisfiable

insignia *n pl* badges, emblems

insinuate *v* hint, convey indirectly; introduce deviously or gradually (e.g. oneself *into* favour)

insipid *adj* dull, tasteless

insomnia *n* sleeplessness

intercede *v* interpose or plead on behalf of another

interminable *adj* endless

introvert *n* (or *v*) self-absorbed person

irascible *adj* prone to anger

irrational *adj* unreasonable, illogical, absurd

irrevocable *adj* beyond recall, unalterable

lethal *adj* deadly

lethargy *n* lack of energy and interest

levity *n* 'light' behaviour, frivolity

lithe *adj* supple, limber

loquacious *adj* very talkative

lucrative *adj* profitable

ludicrous *adj* ridiculous

lyrical *adj* suggestive of expression through singing or poetry

malignant *adj* having ill-will; virulent, infectious

malinger *v* pretend illness to escape duty

manifestly *adv* clearly, obviously, plainly

marshal *v* arrange, assemble

martial *adj* of war, military

maudlin *adj* mawkish, over-sentimental, tearful

mockery *n* derision, ridicule

monologue *n* long speech by one person; soliloquy

moribund *adj* about to die

nostalgia *n* sentimental longing for the past

nostrums *n pl* quack remedies; pet schemes for improvement

nurture *v* (or *n*) nourish, bring up, foster

odious *adj* hateful, repulsive

ominous *adj* threatening, foreshadowing disaster

pallid *adj* pale, wan

pandering *pr p* appealing *to* base instincts (of others)

paranoid *adj* psychologically deranged with delusions of persecution

passive *adj* not active, inert, submissive

perennial *adj* (or *n*) long-lasting or recurrent

permeate *v* penetrate, diffuse through, pervade

perpetually *adv* eternally, unceasingly

pervade *v* diffuse or extend through, permeate

petty *adj* trivial, minor; small-minded

petulant *adj* easily roused to small outbursts of temper

placid *adj* peaceful, calm

poignant *adj* painfully sharp, moving, touching

pompous *adj* self-important, inflated, pretentious

predatory *adj* preying upon others

premonition *n* forewarning

prerogative *n* particular right or privilege

proclaim *v* announce publicly or officially

prolific *adj* abundantly productive

prostrating *pr p* casting (oneself) flat on ground in reverence or submission; overcoming with exhaustion or disease

provocative *adj* arousing controversy, anger, lust, etc

provosts *n pl* senior officials or administrators (e.g. of military police)

prowess *n* outstanding skill or courage

prudent *adj* wise, careful

puberty *n* stage at which an individual becomes capable of sexual reproduction

racist *n* one who espouses racial discrimination or antagonism

ratify *v* make valid, confirm formally

recounted *pp* narrated, told

recuperate *v* recover (from illness, loss, etc.)

regime *n* system of rule

relegating *pr p* consigning to an inferior position [*to*]

replenish *v* fill up again

repudiate *v* reject, disown

repugnant *adj* offensive, distasteful

resilience *n* capacity to spring back or recover

retrograde *adj* tending to revert or backwards; not progressive

rhetoric *n* impressive and persuasive (use of) language

sadist *n* one who enjoys inflicting or observing pain

scant *adj* barely sufficient

scepticism *n* attitude of doubt, critical questioning

secluded *adj* solitary, quiet, separate, private

sedate *adj* (or *v*) calm, composed, tranquil

sinecure *n* position yielding gain but requiring no work

solace *n* (or *v*) comfort in distress or trouble

sombre *adj* dark, gloomy

sordid *adj* squalid, impure

spawning *pr p* producing offspring; depositing eggs

spontaneous *adj* voluntary, not induced by external forces; natural, unprompted, instinctive

squalor *n* dirty, miserable conditions or surroundings

staid *adj* sedate, settled

static *adj* not moving, at rest

stipulate *v* specify as essential part or condition of agreement

succumb *v* yield, be overcome

superficial *adj* on or of the surface only, lacking depth

surveillance *n* close watch

syndrome *n* set of symptoms typically found together; distinctive pattern

taciturn *adj* reserved, not inclined to talk

tangible *adj* real or definite; touchable

taut *adj* tight, trim

tenacious *adj* holding fast, persistent, resolute

terse *adj* concise (in language); curt, abrupt

tier *n* row, rank, level

totalitarian *adj* of a political system based on absolute power of a single party or dictator

transient *adj* not lasting

trite *adj* commonplace, stale through overuse

truculent *adj* aggressive, bellicose, fierce

turbulent *adj* in commotion, violent, disturbed

turgid *adj* swollen, enlarged; pompous, inflated (e.g. prose)

ultimate *adj* (or *n*) final; beyond which no advance or progress is possible

undulate *v* have a wave-like motion or appearance

unscathed *adj* uninjured

unutterable *adj* beyond description, unspeakable

vacillate *v* waver, hesitate

venerate *v* respect deeply, revere, hold in awe

veracity *n* truthfulness; truth

versatile *adj* having varied abilities or interests and able to switch readily among them, many-sided

vestige *n* trace, remnant

vexation *n* irritation, worry, annoyance

vindictive *adj* vengeful, spiteful

violation *n* transgression, non-observance; rough disturbance, breaking in upon

vulnerable *adj* open to attack, able to be hurt

writhe *v* squirm, twist

zealous *adj* enthusiastic, fervent, eager